BUSH'S WAR

Communication, Media, and Politics

Series Editor
Robert E. Denton, Jr., Virginia Tech

This series features a range of work dealing with the role and function of communication in the realm of politics, broadly defined. Including general academic books and texts for use in graduate and advanced undergraduate courses, the series encompasses humanistic, critical, historical, and empirical studies in political communication in the United States. Primary subject areas include campaigns and elections, media, and political institutions. *Communication, Media, and Politics* books will be of interest to students, teachers, and scholars of political communication from the disciplines of communication, rhetorical studies, political science, journalism, and political sociology.

Recent Titles in the Series

Political Campaign Communication: Principles and Practices, Fifth Edition
    Judith S. Trent and Robert V. Friedenberg
The Rhetoric of Redemption: Kenneth Burke's Redemption Drama and Martin Luther King, Jr.'s "I Have a Dream" Speech
    David A. Bobbitt
Reelpolitik II: Political Ideologies in '50s and '60s Films
    Beverly Merrill Kelley
New Frontiers in International Communication Theory
    Edited by Mehdi Semati
News Narratives and News Framing: Constructing Political Reality
    Karen S. Johnson-Cartee
Leading Ladies of the White House: Communication Strategies of Notable Twentieth-Century First Ladies
    Edited by Molly Meijer Wertheimer
Entertaining Politics: New Political Television and Civic Culture
    Jeffrey P. Jones
Presidential Candidate Images
    Edited by Kenneth L. Hacker
Bring 'Em On: Media and Politics in the Iraq War
    Edited by Lee Artz and Yahya R. Kamalipour
The Talk of the Party: Political Labels, Symbolic Capital, and American Life
    Sharon E. Jarvis
The 2004 Presidential Campaign: A Communication Perspective
    Edited by Robert E. Denton, Jr.
Women's Political Discourse: A 21st-Century Perspective
    Molly A. Mayhead and Brenda DeVore Marshall
Making Sense of Political Ideology: The Power of Language in Democracy
    Bernard L. Brock, Mark E. Huglen, James F. Klumpp, and Sharon Howell
Transforming Conflict: Communication and Ethnopolitical Conflict
    Donald G. Ellis
Towel Snapping the Press: Bush's Journey from Locker-Room Antics to Message Control
    James E. Mueller
The Internet Election: Perspectives on the Web in Campaign 2004
    Edited by Andrew Paul Williams and John C. Tedesco
Bush's War: Media Bias and Justifications for War in a Terrorist Age
    Jim A. Kuypers

BUSH'S WAR

Media Bias and Justifications for War in a Terrorist Age

Jim A. Kuypers

ROWMAN & LITTLEFIELD PUBLISHERS, INC.
Lanham • Boulder • New York • Toronto • Plymouth, UK

*69594031

ROWMAN & LITTLEFIELD PUBLISHERS, INC.

Published in the United States of America
by Rowman & Littlefield Publishers, Inc.
A wholly owned subsidiary of The Rowman & Littlefield Publishing Group, Inc.
4501 Forbes Boulevard, Suite 200, Lanham, Maryland 20706
www.rowmanlittlefield.com

Estover Road
Plymouth PL6 7PY
United Kingdom

British Library Cataloguing in Publication Information Available

Library of Congress Cataloging-in-Publication Data

Kuypers, Jim A.
  Bush's war : media bias and justifications for war in a terrorist age / Jim A.
Kuypers.
    p. cm. — (Communication, media, and politics)
  Includes bibliographical references and index.
  ISBN-13: 978-0-7425-3652-4 (cloth : alk. paper)
  ISBN-10: 0-7425-3652-1 (cloth : alk. paper)
  ISBN-13: 978-0-7425-3653-1 (pbk. : alk. paper)
  ISBN-10: 0-7425-3653-X (pbk. : alk. paper)
  1. United States—Politics and government—2001—Press coverage. 2. War
on Terrorism, 2001—Press coverage—United States. 3. Journalism—
Objectivity—United States. 4. Press and politics—United States. I. Title. II.
Series.
  E902.K89 2006
  973.931—dc22

                                                                2006017412

Printed in the United States of America

∞ ™ The paper used in this publication meets the minimum requirements of
American National Standard for Information Sciences—Permanence of Paper
for Printed Library Materials, ANSI/NISO Z39.48-1992.

To Theodore O. Windt,
may he peacefully rest,
and to my wife Tammy
for the best of reasons

Contents

List of Tables   ix

1   Media Bias and Presidential Justifications for
    War in the Age of Terrorism   1

2   A New Justification for War?   17

3   President Bush Speaks to the United Nations,
    November 2001   35

4   The State of the Union, 29 January 2002   51

5   Remarks by the President from the USS
    Abraham Lincoln, May 2003   75

6   President Bush Addresses the United Nations
    General Assembly, September 2003   99

7   President Bush Commemorates Veterans Day and
    Discusses the War on Terror, 11 November 2005   113

8   News Media Reporting of the War on Terror   135

Notes   167

Index   195

About the Author   199

Tables

8.1   9/11 to Afghanistan   143
8.2   President Bush Speaks to the United Nations,
      November 2001   143
8.3   State of the Union, January 2002   145
8.4   Remarks by the President from the USS
      Abraham Lincoln, March 2003   147
8.5   President Bush Addresses the United Nations
      General Assembly, September 2003   148
8.6   President Bush Commemorates Veterans Day and
      Discusses the War on Terror, November 2005   150

1

Media Bias and Presidential Justifications for War in the Age of Terrorism

Given their stunning and incomprehensible nature, it is easy to see why thousands of books, articles, and essays followed in the wake of the events of 9/11. Immediately after the attacks, Americans looked to their president for words of leadership, and on the evening of 9/11 President George W. Bush gave his most formal reply of the day. In part, he said:

> Today, our fellow citizens, our way of life, our very freedom came under attack in a series of deliberate and deadly terrorist acts. The victims were in airplanes, or in their offices; secretaries, businessmen and women, military and federal workers; moms and dads, friends and neighbors. Thousands of lives were suddenly ended by evil, despicable acts of terror.[1]

The stark tone of President Bush's words hinted at the impact these attacks had upon the United States. The tone also suggested the promise of more words to come from the president. It is with these subsequent words that this book is concerned. Although the attacks of 9/11 and their impact upon American society are discussed in numerous publications, there is one area that has been comparatively ignored: presidential justifications for war in the age of terrorism. Specifically, how do presidents since the ending of the Cold War convince Americans that a certain foreign policy is justified? Put another way, how did President Bush justify U.S. military actions in the post-9/11 world? For example, whereas the invasion of Afghanistan seemed justified, what

1

about the invasion of Iraq? What of forthcoming military strikes, and the continuing military presence in Afghanistan and Iraq? To answer these questions, it is simply not enough to find out how the Bush administration explains these actions to the American people. There is an important intermediary element to examine, one that lies between what President Bush says and what Americans actually understand him to say.

Consider that only a very small minority of Americans listen to a president's speech or later read a transcript of that speech; the lion's share of Americans receive their information filtered through their daily news. In this book, I examine both *what the President says* and *what the mainstream press reports the President says*, in order to determine *what the public is told to believe* about America's new post-9/11 role in the world.[2] In short, in this book you will see how media bias shapes our perceptions of what the president says within the context of having entered into the age of terrorism.

To better understand this process, start by considering the modern presidency as a *rhetorical presidency*.[3] Viewed in this light, the "presidency is an office, a role, a persona, constructing a position of power, myth, legend, and persuasion. Everything a president does or says has implications and communicates 'something.' Every act, word, or phrase becomes calculated and measured for a response."[4] From this point of view, the president has enormous power to set national goals and provide solutions for the nation's problems. Additionally, the mass media *dramatize* the content of what presidents say, thus moving the emphasis away from what presidents *do* to what they *say*. Finally, the continual campaigning by U.S. presidents encourages an emphasis upon presidential character, image, and personality, while deemphasizing deliberation on the particular issue in question.

It is a well-known American cultural fact that following closely upon the heels of World War II, a forty-five-year Cold War ensued. Each year, from 1947 until 1991, the collective weight of U.S./Soviet experiences made it easier for American presidents to construct foreign policy arguments and to take political and military action; however, as each year passed, it became more difficult to break the established cycle. This *Cold War metanarrative* permeated every aspect of U.S. foreign policy decisions during those forty-five years.[5] By *metanarrative*, I mean the combined totality of all U.S./Soviet communication interactions during this period. This metanarrative involved the general American cultural perception of the Soviets as bad or evil, as opposed to the United States, which was identified with being good or moral. It is a narrative that is found throughout almost all U.S. government communications about the Soviets—thus, its "meta" nature.

There existed prior to the ending of the Cold War a "contest of force vs. freedom, irrationality vs. rationality, and aggression vs. defense [that permeated] the substance and style of the call-to-arms throughout American history."[6] Cold War rhetoric draws upon this tradition, and presidents were able to construct arguments appealing for public support using the values and cultural myths lived by the American people. Usually, this strategy involved the indirect construction of an image of the enemy through the use of contrasting references: the enemy as "coercive, irrational, and aggressive," attempting to "subjugate a freedom-loving, rational, and pacific victim."[7]

Importantly, those who study this area argue convincingly that the primary strength of Cold War rhetoric *as a policy-making rationale* lay in its "prevailing image of the Soviet threat."[8] This perception of threat allowed the U.S. government to characterize antagonistic states, most notably the Soviet Union, in a certain manner: "The nation's adversary is characterized as a mortal threat to freedom, a germ infecting the body politic, a plague upon the liberty of humankind, and a barbarian intent upon destroying civilization."[9] In short, most Americans *knew* that the Soviets were evil, aggressive, and not genuine. Knowing such, it would be natural for U.S. presidents to suggest policies that took those believed characteristics as a given.

The Cold War metanarrative additionally functioned as a resource for the American public. We can think of the public as a group of persons "united in interests, aspirations, traditions, and experiences."[10] As a public, Americans possess "a fund of truths, principles and values."[11] In a sense, the Cold War metanarrative was part of American collective *public knowledge*, which is the "accumulated wisdom of the people" that "serves as the authoritative ground for political discourse."[12] Particularly in an atmosphere of crisis (and 9/11 certainly qualifies), the public would rely upon this "accumulated knowledge to define the situation."[13] Additionally, the public and its knowledge act to *authorize* policy decisions from those who are acting as representatives for the public—the president, for example. Although case-specific authorization is not always needed for day-to-day activities, many political and military acts occur within a crisis context and thus require authorization, because "authorization is needed when a proposed act or message might seriously affect the well being of others."[14]

However, with the ending of the Cold War, U.S. presidents now find themselves hard-pressed to justify international political and military action—no Cold War metanarrative exists—so to what common knowledge do presidents turn to invent (ground) their arguments? Presidents can no longer simply assume that Americans will agree that a certain course of action is justified just because in the past such action would have been explained (or authorized) by the Cold War metanarrative. Presidents have lost the settled arguments comprising the Cold War metanarrative, so how do they "invent" arguments?

The Bush administration's response to 9/11 certainly needed justification on some level. Americans needed the attacks explained, but also needed the administration's response explained. As it turned out, 9/11 was an event that allowed the Bush White House the opportunity to begin to develop a new metanarrative: the "War on Terror."

Definition of Crisis

Communication researchers who study presidential crises generally view them as *rhetorical constructions*. That is to say, outside of direct military attack, the situation does not create the crisis; instead, the president's *response* to the situation—how he *describes* it—creates our understanding of the situation as a crisis or not. Although the reality-based features of crises are not denied, these researchers argue that the public's understanding of the crisis—its seriousness, its scope, and its impact—is directly affected by what a president says and does. For example, a crisis is generally announced by the president as such, and then an assertion is made that the situation demands that he "act decisively."[15] During this time, the president asks not for debate, but for his response to be supported. So long as the crisis is not one of a military attack upon the United States, it is to be considered a political event "rhetorically created by the president."[16] Be that as it may, the president is not free to say what he pleases when responding to a crisis; his rhetorical options are limited by "precedent, tradition, and expediency."[17] The events of 9/11 were, of course, a terrorist attack. Even though the United States had been attacked, it was not a military assault by another country, so Americans had yet to form their collective interpretation of the event. Just what type of crisis was this, and how should Americans respond?

International crises often appear suddenly, are usually complex, and do not allow easy interpretation by the public. Presidential statements act to create a stable context from which to interpret the crisis. Generally, presidential speeches announcing a crisis "begin with an assertion of the President's control of the facts of the situation and an acknowledgement that the New Facts which occasion the speech constitute a New Situation—a crisis for the United States."[18] Prior to the ending of the Cold War, researchers in the area of crisis communication suggested three basic items distinguishing presidential crisis rhetoric from other types of presidential utterances.[19] First, there was the obligatory statement of facts. Second, there was the establishment of a "melodrama" between good (the United States) and evil (traditionally the Soviets). Third, the policy announced by the president and the asked-for support were framed as moral acts.

Although this structure held true for post–World War II presidents up to President George H. W. Bush, presidents Bill Clinton and George W. Bush have been unable to frame their responses to international crises exactly in this manner due to the ending of the Cold War. The Evil Empire of the Cold War no longer exists; the Cold War metanarrative (which provided reassuring knowledge for Americans) no longer exists. So then, how may a president frame international crisis situations? More specifically, how was President Bush to frame the terrorist attacks of 9/11?

These attacks most certainly represented a grave crisis for the United States, the fact of which the public was well aware. Initially the public needed reassurance that its safety was at hand and that no further attacks were on the near horizon. The public demanded information: What should we do? What happened? There existed an immediacy to the crisis, and the president's first responses on 9/11 sought to answer these concerns. After the initial shock of the attack wore off, the second stage of response to this crisis occurred, involving a greater degree of interpretation on the part of the Bush administration. Just how was the United States to respond to these attacks? Just as importantly, how were these responses to be justified to the American public? In short, how could the Bush administration tap into American public knowledge in a similar manner to Cold War presidents?

During a crisis, the president is not completely free to act in any way he wishes; presidential responses to crises are culturally and historically based. Specific to international crisis, the president must build certain images of the enemy or must make links with the values embedded within American culture and history, if he is to successfully mitigate the crisis. In short, "leader[s] must find the acceptable images of political reality suitable for his/her people."[20] Following 9/11, the

Bush administration, knowingly or not, began laying the framework for a new metanarrative to ground arguments for America's action in the world: the War on Terror.

Crises may be immediate, as with 9/11, or they may slowly evolve, presenting presidents with the opportunity to respond to the budding rhetorical situation.[21] Either way in "clear cases of crisis, the context—and, hence, the [president's] reaction—is less ambiguous. When national interests are not so directly involved, however, the context is more dubious and conflicting perceptions may weaken the public's understanding of the event. In these instances, the public seeks additional guidance."[22] When the public seeks additional information from the president, and it is provided, the overall situation again changes. For with each new round of information disclosures, the amount and primacy of information that constitutes public knowledge change, and with this comes a change in the context through which the public views the crisis. A crisis atmosphere disrupts the usual stability of public knowledge; a state of flux ensues. A crisis, by its very transitional nature, generates new knowledge; it subverts or contests old knowledge about the situation.[23]

It is at this critical juncture that the role of the news media takes on extreme importance to the creation of public knowledge. For in these crisis situations, the president's message is relayed through the interpretive lens of the press; together, president and press act as providers of *preknowledge* (knowledge as yet unassimilated into the public consciousness, not yet formally part of American public knowledge). Eventually, portions of this preknowledge will evolve into public knowledge, while other portions will simply fade away like remnants of a dream. However, the public's perception of the situation and the initial presidential utterances are viewed through the public's initial knowledge held in general: common American historical and cultural knowledge.

With the disappearance of the Cold War metanarrative, however, public knowledge concerning international crisis situations was thrown into flux. The absence of this metanarrative made the rhetorical interpretation and response to crises problematic for both presidents and the public. Americans knew that 9/11 needed a response—but what constituted a *fitting* response? More to the point, following 9/11, how could Americans judge the responses of presidents to crisis situations?

Discovering the answers to these questions is the point of this book. Essentially, I will examine statements made by President Bush about the War on Terror and then compare them to the reports made by the mainstream news media about the president's statements. In this way, we can see how presidential/press utterances contended in their efforts both to offer preknowledge and then to facilitate the change from preknowledge into public knowledge. In the president's case, we see the attempt to develop a new metanarrative to ground arguments for U.S. action in the world.

Looking for Frames

One way to discover how a president and press advance an understanding of any situation is to look for how they *frame* that situation. A "frame is a central organizing idea for making sense of relevant events and suggesting what is at issue."[24] Although facts do remain neutral until framed, they "take on their meaning by being embedded in a frame or story line that organizes them and gives them coherence, selecting certain ones to emphasize while ignoring others."[25] When we frame facts or events in a particular way, we encourage others to see those facts and events in that same particular way. In this sense, framing can be understood as taking some aspects of our reality and making them more easily noticed than other aspects.

Frames have enormous power to shape the way we view certain issues and situations; for example, researchers using mandatory testing for HIV as the issue for their study found that the effect

> of framing is to prime values differentially, establishing the salience of the one or the other. [A] majority of the public supports the rights of persons with AIDS when the issue is framed to accentuate civil liberties considerations—and supports . . . mandatory testing when the issue is framed to accentuate public health considerations.[26]

Another study used a local news story about a Ku Klux Klan march as the controlled frame. Audiences were shown one of two videotaped stories. The first story stressed a *free speech* frame; viewers were presented with a theme that stressed Klan members and protesters wanting to share their respective messages. Quotes shared in the taped stories included a protester with a sign saying "No free speech for racists." Another quote came from a Klan supporter: "I came down here to hear what they have to say and I think I should be able to listen if I want to." Images shown included the chanting of protesters and a

Klan leader speaking into a microphone. Finally, four interviews were presented, three of which were Klan supporters wishing to hear the Klan message. The second story stressed a *disruption of public order* frame. Viewers were presented with a theme that stressed that Klan marches tend to be disorderly and potentially violent. Quotes given included an observer: "Here you have a potential for some real sparks in the crowd." Another quote came from a reporter: "The tension between Klan protesters and supporters came within seconds of violence." Accompanying images included police officers in front of Klan members, protecting them from the crowd. Finally, three interviews were presented, each of which mentioned potential violence and disruption of public order. The results of this study are instructive: "Participants who viewed the free speech story expressed more tolerance for the Klan than those participants who watched the public order story."[27] These studies demonstrate that even on topics requiring serious thought, the power of frames to shape our perceptions of an event or action is great.

Frames are so powerful because they are able to make some information more *salient* than other information; that is, they "highlight some features of reality while omitting others."[28] Unless we are actively looking for it, we rarely notice this process because our public attention is highly selective and often relies solely upon the information the press decides to share with us. That is, we read our local papers and watch the evening news; rarely do we actively seek additional information that might challenge what the press presents to us.

Framing is a process whereby communicators, consciously or unconsciously, act to construct a point of view that encourages the facts of a given situation to be interpreted by others in a particular manner. Frames operate in four key ways: they define problems, diagnose causes, make moral judgments, and suggest remedies. They reside in the communicator, the receiver of the message, and the culture at large. Frames are often found within a narrative account of an issue or event and are generally the central organizing idea. Frames are all around us and are a normal part of the communication process; we need ways to negotiate the massive amounts of information that comes to us every day, and frames provide the interpretive cues for otherwise neutral facts. Large and complex ideas and events need framing since they have so many elements upon which we could focus our attention. Framing analysis can help us to see how we construct interpretations of our environment. Additionally, and central to this book, framing analysis is a particularly useful way to understand the effects the news media have upon our understanding of the world.

Framing and the Media

There is little doubt that the media are able to focus the attention of the public on particular issues merely by giving that issue more attention than another. Consider the 2004 coverage of the Abu Ghraib prison situation. During three weeks of intense front-page coverage and nightly news reports, America was force-fed this event to the exclusion of others. Even other aspects of the U.S. involvement in Iraq were virtually ignored. For instance, how many schools, hospitals, or water-treatment plants were reopened during this time? How many successful counterterrorism operations did the U.S. military conduct? If you were like the overwhelming majority of Americans, you would have no idea, since the news media had focused your attention elsewhere. This process, whereby the news media focus our attention on an issue or event, is called *agenda setting*.

In addition to focusing our attention on a specific issue or event, the media can also focus public attention on particular attributes within that topic.[29] Since a particular facet of the issue would be foremost in the public eye, it seems likely that the public would use that particular attribute to evaluate, for instance, how a politician performs in a certain situation. The public becomes *primed* to evaluate someone—the president, for example—by how well he or she handles the particular issue covered by the press. The more the press covers an issue, the more the public will evaluate *the president's success or failure in relation to the content of media coverage*, as opposed to the actual actions of the president.

By focusing upon one event over another, or upon a particular attribute within an event, the media set an agenda for our attention. Beyond this, though, *how* the media invite us *to think about* a particular event or issue moves beyond setting an agenda. The media are now providing "contextual cues or frames in which to *evaluate* those subjects."[30] If the media continue to focus on an issue, that issue is thrust into the forefront of national thought; it is here that the media-generated context becomes crucially important. *When the media move beyond establishing a neutral context for understanding an event or issue, they move beyond neutral reportorial practices and into the realm of agenda extension.*

By way of example, we saw agenda extension operating during the Watergate hearings, and it began when media gatekeepers decided to publish that particular story.[31] Although deciding what story to tell is the first step in all news reporting, the press takes a second step when determining how much attention to give to the story and for how long.

This is agenda setting. Next, station managers, producers, and editors frame a story by *how they decide to tell that particular story*, and it is here that the notion of agenda extension gains pertinence. In the Watergate example, coverage was first framed in terms of the 1972 election. The nation became obsessed, however, as soon as the media switched frames (agenda extension), moving from the framework of the election to the framework of continual Washington corruption—and a presidency soon crumbled.

A Neutral Press?

I am inclined to believe that most Americans want the news media to provide contextual cues for proper interpretation of events and issues. I also feel that most would believe that when the media place their partisan context over the neutral one needed by the people, an abuse of press privilege has occurred. Traditionally Americans have thought of the mainstream news media in America as being objective sources for the news needed to make informed decisions. Objectivity involves both impartiality and the reflection of the "world as it is, without bias or distortion of any sort."[32] We expect the news to present a true image of the world, even though we know this is an extremely difficult ideal to achieve.

The notion of agenda extension allows us to discover the ways in which the media report outside of the aforementioned norms of reportorial objectivity. When the news media frame an issue or event, they may do so in one of three ways: They can frame it to reflect their view of the world; to reflect what they think their audiences wish to hear; or, as accurately as possible, to impart the meaning of the issue or event by allowing the issue or event to speak for itself. It seems to me that the third represents the best attempt at a fair and responsible press. I would agree with Louis A. Day, who writes that news media outlets should "strive to keep their personal preferences and opinions out of news stories"; they should be "concerned with facts and impartiality in the presentation of those facts."[33] Framing analysis can help us determine if journalists are living up to these standards or are framing the news to impart a meaning in keeping with their own view of the world.

How to Look for Frames and Bias

I think it's safe to say that the news media exercise *enormous* political and social power because they establish the relevance of some issues and events vis-à-vis others. This allows them to control the content and direction of public discussion. Through framing, the central organizing principle of continued news coverage, the news media are able to tell us *how to think about* a particular issue or event. The question now is, how can we use this concept to fruitfully analyze news media products?

Perhaps the easiest way to detect frames is through comparison. Given that "frames reside in the specific properties of the news narrative that encourage those perceiving and thinking about events to develop particular understandings of them,"[34] the differences in frames for similar events should easily be detected. Specifically, framing elements reside in the press narrative accounts of events; they consist of key words, metaphors, concepts, symbols, and visual images. They consistently appear within a narrative and "convey thematically consonant meanings across . . . time."[35] Once the framing process is set in motion by the interaction of sources and journalists, the established frame guides the thinking of both audience and journalist. This type of frame is called *event-specific* since it was a frame generated in response to a specific event. Once in place, event-specific schema—frames—encourage journalists to "perceive, process, and report all further information about the event in ways supporting the basic interpretation encoded in the schema."[36]

By way of example, one study comparatively analyzed the narratives within news stories about two commercial jets, KAL (Korean Airlines) 007 and Iran Air 655, both shot down by military forces in separate incidents.[37] In 1983, Soviet fighter jets shot down the Korean passenger airliner, which had flown into Soviet airspace, and in 1988 the USS *Vincennes*, while operating in the Persian Gulf, shot down an Iranian airliner. This study used news items appearing in *Time, Newsweek, CBS Evening News,* the *Washington Post,* and the *New York Times.* During the two-week period following the KAL 007 shootdown, the *New York Times* printed 286 stories and the *Washington Post* printed 169. During a similar two-week period following the shootdown of Iran Air 655, the *New York Times* printed 102 stories and the *Washington Post* 82. In terms of agenda setting, the volume of coverage helped to determine the importance of the event. What frames were generated, though? The destruction of KAL 007 was framed as a moral outrage, whereas the downing of Iran Air 655 was framed as a technical problem.

These findings demonstrate how frames impose a specific interpretation onto events. They often obscure contrary information that may be presented in a particular case: "for those stories in which a single frame thoroughly pervades the text, stray contrary opinions . . . are likely to possess such low salience as to be of little practical use to most audience members."[38] For the KAL and Iran Air shootdowns, this meant that it was perfectly acceptable for political elites to describe the KAL shootdown as a brutal attack; however, it was much less likely for them to describe it in terms of a tragedy because the established frame prevented that: the Soviets were evil and at fault. To think of the shootdown in terms of tragedy would have run against the frame. In stark contrast, the Iran Air 655 shootdown was framed as a technical glitch. To call it other than an accident or tragedy, or to suggest that U.S. Gulf policy was at fault, would have run counter to the established frame.

When examining the news media, a comparative analysis is performed by examining the primary event and the subsequent press coverage of that event; for example, examine a speech given by President Bush and then examine the press reports that follow about that speech. By looking at how the president framed the issue or event in his speech, and then looking at how the press framed the same issue or event, one may easily detect differences in frames and thus see how the press might be inserting bias into the news. For example, in *Presidential Crisis Rhetoric and the Press in a Post–Cold War World*, I examined the contending frames of the Clinton administration and the printed press when discussing crisis situations in North Korea, Bosnia, and Haiti.[39] Specifically, I sought to discover how the Clinton administration framed the situations and how the press framed the situations as a response to the administration's statements. I examined news stories and editorials printed in the *Washington Post* and the *New York Times* during a ten-day period following each of the administration's public statements concerning the above crises.

In order to discover frames, I began by analyzing the administration's statements for narratives; next I specifically looked for various framing devices that could have been used by the Clinton administration: key words, metaphors, and concepts.[40] Having accomplished this, I repeated the analysis on the news stories and editorials. Three questions guided my investigation: (1) How did the Clinton administration frame the crisis situations in Haiti, North Korea, and Bosnia? (2) When responding to the Clinton administration, how did the press frame the respective situations? (3) Did the frames of the president and the press ever coalesce to present a unified contextual whole? I reasoned that unless the reader had firsthand access to transcripts of the Clinton administration's utterances, all public knowledge about the crises was filtered through the frame of the press. However, I also found that while the *content* of presidential messages was being reported, the *context* in which the messages were originally uttered often was not conveyed. In this manner the administration was not treated as a news source, providing informative utterances about the situation, but rather it was forced into an oppositional role to that of the press.

For example, during the North Korean situation, the press framed the crisis in a manner that highlighted the potential drama of a North Korean withdrawal from the nuclear nonproliferation treaty, while the Clinton administration framed the crisis in a manner that stressed calm negotiation and the budding reconciliation of North and South Korea. For another example, in 1995 President Clinton declared he would send 20,000 U.S. troops to Bosnia for peacekeeping missions; the press was predisposed to accept his decision to send troops.[41] Because of this, perhaps the most important frame the administration advanced—that the mission was acceptable to the American people and relatively risk free—was actually adopted in whole by the press. Such was not the case in other areas, however. For instance, I found that the press framed the issue of congressional support for the mission differently than the Clinton administration framed it. According to the press, the Republican-controlled Congress was openly hostile and partisan in its deliberations. This frame was so well structured that it made contrary opinions, such as President Clinton's, irrelevant. At a time when calm deliberation and consensus were extremely important for the U.S. government to project, the press was advancing a contradictory impression of the continuing discussion between Congress and the White House over U.S. involvement in Bosnia. In this instance, then, *the press was intentionally miscommunicating the direct assertions of the President of the United States.*

In yet another example of oppositional framing, consider that when President Clinton took office in 1993, the country was threatened with a flood of Haitian refugees. Prior to taking office, Clinton had promised fleeing Haitians political asylum, but after taking office, and seeing a massive humanitarian tragedy in the making, he instead continued his predecessor President Bush's policy of repatriation on the high seas. Eventually this turned into a yearlong crisis for the Clinton administration. I found that the press framed the situation as a domestic issue, while the administration framed it as a foreign policy issue. The Clinton White House was stressing a foreign policy that had as its focus the return of democracy to Haiti and the aversion of a massive humanitarian tragedy. The press frame, however, stressed a domestic focus that highlighted its perception of an "inhumane" administrative policy of returning all Haitian boat people to Haiti. Although the press did report what the administration said, the *context* surrounding statements made by the administration was modified by the frame of the press. Not restoration of Haitian democracy, but rather the domestic U.S. legal issue of the administration's policy became the press focus. In such a setting, the administration was presented not as a source of news, but as one side of a partisan battle with the press. This oppositional framing by the press is widespread; in other projects, I found that the press advanced its own interpretation of events over that of the speaker if that speaker's comments went against press-supported positions.[42]

The words chosen by a news reporter reveal the way that reporter categorizes the subject on which he or she is reporting.[43] In this sense, word choice often "signifies the presence of a particular frame."[44] One other important aspect of framing involves how the press uses labels or names. Some researchers cite the descriptions of Saddam Hussein given by American reporters during the first Gulf War. Hussein was described as the "Iraqi dictator," a description that placed him in the same category, in the minds of Americans, as Hitler, Mao, Stalin, and other loathsome totalitarians. Contrast this with describing him as the "Iraqi leader," "Iraqi president," or "Iraqi commander-in-chief." From this example, we can see that the lexical choices made within the various frames (names used to describe an individual), act to frame the news story in such a manner that a dominant reading is suggested. Similarly, consider the American press descriptions of Yugoslavian president Slobodan Milošević given during the NATO bombing of Serbia. He was described as an "evil dictator, " "a cruel and determined enemy," and "a brutal dictator" to name only three. Frequent comparisons were made with Hitler as well: "Adolf Hitler had a 'final solution.' Slobodan Milošević has 'ethnic cleansing.' Each leader's term gives a brilliant, if not positive, spin to his massacres."[45] If the press described Milošević as the "Yugoslavian leader," "Yugoslavian president," or "Yugoslavian commander-in-chief," considerations about Milošević's legitimacy would have been quite different.[46]

In the next chapter, the speeches given by President Bush immediately following 9/11 will be examined, along with the press coverage of those speeches. In each of chapters 3 through 7, at least one major speech by the president is examined, again with the press coverage of that speech. The idea is to look for themes about 9/11 and the War on Terror that the president used, and then to look at what themes the

press used when reporting on what the president said.[47] The idea behind this is that themes can provide a "measure of the presence of
frames."[48] After identifying themes, I will describe how those themes
are framed. Through this comparative analysis, we can detect differences in the frames presented to the American people and determine
the nature of any press bias. Except in chapter 2, the major networks
covered are ABC, CBS, and NBC. The major newspapers covered include the *New York Times*, *USA Today*, and the *Washington Post*.

2

A New Justification for War?

Following the 9/11 terrorist attacks, Americans desperately needed information so they could comprehend and respond appropriately to the horrendous event thrust upon them. This was a direct attack upon the United States, so President Bush had no need to convince the public of the necessity of a response. He did, however, have three tasks before him: he had to prevent panic, guide the emotional responses of Americans, and guide the development of America's interpretation of the attack.

The president spoke to Americans three times on September 11, 2001 (his Emma Booker Elementary School comments, the Barksdale Air Force Base comments later that day, and his address to the nation that evening), and twice on September 12 (his comments during a Pentagon visit and remarks at a photo opportunity with his national security team). Collectively, these statements laid the groundwork for the administration's initial framing of the 9/11 attacks.

As mentioned in chapter 1, with end of the Cold War, America's role in the world entered a state of flux and also made the job of justifying foreign policy action more difficult for U.S. presidents. The events of 9/11 exacerbated this situation, immediately creating a new situation in which America's public knowledge about how to act in the world was all but destroyed. With this context in mind, I examine in this chapter both the Bush administration's public response to the 9/11 tragedy and the news media's role in reinterpreting and conveying that response to the American people.

In this chapter we see how the Bush administration, combined with the reporting of the mainstream media, created a unique combination of elements that formed a *stable preknowledge*. In the present case, the initial press reaction to President Bush was generally supportive and rather accurately relayed his statements to the American public. Accordingly, the frames and themes used by the president were relayed to Americans by the press; because of this, the Bush administration was able to create a stable contextual frame through which information-hungry Americans could view both the 9/11 crisis and future administration responses. The press and the president repeatedly provided the same facts and, more or less, the same interpretation of those facts, so Americans were allowed a period of relative stability regarding how they interpreted events surrounding 9/11.

Americans and the press often exhibit a "rally 'round the president" attitude in times of crisis, although since the ending of the Cold War this practice is increasingly infrequent and short lived. It is very likely that President Bush was in part supported initially due to the extreme shock of the events on 9/11. Consider, too, that many in the mainstream press call New York City home; it is likely that they felt some need to look for help as well. Nevertheless, both the press and the American public were knocked hard out of a sense of safety by 9/11; the combined president-press coherent response aided Americans during these crucial first weeks.

The immediate emotional impact of the attacks upon the American psyche should not be overlooked. Entire generations of Americans had never experienced a major war, much less an attack on U.S. soil; the attacks pushed Americans into new emotional territory. Graphic images were repeatedly seen on television and in print, searing them into the collective consciousness of Americans who were hour by hour increasingly wondering about their safety: were more attacks lurking around the corner? This combined emotional and physical setting forms the background of the rhetorical situation in which President Bush and the press were to act.

9/11 created a completely new category of events—foreign terror attacks on U.S. soil—and on this issue, Americans had no set sense concerning proper response. Usually, when presidents frame a foreign policy crisis, it is "a crisis that does not involve an external military attack on the United States" and can be viewed as "a political event rhetorically created by the President."[1] But 9/11 *was* an attack, so from this perspective it could seem that the president would not have as much latitude in framing the crisis (certainly it is a given that the president had little control over the facts that surrounded the attacks). However, there existed so much confusion, growing outrage, and desire for unity that the president was able to frame the facts surrounding 9/11 to initially rally the pubic to support his actions. Although at the outset the president and press had to respond to the immediate concerns of the American public, once the situation had stabilized, the 9/11 attacks gave the president and the press a unique opportunity to begin the creation of a new metanarrative and reshape public knowledge concerning America's role in the world.

In his speeches of September 11 and 12, President Bush introduced a number of themes that he would further develop into major frames during the months and years that followed. These themes provided the press, and therefore the American public, with the beginnings of a larger frame through which to understand, discuss, and respond to the events of 9/11: the War on Terror. Through repetition of the themes in almost all of his major addresses between September 11 and October 6, Bush effected a stable frame through which he could contextualize and interpret new events related to 9/11. Eventually, the frame the president used would develop into a master frame and attempt a transformation into a new metanarrative.[2] The press initially supported President Bush and helped to relay accurately his words to the American public. Although this chapter shows that at first the press accurately imparted the meaning of the president's speeches to Americans, the chapters that follow reveal an increasingly oppositional press, one set on countering presidential statements.[3]

The President Speaks

President Bush's earliest remarks at 9:30 A.M. on the morning of 9/11 were little more than an attempt to reassure the nation that the government was aware of the situation and that proper action would be taken. Asserting that the government was mobilizing, the president said that he had "spoken to the Vice President, to the Governor of New York, to the Director of the FBI" and promised that the government would aid those affected by the attacks with the "full resources of the federal government [going] to help the victims and their families."[4] These remarks acted to assure the public that their government was fully aware of the crisis and its consequences and was currently working to address the situation. As more details about the attacks emerged later in the day, Bush was able to speak from a better informed position. This allowed him to send a more reassuring message, in which he emphasized the strength of the government. On the evening of the 11th, the president told the nation that "the functions of our government continue without interruption" and that "federal agencies . . . will be open for business tomorrow. Our financial institutions remain strong, and the American economy will be open for business as well."[5] The implication, business-as-usual, was also heard operating the next day when he said that the "Federal government and all our agencies are conducting business."[6] Hearing this, the public was invited to believe that its government was strong, resilient, and working to protect the American people.

The president's central message of encouragement to the American people was that they would be effectively protected from more terror attacks, so panic was not an appropriate response to the 9/11 attacks. Bush repeatedly emphasized the role of the government in protecting Americans: "We have taken all appropriate security precautions to protect the American people. . . . We will do whatever is necessary to protect America and Americans,"[7] and our "first priority is to . . . protect our citizens at home . . . from further attacks."[8] The government was not only portrayed as actively working to protect Americans from future attacks but also as aiding those affected by the acts of terror committed on 9/11. The president wanted "to reassure the American people that the full resources of the federal government are working to assist . . . to save lives and help victims"[9] and told them that "our emergency teams are working in New York City and Washington, D.C. to help with local rescue efforts."[10] With these messages, President Bush helped Americans start to believe that they were being protected from future attacks and that those most affected by the attacks would be helped.

Additionally, Bush both acknowledged and sympathized with the public's emotional reaction to the attacks. He characterized this emotional response as "disbelief, terrible sadness, and a quiet, unyielding anger" and explained that the "acts . . . were intended to frighten our nation into chaos and retreat." He urged the public to avoid responding with fear and described the "terrible sadness" of Americans in such a way that it could be transferred into an "unyielding anger." America and its people would persevere because they would not panic and escalate the "chaos."[11]

Although it was natural in this crisis atmosphere for the president to work to avert panic and to be sensitive to the emotional impact of the attacks, he also needed to establish a frame through which to view both the attacks and America's new enemy. Given the unique nature of 9/11, the public had little experience upon which to draw. Its public knowledge was lacking, so the president had to characterize the attacks for them. The framing of the attacks clearly progressed through the president's first speeches, moving from a "national tragedy," to considerably more severe characterizations.[12] By late afternoon of the 12th, the characterization was set:

> Coming here [to the Pentagon] makes me sad, on the one hand; it also makes me angry. Our country will, however, not be cowed by terrorists, by people who don't share the same values we share, by people who are willing to destroy people's lives because we embrace freedom. The nation mourns, but our government will go on, the country will function. We are on high alert for possible activity.[13]

On the night of 9/11, Bush indicated that the response to the attacks would be considered a "war on terrorism,"[14] and by the following morning, the attacks were to be understood in a particularly expansive way. Whereas simple terrorist attacks would necessitate a police response, the president framed the 9/11 attacks as "more than acts of terror. They were acts of war."[15] Furthermore, this war involved finding "those responsible and to bring[ing] them to justice."[16] In terms of the scope of the war, the president stated that "we will make no distinction between the terrorists who committed these acts and those who harbor them."[17] In this way, then, 9/11 was now framed not as isolated terrorist acts but as the first strike in a war against "freedom and democracy."[18] The president explained that America would "go forward to defend all that is good and just in our world," against a powerful, determined, and as yet undefined enemy.[19]

Calling upon imagery deeply embedded within American public knowledge, President Bush advised the nation that this was going to be a war of "good versus evil."[20] Within this context, he began to characterize the nature of America's new and unfamiliar enemy. These terrorists were not a cohesive, identifiable nation openly declaring war on the country, but rather an unseen and unknown force with vague objectives. Thus, we see that in his first addresses on 9/11, the attacks were described as "cowardly acts" and the perpetrators were "folks."[21] Quickly thereafter, the attacks were characterized as "evil, despicable acts"[22] and the attackers as an enemy that "preys on innocent and unsuspecting people, then runs for cover."[23] The refining of the image of the enemy moved from "cowardly acts" executed by "folks" to "acts of war" committed by an enemy who "hides in shadows, and has no regard for human life."[24] Thus, within a 48-hour period, we see the emergence of several themes and the ever refined framing of those themes. Taken together, they represent the first steps toward the formation of the administration's master frame: the War on Terror.

The Press Response

The initial press response facilitated the Bush administration's effort to create the impression that a strong government still protected Americans. In this sense, the press relayed and contextualized the president's message accurately to the public. CBS News stated early in the day on 9/11 that "the first order of business here is to protect yourself against further attack."[25] Along with CBS, other networks emphasized the president's contention that America was strong and its government was properly responsive, usually paraphrasing or employing the president's own words to impart the message of reassurance. For example, NBC News quoted President Bush as saying, "I am sending to Congress a request for emergency funding, so that we are prepared to spend whatever it takes."[26] CBS News highlighted the fact that the president was "promising the full resources of the federal government to . . . help the victims."[27] The *New York Times* also quoted the president: "Our country is strong. Terrorist acts can shake the foundation of our biggest buildings, but they cannot touch the foundation of America."[28]

In addition to supplying numerous quotes and paraphrases, the press also emphasized the significance of the president addressing the nation from the Oval Office. By stressing the symbolic significance of Bush's address on the evening of 9/11, the press added to the president's message of strength and preparedness. According to ABC News, it was "wise for the president to be back at the center of power, showing the world that there was no fear and intimidation."[29] NBC News noted that it was "important to address this nation, on this night, from the Oval Office, the symbol of power and presidential authority."[30] The instant shift in presidential style was not lost on the *Washington Post*:

> For his first eight months in office, President Bush preferred an understated, sometimes subdued style. That presidency ended yesterday. Standing behind his desk in the Oval Office, a strikingly combative and emotional Bush vowed to lead the nation and an allied coalition to victory over . . . terrorists. . . . The moment was part of a sharp pivot Bush has made since Tuesday's attacks from emphasizing

an America "open for business" to portraying himself as commander in chief for what will likely be a long struggle.[31]

Although the press essentially upheld President Bush's framing of the attacks as evil done against freedom and democracy, it was of two minds concerning the adoption of a frame of full-scale war. By September 13, the *Washington Post* editorially wrote:

> President Bush and key members of his administration have begun to articulate some clear principles in response to the unprecedented assault by terrorists on the United States. Yesterday Mr. Bush said the attacks were not just incidents of terrorism but "acts of war" and promised in response a "battle that will take time and resolve." These are the right foundations for what should be the national security policy of an America at war.[32]

The *New York Times* quoted President Bush as he established the frame of good against evil: "today our nation saw evil, the very worst of human nature."[33] NBC News noted this same characterization and pointed out that "the president cast this tonight as a battle between good and evil . . . using the word 'evil' several times."[34] However, the press hesitated to characterize the acts as the initiation of a war. This was one of very few themes the media openly questioned, almost to the point of opposition. Fox News pointed out that the implications of treating those who harbor the enemy the same as those who committed the attacks were far reaching: "[If] this turns out to be Osama bin Laden, [the United States] would also strike at the government of Afghanistan, at the Taliban, for harboring him. And that is . . . much more controversial and a little more dangerous."[35] NBC News also responded to the "harboring" statement made by the president: "The president . . . promised that we would seek out and attack, not just the terrorists, but any nation that harbored them as well. That is—and I'm not belittling what he had to say here—but that is easier said than done."[36]

The President and Press:
September 14 and into Afghanistan

Initially, then, the press questioned the wisdom of the president's attempt to define the war as broadly as he did. Be that as it may, the press did embrace the president's framing on September 14, the National

Day of Prayer and Remembrance. On this day, the president made two major addresses, one at the National Cathedral in Washington, D.C., and the other at "ground zero," the site of the World Trade Center rubble in New York City. That evening, Fox News shifted from hesitancy to support, declaring, "President Bush has emerged today fully as a serious and credible war president. . . . He's getting inspiring."[37] The *New York Times* also bestowed editorial support:

> Mr. Bush has managed to reach out in ways both symbolic and practical. . . . After a shaky start, his speech Friday at the National Cathedral struck the note of somber confidence that the nation was looking for. . . . If in the past he reflected the country's more Manhattan-phobic side, his ability to transcend those feelings represented his ability to unite. . . . By his actions . . . Mr. Bush has won the first battle of the war.[38]

Since the end of the Cold War, the press has assumed an increasingly oppositional role to the president in foreign affairs.[39] Given this trend, what was it that the president did that allowed the press to generally adopt the framing he used after 9/11? For the most part the president simply expanded upon the themes he used on the 11th and 12th: reassurance, allowing for emotional responses, characterization of the attacks as war, and describing the enemy as evil.

President Bush continued to convey a message of reassurance when he said that American grief provided the solidarity with which Americans could face the challenge ahead: "You are not alone," the president told surviving family members. "Today we express our nation's sorrow. . . . We feel . . . the warm courage of national unity. . . . American flags . . . are displayed in pride, and wave in defiance. . . . Our unity is a kinship of grief."[40] Recalling the victims of 9/11, Bush also spoke to the collective American emotional reaction and gently took the nation's hand in this moment of grief: "We will linger over them, and learn their stories, and many Americans will weep." Our "unity is . . . a resolve to prevail against our enemies." Bush expressed the spiritual dimension of the tragedy as well; inviting the public to look to God for guidance, he stated: "God's signs are not always the ones we look for. . . . We learn in tragedy that his purposes are not always our own. . . . Yet the prayers . . . are known and heard, and understood."[41] At Ground Zero he extended his previous remarks: "America is on bended knee in prayer for the people whose lives were lost here."[42]

With the introduction of religion, Bush provided the public with not only a means to process its grief but also a stronger context through which to understand his earlier comments about a war against evil: "Our responsibility is already clear . . . to rid the world of evil. In every generation, the world has produced enemies of human freedom. They have attacked America, because we are freedom's home and de-fender."[43] The president continued to drive home the idea that the United States represented freedom and the enemy represented "stealth and deceit and murder."[44] Of these comments, the *Washington Post* reported that the president had used religious themes, but also that there was concern about that usage:

> President Bush stepped to the lectern . . . last week and promised a packed house of 3,000 people to "answer these attacks" on the Pentagon and World Trade Center and "rid the world of evil." The language was the rhetoric of war, and the speech came . . . from a sacred spot before the altar of a church. That has some religious leaders and scholars wondering whether the president went too far in . . . mixing patriotism with religion to stir up support for military action.[45]

For the press, however, the president's actions were equally as important as his words. For instance, Fox News highlighted a moment when Bush "went to New York City and grabbed that bullhorn and was there with the rescue workers while they're chanting, 'U-S-A!'—I think at that moment, he kind of started defining himself as a president we're all going to rally behind."[46] This Ground Zero moment was a turning point for the press. For example, NBC News reported that the president, in a seemingly impromptu speech at the World Trade Center site, "was able to throw his arms around New York firefighters and New York rescue workers" inspiring cheering and chanting of "U-S-A!" from the crowd.[47] Other networks repeatedly evoked this image of the president speaking "through a bullhorn to the hard hats there clearing out the debris and looking for those who may be alive,"[48] and "raising his thumb to a group of firefighters . . . still working to clear the debris . . . mouth[ing] the words 'I appreciate you.'"[49]

From this point until the commencement of military strikes into Afghanistan, there was little press hesitancy when bringing war rhetoric into reports. In but three days, according to NBC News, President Bush had established himself as "the chief executive, the commander in chief, America's minister, the patriarch, the healer."[50] Additionally, the press imparted to Bush a sense of being a war president through its complimentary framing and generally positive support following the president's addresses on the National Day of Prayer and Remembrance. Be that as it may, it was not uncritical support, as this *New York Times* editorial demonstrates:

> Franklin D. Roosevelt . . . understood the power of words and put them to effective use as [he] rallied America . . . during the bleakest hours of World War II. President Bush, who is waging a different kind of war, must also find the right rhetoric to lead the United States and a coalition of diverse nations in this unconventional battle. Inflating expectations, and shifting tone from day to day, will not serve Mr. Bush or the nation well.[51]

Even though reserved, the press followed Bush's lead in framing the public's conceptualization of the 9/11 terrorist attacks and their aftermath. The president was being looked to more as a source of news than of controversy.

This is not to say that the press was uncritical of administration proposals for dealing with the aftermath of 9/11. The press did present concerns politicians and policy analysts raised about proposed actions in the wake of 9/11. For instance, the *New York Times* wrote, "The Bush administration's plan to rewrite immigration and surveillance laws after last week's terrorist attacks drew new criticism today from both the left and the right after a detailed analysis showed the plan would also create sweeping federal powers to gather evidence and share it within the government."[52]

Maureen Dowd, after failing to resist the puerile temptation to insult the president by writing "Last spring, when the president was letting Dick Cheney run the country," also wrote that on *Meet the Press* "the vice president conceded that the unspeakable air attack had caught the government by surprise, even though 'there had been information coming in that a big operation was planned.'" She then expressed concern that the government had been "so clueless." Dowd continued, decrying the administration's work on missile defense:

> This week, when Bush diplomats should have been riveted on the hard work of building an alliance against terrorism, [a U.S. envoy] went to Moscow to insist that the reluctant Russians come around on missile defense. As long as they cling so tenaciously to their cold-war theology, it will be hard for the Bush crowd to engender the trust we need outside the country and accomplish the radical revamping we need inside.[53]

In terms of changes to both international and domestic information gathering, the *New York Times* editorially wrote:

> The rush has already begun to "unshackle" the Central Intelligence Agency and its fellow spy agencies so that they can better combat terrorism. Some easing of restrictions may be warranted in light of last week's terrorist attacks. . . . But any changes must be carefully weighed by the Bush administration and Congress. The temptation will be great to take steps, including loosening limitations on domestic spying, that could end up compromising important democratic principles without yielding any tangible gain in the fight against terrorism.[54]

The Washington Post ran a story titled "Anti-Terror Push Stirs Fears for Liberties; Rights Groups Unite To Seek Safeguards." The article described how a "coalition of public interest groups from across the political spectrum has formed to try to stop Congress and the Bush administration from rushing to enact counterterrorism measures before considering their effect on" the privacy and civil rights of Americans.[55]

President Bush's address to Congress on September 20 continued the development of his administration's War on Terror frame; at the same time, it further characterized the enemy and better defined the nature of the war ahead. For the first time, too, Bush definitively stated that Osama bin Laden was the man behind the attacks: "Who attacked this country? The evidence we have gathered all points to a collection of loosely affiliated terrorist organizations known as al Qaeda . . . and its leader—a person named Osama bin Laden." The president noted carefully, however, that this named enemy represented "a fringe form of Islamic extremism" and did not represent all "Muslims throughout the world." He continued, "We respect your faith . . . its teachings are good and peaceful, and those who commit evil in the name of Allah blaspheme the name of Allah."[56]

In further clarifying the image of America's new enemy, Bush stated that "al Qaeda is to terror what the mafia is to crime" and employed a historical analogy to connect this unique enemy to enemies of the past: "They are the heirs of all the murderous ideologies of the 20th century. . . . [and] they follow in the path of fascism, and Nazism, and totalitarianism." Although linking the new enemy with the past, the president made clear that this was a different kind of enemy than Americans had seen before—"There are thousands of these terrorists in more than 60 countries"—and that war tactics would be unlike those previously employed: "How will we fight and win this war? Americans should not expect one battle, but a lengthy campaign, unlike any other we have ever seen. It may include dramatic strikes, visible on TV, and covert operations, secret even in success. We will starve terrorists of funding . . . drive them from place to place."[57]

The reporting by the press matched the frame used by the president well; seemingly the press supported President Bush in his continued characterization of the enemy, and it extensively quoted his remarks concerning the distinction between Muslims and the Muslim terrorists. *Good Morning America* summed up the president's congressional speech when the host stated: "President Bush was clear in defining who our enemies are and who they are not . . . he kind of defined what the war is going to look like . . . something different that we've never seen before."[58]

Press expression of concern was not lacking, however. Howard Kurtz of the *Washington Post*, for instance, looked well ahead when he wrote: "As the administration gears up for what President Bush has described as a new kind of war, many journalists are growing concerned that they will have less information and less access to U.S. troops than ever before. Even the use of deliberate disinformation cannot be ruled out."[59] Speaking specifically of the looming campaign in Afghanistan, the *New York Times* reported:

> It will not be like the gulf war, made to order for America's massive bombing, tank and helicopter attacks. And the economic and industrial might that helped carry the United States to victory in two world wars, while still a strength, is also, as the suicide airline hijackers showed, a vulnerability. It's true that the president has a number of options at his disposal, but all are fraught with uncertainty.[60]

Throughout the weeks following the 9/11 attacks, President Bush not only reassured Americans but also developed an increasingly nuanced master frame through which to understand the post-9/11 world in which America found itself: the War on Terror. Within that master frame, he developed a clear conception of the 9/11 attacks as acts of war and a clear characterization of the enemy as evil. Importantly, a strong correlation existed between how the president framed the events and how the press reported the news of those same events. For example, the *New York Times* editorially stated: "The issue is not whether the United States should respond forcefully and decisively to these murderous assaults. With some 6,000 civilians feared lost in the attack on the World Trade Center, America has every right to strike back against its assailants, wherever they may be." The editorial went on to discuss the nature of the proposed actions, ending with this statement: "America is fighting a new kind of war against a new kind of enemy. Military means alone will not assure success."[61]

The War on Terror frame ultimately acted to prepare the nation for a long war that commenced with U.S. strikes against Afghanistan on October 6, 2001. Even so, the press continued to advance contrary voices, indicating that the strength of the administration's War on Terror master frame was not so strong that voices critical went unheard. The *Washington Post* published several stories along these lines, including "The Solitary Vote Of Barbara Lee; Congresswoman Against Use of Force"and "Proposed Anti-Terrorism Laws Draw Tough Questions; Lawmakers Express Concerns to Ashcroft, Other Justice Officials About Threat to Civil Liberties."[62] And although the press would share praise, it was often grudgingly given, as this example from Tom Shales, commenting on the president's speech to Congress, demonstrated: "Considering his limitations as a public speaker, Bush accomplished what was presumably his main goal, reassurance—reassuring the American people that the country is safe, that action will be taken against the perpetrators, and that he is firmly in command of the situation."[63] Generally speaking, however, by October 6, the president's explanation for war was received and accepted by the American public and the press:

> On my orders, the United States military has begun strikes against al Qaeda terrorist training camps and military installations of the Taliban regime in Afghanistan.
>
> This military action is a part of our campaign against terrorism, another front in a war that has already been joined through diplomacy, intelligence, the freezing of financial assets and the arrests of known terrorists. . . . Given the nature and reach of our enemies, we will win this conflict by the patient accumulation of successes, by meeting a series of challenges with determination and will and purpose.
>
> Today we focus on Afghanistan, but the battle is broader. Every nation has a choice to make. In this conflict, there is no neutral ground. If any government sponsors outlaws and killers of innocents, they have become outlaws and murderers themselves.
>
> The battle is now joined on many fronts. We will not waver; we will not tire; we will not falter; and we will not fail. Peace and freedom will prevail.[64]

Summary of President and Press Interaction

The Public's Knowledge

This section is actually a summary of chapters 1 and 2. My idea here is to provide the context through which to view the remaining chapters in this book. In chapter 1, I discussed the concept of *public knowledge*. The public is able to make decisions about and make sense of public messages based upon the knowledge, ideas, and values its members possess and hold in common. Public knowledge is therefore more than the latest news stories we receive from broadcast or print news; it also consists of the shared values, doctrines, and beliefs that characterize a culture. Communication scholar Lloyd Bitzer described public knowledge as the

> principles of public life to which we submit as conditions of living to-
> gether; shared interests and aspirations; values which embody our
> common goals and virtues; our constitution, laws and rules; defini-
> tions and conceptual systems; truths expressed in literatures of po-
> etry, criticism, philosophy, aesthetics, politics, and science; the
> accumulated wisdom proffered by our cultural pasts. . . . This con-
> ception of public knowledge very nearly coincides with what Michael
> Polanyi names "superior knowledge." He writes . . . , "Only a small
> fragment of his own culture is directly visible to any of its adherents.
> Large parts of it are altogether buried in books, paintings, musical
> scores, etc., which remain mostly unread, unseen, unperformed. The
> messages of these records live, even in the minds of those informed
> about them, only in their awareness of having access to them and of
> being able to evoke their voices and understand them."[65]

Understood in its fullness, it is public knowledge that allows members of a public to make sense of a given message; in our case, those messages about 9/11 coming from the Bush administration and the press.

Also in chapter 1, I discussed the concept of *framing*. I am of the opinion that metanarratives (certainly the Cold War metanarrative) are well-assimilated, expansive *master frames* that the president, press, and American public all use; moreover, these metanarratives reside in our public knowledge.[66] The Cold War metanarrative is a classic example of this. In order to generate support for their policies, presidents and other politicians of that period would draw upon the shared public knowledge Americans possessed about the Soviet Union (and commu-nism in general). As a result, any interaction between Soviets and

Americans was framed so that the established Cold War metanarrative remained in place and supported the more specific frame used in the given circumstances. In one sense, the Cold War metanarrative was a larger-than-life frame so dominating that its roots in American patriotism and anticommunism had been deeply assimilated into the American pool of public knowledge.

The American response to the 9/11 attacks also shows how public knowledge is related to framing. President Bush and the press drew on public knowledge to frame the 9/11 crisis. Since this was an unprecedented event, parallels to experiences with which Americans were familiar (public knowledge) had to be drawn. For instance, in his address to Congress on September 20, 2001, Bush described the attackers thus: "We have seen their kind before. They are the heirs of all the murderous ideologies of the 20th century . . . they follow in the path of fascism, and Nazism, and totalitarianism. And they will follow that path all the way, to where it ends: in history's unmarked grave of discarded lies."[67] The president here touched upon thinking deeply ingrained in American public knowledge—disdain for America's historical enemies—and linked it to the current crisis. An additional example occurred when he invoked the American reverence for freedom: "America was targeted for attack because we're the brightest beacon for freedom and opportunity in the world."[68]

The initial framing attempts of the Bush administration take on new meaning when the terrorist enemy is depicted as set on destroying not just Americans but also a special part of American public knowledge—freedom and opportunity. Additionally, the press was initially part of the process of developing a new frame through the use of existing public knowledge. CBS News, for instance, made the following point: "This is certainly comparable to Pearl Harbor and the death toll is going to be much higher, and when we rally international support behind us, we have always prevailed."[69] The *New York Times* also used the Pearl Harbor touchstone embedded within American public knowledge. Drawing parallels between father and son, the paper reported: "'In every generation, the world has produced enemies of human freedom,' the president said, glancing at his father, a fighter pilot in the Pacific in World War II and a symbol of another generation's heroic battles."[70]

When looking at the 9/11 responses of president and press, I see that framing functions through its use of public knowledge. Additionally, far from being a static body of information, public knowledge is a dynamic, interanimated grouping of ideas. President Bush and the press drew connections between 9/11 and past attacks, but did so within a context of the values that put the United States under attack; in so doing, they formed a new set of beliefs that combined current events with deeply held convictions. In this sense, then, we see public knowledge deployed to create more public knowledge.[71]

Preknowledge

President Bush's speeches not only drew upon public knowledge but also acted to create a frame through which America's impending War on Terror could be understood. It became clear through press conferences, news reports, and presidential speeches that there exist certain recurring themes that the public is supposed to assimilate. However, following so closely upon the crisis, the themes and general information had yet to be assimilated into public knowledge, although the public was being constantly exposed to new information about the crisis and America's response. One way of understanding the situation is to consider this mass of new information a type of *preknowledge*, a term coined by Marilyn Young and Michael Launer, who wrote:

> Intense media coverage provides new and often discrepant information, shaping public perception, adding to the rhetorical mix and contributing to the dynamism of public knowledge. The result is a mass of detail that overlaps, affects, and perhaps introduces *incremental changes* to public knowledge but is not yet a part of it . . . this information may be termed "pre-knowledge."[72]

This function of producing incremental change is what is crucial about preknowledge; it is a middle ground between the news stories or other information to which Americans are constantly exposed and the information that finally makes it into their collective and more permanent public knowledge.

Another crucial facet of preknowledge is that, because it reflects—in our present case—a whirlwind of media reports and administrative documents, it is usually disorganized, fragmented, and at times conflicting. How the public sorts everything out is in part answered by how the information is framed. Although there is very likely some intermediate level of values and knowledge imparted to and attributed to the public, in the case of crises, this situation differs. With regard to 9/11, the information coming from the Bush administration and conveyed by the press was not consistently fragmented and contradictory. Instead, the press relayed accurately the initial framing of the administration and seemed to support the president's actions. I am inclined to believe that this is in part due to the unprecedented nature of the attacks, which triggered a short-lived and "mild rally 'round the president" attitude in the press; the press was in agreement with or unwilling to directly attack the president in a time of crisis.

These differences above are explained if one modifies the concept of preknowledge. Essentially Bush created, and the media facilitated the creation of, *stable preknowledge* concerning the state of the knowledge surrounding the attacks of 9/11. The president and press agreed on the content that needed to be conveyed. There seemed to be a stable body of knowledge/values that the public was receiving, yet because of the unprecedented and unexpected nature of the events that created it, this body of knowledge was malleable, unlike public knowledge which has taken on some degree of consistency and permanency. Viewed in this manner, the notion of a stable preknowledge provides an intermediate stage between preknowledge and public knowledge.

Metanarrative/Master Frame

Additionally, when viewing the interaction of the press and president, one can detect the development of a nascent metanarrative/master frame. Far from being a simple frame through which to view the immediate responses to 9/11, this nascent metanarrative—the War on Terror—presented common themes that were solidified among both the administration and the press. Clear distinctions were drawn between who was good and who was evil; who were the lovers of freedom and who embraced tyranny; who were civilized and who were barbaric. Although there was a distinct harmony of voice between the president and the press, the period covered in this chapter is simply too short to call this *stable preknowledge* a master frame, and it is certainly not a metanarrative. And as a hint to the content of upcoming chapters, one should view the rhetorical consensus skeptically and perhaps think of the stable preknowledge emerging from this period as a sprouting seed that hopes to grow into the master frame or metanarrative of the War on Terror.

Public Knowledge and Framing

The aftermath of 9/11 demonstrated a distinct relationship between public knowledge and the framing process. The way speakers draw upon public knowledge to construct a specific interpretation of events, and then apply that interpretation to a current situation, is the framing process. Furthermore, the interanimation between current events and public knowledge creates new knowledge that can be assimilated into public knowledge. This assimilation is not immediate, however, but occurs over long periods of time—years. The short-term effects of current events and their lingering memories are seen in an unstable, shifting preknowledge. In times of immediate and extreme crisis, though, preknowledge may take the form of a stable preknowledge.

9/11 created a unique rhetorical situation. The shock that followed gave the president a public and press willing to listen to and follow the message he conveyed. The message presented in the weeks that followed was one in which the president drew heavily upon America's shared public knowledge. The constant and consistent press coverage of the messages of the administration acted to create a preknowledge that, rather than being fragmented and contradictory, seemed more or less unified. This contributed to the development of a frame through which to view 9/11, its aftermath, and future actions of the administration: the War on Terror. Whether or not the term *war on terror* blooms into a useful tool for presidents to create and manage future crises will be investigated in the chapters that follow.

3

President Bush Speaks to the United Nations, November 2001

> We did not ask for this mission, yet there is honor in history's call. We have a chance to write the story of our times, a story of courage defeating cruelty and light overcoming darkness. This calling is worthy of any life, and worthy of every nation. So let us go forward, confident, determined, and unafraid.
>
> —George W. Bush

> Bush wants patience, but are the American People willing to wait?
>
> —*This Week*

> Johnson wanted to teach the Vietcong a lesson, but in the end it was the American people who were forced, to their sorrow, to learn a new way of looking at the world. We can't shake those memories.
>
> —*New York Times*

The President's Speech

World leaders waited anxiously for President Bush's speech to the United Nations on November 10, 2001. The military action against the Taliban in Afghanistan had been largely successful, even though

Osama bin Laden remained at large. The world and the American public needed to know what future actions to expect from the Bush administration during its War on Terror.

The president's speech addressed these concerns and also continued his development of the War on Terror frame. The obvious purpose of this speech was to discuss the situation in Afghanistan, since the invasion was in some sense the official beginning of America's War on Terror; as President Bush stated, "The time for sympathy has now passed; the time for action has now arrived."[1] This speech also touched upon America's recovery from 9/11:

> Time is passing. Yet, for the United States of America, there will be no forgetting September the 11th. We will remember every rescuer who died in honor. We will remember every family that lives in grief. We will remember the fire and ash, the last phone calls, the funerals of the children.

Essentially this speech offered nothing new concerning *how* the administration was framing the War on Terror; its importance lay instead in offering the world an increasing sense of refinement of the meaning of the War on Terror. We still see the themes discussed in chapter 2: good versus evil, civilization versus barbarism, working with other nations, freedom versus tyranny, the nature of the enemy, and the nature of the war.

Good vs. Evil, Civilized vs. Barbaric, and Working with Other Nations

One area the president clarified involved working with other nations. The War on Terror was to be a international effort spanning the globe. Commingled with this idea of international cooperation was the theme of civilization versus barbarism. The United States would work with the civilized portions of the world to eradicate terrorists and the barbarism which the terrorists exemplify:

> The United Nations was founded in this cause. In a second world war, we learned there is no isolation from evil. We affirmed that some crimes are so terrible they offend humanity, itself. And we resolved that the aggressions and ambitions of the wicked must be opposed early, decisively, and collectively, before they threaten us all. That evil has returned, and that cause is renewed.

Not just the United States, then, but civilization itself was called upon to fight this new war:

> We're asking for a comprehensive commitment to this fight. We must unite in opposing all terrorists, not just some of them. In this world there are good causes and bad causes, and we may disagree on where the line is drawn. Yet, there is no such thing as a good terrorist. No national aspiration, no remembered wrong can ever justify the deliberate murder of the innocent. Any government that rejects this principle, trying to pick and choose its terrorist friends, will know the consequences.

Expanding upon the meaning of the War on Terror, and foreshadowing his concept of preemptive strike, the president said: "Every civilized nation here today is resolved to keep the most basic commitment of civilization: We will defend ourselves and our future against terror and lawless violence." Moreover, he noted, the "civilized world" was responding already to the attacks, acting to defend itself against this new enemy, and delivering its "children from a future of fear." Bush stated his belief that those acting against terrorism were choosing "the dignity of life over a culture of death." He added that civilized nations "choose lawful change and civil disagreement over coercion, subversion, and chaos. These commitments—hope and order, law and life—unite people across cultures and continents. Upon these commitments depend all peace and progress. For these commitments, we are determined to fight."

Freedom vs. Tyranny

Another theme closely related to those above is freedom versus tyranny: "There is a current in history and it runs toward freedom. Our enemies resent it and dismiss it, but the dreams of mankind are defined by liberty." As civilization fights for freedom, it will be on the side of good in the struggle:

> We did not ask for this mission, yet there is honor in history's call. We have a chance to write the story of our times, a story of courage defeating cruelty and light overcoming darkness. This calling is worthy of any life, and worthy of every nation. So let us go forward, confident, determined, and unafraid.

The Nature of the Enemy and the War

Perhaps the most difficult theme touched upon by the president involved the nature of the new enemy. Here Bush acted to further strengthen America's conception of its terrorist enemy, but this also allowed the world know how America was to officially conceive of its opponents in the War on Terror. The enemy were those "hateful groups that exploit poverty and despair. . . . [They] hate not our policies, but our existence; the tolerance of openness and creative culture that defines us."

Although Americans were not ignorant of the general existence of terrorists or their methods, they had never truly experienced foreign-sponsored terrorism so intimately as on 9/11. Certainly the Oklahoma City bombing had had an effect, but, framed as a police matter, it involved disenchanted Americans acting against their own government. 9/11 presented a new type of enemy, one that would require new action against it. Because of this, President Bush needed to define the nature of this unknown enemy well:

> The terrorists call their cause holy, yet, they fund it with drug dealing; they encourage murder and suicide in the name of a great faith that forbids both. They dare to ask God's blessing as they set out to kill innocent men, women and children. But the God of Isaac and Ishmael would never answer such a prayer. And a murderer is not a martyr; he is just a murderer.

Foreshadowing the nature of the new war, and contemplating Americans' dawning realization of the nature of the enemy, President Bush stated: "And the people of my country will remember those who have plotted against us. We are learning their names. We are coming to know their faces. There is no corner of the Earth distant or dark enough to protect them. However long it takes, their hour of justice will come." In defining the nature of the terrorists, the president spoke not only to Americans but also enjoined the civilized world to accept the face he was putting on the new enemy: "Every nation has a stake in this cause. As we meet, the terrorists are planning more murder—perhaps in my country, or perhaps in yours. They kill because they aspire to dominate."

The overwhelming danger of the terrorists was well stressed:

> They seek to overthrow governments and destabilize entire regions. Every other country is a potential target. And all the world faces the

most horrifying prospect of all: These same terrorists are searching for weapons of mass destruction, the tools to turn their hatred into holocaust. They can be expected to use chemical, biological and nuclear weapons the moment they are capable of doing so. No hint of conscience would prevent it.

The very seriousness of this possibility acts as a hint at preemption:

For every regime that sponsors terror, there is a price to be paid. And it will be paid. The allies of terror are equally guilty of murder and equally accountable to justice. The Taliban are now learning this lesson—that regime and the terrorists who support it are now virtually indistinguishable.

Speaking again to civilization, the president declared:

We did not ask for this mission, yet there is honor in history's call. We have a chance to write the story of our times, a story of courage defeating cruelty and light overcoming darkness. This calling is worthy of any life, and worthy of every nation. So let us go forward, confident, determined, and unafraid.

The Press Response

Considering the above, together with what we saw in chapter 2, the Bush administration was notably consistent with both the themes it addressed and the framing of those themes; however, the previously observed press tendency to echo the president deteriorated during this time. There are considerably fewer direct quotations of the president and his administration, and increasingly more press commentary and redirection of focus. Although the press was still supportive of the president's efforts, following his speech it began to show signs of departing from previously established reportorial themes and frames. In a sense, we see a continued discussion of the president/press frames discovered in chapter 2, yet at the same time, we see the weakening of the bond of those frames, as well as the introduction by the press of new themes. The majority of press reports touched upon six major themes, some of which were framed in opposition to the White House frames.[2] I discuss each of the six themes and their framing below. The six themes are the nature of the War on Terror; World War II and Vietnam; patience; the nature of the enemy; international effort; and the question of war or police action.

Nature of the War on Terror

Although the War on Terror was a "national crisis,"[3] the White House also called together an international alliance. The *Early Show,* for example, stated that the president had "met with dozens of other leaders seeking support for the alliance against terrorism."[4] The *New York Times* noted that "state and local law enforcement officials" had found themselves forced onto the front lines of a global war on terrorism.[5] *CBS Morning News* described a "nation swept by both patriotism and fear."[6] The *Washington Post* stressed that "the war on terrorism touches all of our lives in one way or another, whether it be something simple like the inconvenience of dealing with increased security checks at work or the fear of the unknown facing armed forces personnel in Afghanistan."[7]

Echoing the administration, the *Washington Post* editorially stated:

> Even after the Taliban is gone, the war against terrorism will continue. The challenge is for people to continue ordinary life in the face of this threat. "That is the ultimate repudiation of terrorism," President Bush said. . . . But how will the world cope with a terrorism problem that may get worse rather than better for the next few years? Part of the answer . . . will lie in aggressive military actions that make the terrorists pay a severe price for their assaults. And they should be coupled with new diplomatic and economic initiatives that offer a better life for ordinary people in the Muslim world.[8]

Also expanding upon the international dimension, *This Week* said that President Bush was "talking tough to the world community . . . [with] a very solemn, very direct speech . . . yesterday in which he ratcheted up the pressure on world leaders to crack down on terrorists."[9] And pointing out the negative international dimension, the *Saturday Early Show* stated that Bush concluded "his speech saying 'the only alternative to victory in the war against terrorism is a nightmare world where every city is a potential killing field.'"[10]

Others acknowledged the administration's claim that the war was different than any other. For example, *CBS Sunday Morning News* observed that "the front lines seem to . . . coil around the world."[11] That the war would be unconventional and lengthy was acknowledged by the *Washington Post* when it editorialized that the White House "has said all along that the war on terrorism must be conducted on a number of fronts simultaneously. [Defeating] terrorism will require a . . . bold and creative commitment to long-term political change [in the Middle East]."[12] The

New York Times reported that Americans felt the administration "had effectively prepared them for a lengthy and unconventional conflict and had stirred enough patriotic fervor to build substantial support for its efforts."[13] The *Washington Post* also ran an opinion piece by Senator John McCain, in which he wrote: "America is at war, which should mean that parochial agendas are set aside for the national goal of destroying terrorism. [The] administration has stated that the war against terrorism will be protracted and will require significantly more funding for defense."[14] Editorially the *Washington Post* stated that the "real lesson is that the United States has embarked on a long, complex struggle against terrorists operating under the banner of Islamic fundamentalism who are determined to do this country grave harm."[15]

World War II and Vietnam

Demonstrating the human tendency to put the unfamiliar into familiar terms, the press asked whether the War on Terror should be framed in the same terms as World War II or Vietnam. Here, the press was actively beginning to contest the framing of the theme of the nature of the war. For instance, Cokie Roberts on *This Week* asked outright: Is the War on Terror "Vietnam or is it World War II?" After receiving an answer from George Will, who put Americans' views of war into a wider historical perspective, Roberts redirected the question: "Let's [come] back to more modern times because George raised this question of the goals becoming unclear in Vietnam. Are the goals clear here? Do you think that people know what we're after in this war, and does that make a difference?" This question came shortly after Roberts had announced the results of a recent Gallup poll showing that with regard to "the current war on terrorism: 89 percent say they have a clear idea of what this war is about. That compares with only 49 percent in Vietnam."[16]

In exploring World War II analogies, the press ran numerous stories on the recent White House overtures to Hollywood. The purpose was to find out "how the entertainment industry can contribute to the war effort, replicating in spirit if not in scope the partnership formed between filmmakers and war planners in the 1940s."[17] Additionally, the press considered whether or not Americans should feel at home with a World War II mindset: "Food rationing, tin foil drives, victory gardens. . . . Now debate has been rising over exactly how much sacrifice is really needed and how those at home should respond to what Mr. Bush calls 'a different kind of conflict.'"[18]

The discussion was wide ranging, and the *New York Times* stated that it was "less clear how people can respond at home to the conflict that may be more akin to the cold war [than to World War II]."[19] Sacrifice was the answer in World War II, and according to President Bush, sacrifice comes today not through food rationing but through volunteerism. Here the *New York Times* shared the understanding of the Bush administration: "Americans willing to volunteer now were . . . making a sacrifice. 'They are taking time away from their family and their profession.'"[20]

Taking a decidedly negative view of the World War II analogy, Richard Cohen of the *Washington Post* stated flippantly that the "impetus to make the present situation the rough equivalent of World War II has already led the Bush administration to embark on a clutch of programs lacking only the Andrews Sisters for chirpy accompaniment." Given this position, I found it interesting that Cohen chose to use an analogy with Vietnam when he stated that the "declaration of war against all terrorism anywhere is becoming a liability. It's a laudable aim but one that's clearly beyond us. It may well involve us in a quagmire not unlike the one in Vietnam and obfuscate our war aims—once again, as happened in Vietnam."[21]

Presaging Cohen's comments about Vietnam, the *New York Times* editorially stated that "we assure ourselves that this conflict is . . . different from the one we carried out [in Vietnam]. Yet Vietnam's ghosts are still here. They do not tell us that our current fight is less than just or necessary. But they steal away the old certainty that the end will inevitably be triumphant." Implying that President Bush might lie about the war, the paper made a lengthy analogy with Lyndon Johnson's handling of the Vietnam War. This included a "reminder of what can happen when a president lies to the people for what he believes is their own good." The paper continued: "Johnson wanted to teach the Vietcong a lesson, but in the end it was the American people who were forced, to their sorrow, to learn a new way of looking at the world. We can't shake those memories."[22]

Patience

The issue of patience, periodically stressed by the Bush administration, was one which also caught the eye of the press. Generally speaking, the press relayed this call. For instance, *World News Now* briefly mentioned Vice President Dick Cheney's words at Arlington National Cemetery, saying that he "promised victory in the war on terror, but cautions it may not happen quickly."[23] The press, however, defined patience in such a manner that it seemed but a small and dwindling fund from which Americans could draw: "In a sign of potential trouble for the administration, many of those interviewed made it clear that their patience was not endless, and that they had become somewhat more questioning of the government line in recent weeks."[24] What makes for patience? As one person put it, "I think it's easy to be patient . . . when there aren't casualties of war."[25] Another press-generated reason given for the eroding sense of patience was the government's need for secrecy: "Americans would tolerate a degree of secrecy about the war if they sensed it was being waged competently. 'But the government has not effectively gotten across that they are competently handling it on every front.'"[26]

At the time of President Bush's speech to the United Nations, 9/11 was a living memory eight weeks old, and the campaign in Afghanistan was just picking up; success on the ground had recently occurred with the capture of Mazar-i-Sharif in northern Afghanistan. The press, though, raised the issue of the patience of the American people concerning the War on Terror. For example, during the introduction to *This Week*, Bush was shown stating, "Patience. Patience. Patience." Cohost Cokie Roberts followed with: "Bush wants patience, but are the American people willing to wait?" The answer, based on the interviews of Americans shown, seemed to be a weak yes, although that was followed by this follow-up question: "But how long will that last with no signs of a swift victory?"[27]

The press made certain that the conception Americans took away from the news was that no swift victory in either the War on Terror or the war in Afghanistan was forthcoming, while at the same time Americans were shown as losing patience. For example, the *New York Times* insisted "much hard fighting remains before the Taliban can be ousted from power nationwide."[28] One *New York Times* headline read: "Patience, for Now, With Flow of Information." Highlighting the mood of the public, as expressed by several opinion polls and its own interviews, the *Times* stated that those interviewed believed the White House "had effectively prepared them for a lengthy and unconventional conflict and had stirred enough patriotic fervor to build substantial support for its efforts." However, the article also highlighted this: "[In] a sign of potential trouble for the administration, many of those interviewed made it clear that their patience was not endless, and that they had become somewhat more questioning of the government line in recent weeks." Summing up what may well have been the newspaper's own point of view, the story ended with a quote from a political scientist who said that the Bush administration and Congress were "being given a great deal of leeway because people are so stunned by this confrontation . . . they feel that we have to somehow suspend our questioning and our critical eye. But that honeymoon . . . is not going to last."[29]

Striking a solitary and different tone, the *Washington Post* editorialized that the eight weeks since 9/11 had "been barely enough time to recognize all the challenges that face the country, much less come to grips with them. America is still finding its way."[30] Three days later, the same paper, speaking about the war in Afghanistan, highlighted the nature of the press view of the passage of time. Roughly four weeks after the bombing of Afghanistan began and following the fall of Mazar-i-Sharif, the *Post* stated that initially, when military bombing commenced,

> many commentators assumed a quick victory and chose to debate which target President Bush should move to next. . . . [When] the first three weeks of military action brought few visible results . . . a new consensus began to gel: U.S. policy was failing. . . . There's a lesson in all of this. . . . [America] has embarked on a long, complex struggle against terrorists . . . who are determined to do this country grave harm. The struggle is more difficult now because [America] has often cut and run rather than stay and fight.[31]

This fight, according to the editors, was to be conducted with both "urgency" and "patience," the combination of which "poses a continuing challenge."[32]

Nature of the Enemy

Although Americans had heard of terrorist acts before 9/11, such acts were always outside of immediate experience, always something involving some other nation. Those terrorists were not disgruntled citizens, nor were they enemy combatants. They were a vague and shadowy danger that lurked in someone else's backyard. With 9/11, the Bush administration made a consistent effort to educate Americans concerning the nature of their new enemy. This theme of the nature of the enemy was again hammered home in Bush's UN speech, and the press picked up on this theme. Highlighting the nebulous nature of the enemy, the *New York Times* quoted a criminologist who said, "We know there's an enemy but we're not exactly sure who they are, we don't exactly know how to find them, and we don't exactly know how to defeat them."[33]

In better defining the nature of the enemy, *NBC Nightly News* showed President Bush saying: "The suffering of September 11th was inflicted on people of many faiths and many nations. All of the victims, including Muslims, were killed with equal indifference and equal satisfaction by the terrorist leaders." The follow-up by the news report stressed that the president "warned if bin Laden and al-Qaeda acquire weapons of mass destruction, they will use them, arguing the future of civilization itself is threatened."[34] The *Saturday Early Show* also brought up the assertion that the terrorists would have no compunction about using nuclear devices, stating that the president had "made it clear . . . that bin Laden has made absolutely no attempt to hide the fact that he has been trying to acquire such weapons."[35] The following day, on *Face the Nation*, Secretary of Defense Donald Rumsfeld was asked a question that allowed him to reply: "There is no doubt in my mind but that [terrorists] would use chemical, biological, radiation . . . or nuclear weapons if they have them. . . . [They] don't worry about the loss of life."[36] The *Early Show* played a clip of President Bush calling the terrorists "the evil ones" and saying that "the terrorists are planning more murder."[37]

The *Washington Post* also relayed the White House framing of the terrorists, stressing that the president had returned "repeatedly" to that "theme" since 9/11: "Bush said that bin Laden and . . . al Qaeda . . . are 'violating the tenets of every religion,' including Islam. 'A murderer is not a martyr,' Bush said, 'he is just a murderer.'"[38] A separate article carried more of the president's words: "'Every nation has a stake in this cause,' Bush said. 'Last week, anticipating this meeting of the General Assembly, they denounced the United Nations. They called our secretary general a criminal and condemned all Arab nations here as traitors to Islam.'"[39] In subsequent days in the *Post*, William Raspberry described the terrorists as a "small but influential cadre of Muslim extremists . . . bent not just on installing Islamic theocracies in those countries where Muslims are in the majority but also on crippling and eventually destroying the Great Satan—us,"[40] and Richard Holbrooke linked the nature of the enemy to the operations in Afghanistan when he opined that if the United States had done nothing in Afghanistan, that country "would continue to be used as a sanctuary to foment terror and hatred throughout the world."[41]

International Effort

In general, the press framed the initial War on Terror in part as an international effort. Following President Bush's speech to the United Nations, this frame remained, but considering that the speech was given at the UN and asked strongly for continued international support, the numbers of reports that relayed this frame—thirteen—was limited.

For example, *NBC Nightly News* highlighted the fact that the president had asked that "all the UN nations . . . take action against terrorists."[42] To this sentiment, *Saturday Today* added that the president's focus in his speech was one of "strengthening the international coalition."[43] *CBS Evening News* reported the president's meeting with Pakistan's President Musharraf and summed it up by saying that Bush had "called for broad-based unity in the fighting against terrorism" and had declared that Pakistan's "efforts against terror are benefiting the entire world."[44]

Emphasizing the diplomatic nature of the coalition, the *Early Show* reported that since 9/11, the president had "met with dozens of other leaders seeking support for the alliance against terrorism." Additionally, it said, the Bush administration had "signaled that some are not cooperating as much as it had hoped. In his first address to the UN General Assembly, Mr. Bush declared the war is not only America's battle. 'Every nation has a stake in this cause.'"[45] Stressing the importance of international aid, a *USA Today* article noted, "To pursue its war, the United States has set up a worldwide coalition."[46] The *Washington Post* observed that although it is a "worldwide war on terrorism,"[47] what the president had put together was an "unwieldy coalition."[48]

A War or a Police Action?

Following President Bush's speech, the framing of the nature of the war *as a war* began to be called into question. Some in the press continued along with the old frame. For instance, *Saturday Today* used the phrase "to fight this war" and the *Saturday Early Show* called it a "fight against terrorism."[49] *World News This Morning* spoke of the "war on terror," while *CBS Evening News* spoke of "the war on terrorism" as did the *New York Times*, the *Washington Post*, and *USA Today*.[50] The use of these descriptions is but a continuation of both the terms and the framing of those terms by the Bush administration.

What is of note is the press development of an oppositional frame, in this case, contesting the definition the nature of the war and thus an important component of the meaning of the War on Terror. This was initiated by recharacterizing the War on Terror not as an active war but rather as a police action. This reframing began to develop after the president's executive order authorizing military tribunals for noncitizen combatants. For instance, Jim Wallis wrote in the *Washington Post* that the only goal for the United States was to bring terrorists to "justice." According to him, one must work in a manner conducive to "nonviolence" by returning "to the path of restraint" that was seen in the first several weeks after 9/11:

> The most effective and morally defensible strategy . . . would be one focused clearly on feeding starving people, bringing terrorists to justice and utilizing the rule of law and international forces. Our focus should be on . . . intensifying worldwide police and intelligence activity and using international law to convict, isolate and discredit the terrorists—and then carefully targeting search and capture operations to find and stop them.[51]

USA Today carried a front-page article claiming that "Bush's order [on military tribunals] is a signal that the next battlefield in the war on terrorism will be the courtroom [over the policy]."[52] The *Washington Post* declared that President Bush's executive order on military tribunals would actually "undermine the rule of law" and that "the government [had] come down . . . decisively on the anti-liberty side." In short, the editors said, "domestic security [had] clash[ed] with traditional American reverence for civil liberties."[53] Essentially saying that all nations use terrorism as a tactic, Uri Avnery wrote in *USA Today* that "terrorism is always a political instrument [and] the right way to combat it is always political."[54]

Summary

Due to repetition and refinement over time, the initial themes used by President Bush to describe the War on Terror have now taken on the nature of frames. The War on Terror is now composed of five semidistinct, yet interanimated, frames:

1. good versus evil
2. freedom versus tyranny
3. civilization versus barbarism

4. the nature of the new enemy
5. the nature of the war

Each complements the other, and each acts to better flesh out the meaning of the larger frame, the War on Terror. Note that I wrote "the larger frame." The War on Terror is a complex frame composed of the individual themes mentioned above, and each of those themes, during this time period, are in the process of being framed in a particular way. Whereas good/evil, freedom/tyranny, and civilization/barbarism were framed similarly by president and press, the nature of the war and the nature of the new enemy frames were being contested by the press. Thus, eight weeks after 9/11, the larger frame of the War on Terror had both settled and unsettled meanings attached to it. Whereas for the Bush administration it was a master frame, for the press it was simply a term resonating with numerous themes and meanings.

In some ways, the settled meanings remain because the press simply ignored them. For instance, rarely brought into play were the moral dimensions advanced by the president. The theme of good/evil, for instance, was all but ignored in press accounts of the president's speech or actions. A notable exception occurred when *Good Morning America* relayed the fact that Bush had "signed a memorial wall with the message that 'Good will triumph over evil' when he visited Ground Zero."[55] Although the president repeatedly stressed this and other morally related themes, the media chose to focus on other themes: the nature of the war, the nature of the enemy, analogies between the war on Terror and World War II or Vietnam, patience, and the international aspect of the War on Terror. In this sense, the press was attempting to introduce new themes, with their own frames in place, into the larger frame of the War on Terror. Additionally, by not reporting fully on how the president characterized the War on Terror—that is, morally—the press failed to allow the larger American public the opportunity to accept or reject that claim.

Although no one frame within the larger War on Terror frame dominated, we do see the development of press opposition to the framing of the nature-of-the-war theme. For example, whereas in chapter 2 we saw that the press generally relayed the frames advanced by the Bush administration with little oppositional framing (that is, they tended to report what the president said with little interpretive commentary), in this chapter we see this neutral reportorial practice break down in favor of a strong undercurrent of opposition.

In particular we see the press, within the theme of the nature of the war, intentionally framing a negative point of view about the actions of the administration. These press-generated interpretations pushed beyond what was being said in general about the War on Terror. The *New York Times* provided the clearest example of this, and one area of complaint involved the amount of information flowing from the government to the public. In justifying its demand for more information, the *New York Times* stated that the problem the United States was having with its European allies was due to a "post Vietnam patriotic syndrome." In short, public information was allegedly being "co-opted by the government, or at least swept up by patriotism." According to the *Times*'s Elizabeth Becker, this had caused a "public relations problem" with the Europeans, who as a result felt "they have precious little information they can trust." Alarmingly, Becker made a dangerous and inaccurate analogy to justify her point of view: Because of the situation, Europeans had to "rely on conflicting and equally unverifiable claims from Pentagon briefings and Taliban news conferences, and are increasingly unwilling to believe either side."[56] To equate the Pentagon with the Taliban is, charitably put, an instance of negative framing.

This same article soundly criticized the Bush administration for imposing a "tight lid on sensitive military news, particularly about special operations." Becker stressed that "veteran communicators" with wartime experience were "amazed at the limited" access to information and to the battlefields. Secretary of Defense Rumsfeld was described as a hypocrite who "officially" endorsed the "Persian Gulf war guidelines for new media coverage of combat" but then "enforced policies ensuring that journalists have little or no access to independent information about military strategies, successes, and failures." Then, completely disregarding the press access granted during the first Gulf War, the story line turned to Vietnam: "The desire to keep information and expectations at a minimum stems directly from the experience of the Vietnam war."[57]

In another instance of negatively characterizing the nature of the war, the *New York Times* predicted that "much hard fighting remains before the Taliban can be ousted from power nationwide." Downplaying the major accomplishment the capture of Mazar-i-Sharif represented, the *Times* wrote claimed that with "winter approaching . . . it may be some time before a victory in Mazar-I-Sharif can be translated into the goals the White House has set for Afghanistan, including the capture of Osama bin Laden."[58] In a different editorial, the *Times* again negatively characterized the military action in Afghanistan, making another comparison to Vietnam: "Vietnam's ghosts are still here. [They] steal away our certainty that the end will be triumphant. [The] current fight will be long and frustrating."[59]

In some ways, we see the press reframing the theme of the nature of the enemy. No longer does the Bush administration's frame, exemplified by the quotes below, hold:

- The terrorists kill "with equal indifference and equal satisfaction."
- The terrorists violate "the tenets of every religion, including the one they invoke."
- The terrorists have "exacting standards of brutality and oppression."
- The terrorists are the "authors of mass murder."

While the press *was* relaying, and to some extent echoing, the Bush administration's framing, it was also in the process of reframing the nature-of-the-enemy theme. The enemy, the press seemed to be saying, was no longer limited to terrorists but was also beginning to include the administration. For example, speaking editorially, the *New York Times* scathingly asserted that American civil "liberties are eroding, and there is no evidence that the reason is anything more profound than fear and frustration." Although the editors provided no evidence for their assertions, they boldly proclaimed that "Attorney General John Ashcroft has been careless with the Constitution when it comes to the treatment of people arrested in the wake of Sept. 11." Additionally, the editors noted that there is only a "limited need for secrecy while investigating domestic terrorism" and that detention of suspected terrorists constituted "extreme measures."[60]

Corresponding with the paper's editorial slant on the administration's efforts concerning military tribunals for non-American terrorists, the *New York Times* stated: "The Bush administration has moved swiftly in the last few weeks to expand its national security authority and law enforcement powers in ways that are intended to bypass Congress and the courts, officials and outside analysts say."[61] On this point, the *Washington Post* agreed: "Few predicted that the government would come down so decisively on the anti-liberty side. . . . [This is a] potentially irreversible injury at home if Mr. Bush proceeds . . . to undermine the rule of law."[62]

4

The State of the Union, 29 January 2002

As we gather tonight . . . the civilized world faces unprecedented dangers.

—George W. Bush

[President Bush said that] deficits are needed for now to
fight the war on terrorism, protect the homeland and boost
the economy. But, Bush promised, the return to deficit
spending will be "small and short-term." Don't believe that
for a moment . . . the deficits will be big and will last for
nearly a decade. Only by resorting to accounting gimmicks
that would make Enron blush can Bush claim otherwise.

—*USA Today*

A State of the Union address involves certain generic obligations that
presidents must observe. For example, presidents who wish to give a
speech that fits the occasion must focus on issues that are important to
Americans, must tap into the values Americans hold in common, and
must give specific policy recommendations. Given that it fell approximately four and a half months after 9/11, it comes as no surprise that
the ongoing War on Terror would be a large component of President
George W. Bush's 2002 State of the Union address. Additionally, given
the president's earlier calls for Americans to maintain their daily rou-
tines, it would be expected that the president would discuss the domestic concerns of Americans. The president touched on all of these
ideas when he laid out the basic outline of his speech: "As we gather

tonight, our nation is at war, our economy is in recession, and the civilized world faces unprecedented dangers, yet the state of our union has never been stronger."[1]

President Bush's speech met the generic obligations and also acted to extend and strengthen the frames his administration was forming about the War on Terror. Once one separates out the generic elements and the comments about domestic budgetary issues, what remains are the War on Terror themes (and the framing of those themes) seen during the previous four and a half months. According to the president, the time for emotional concerns was past: "Our nation has comforted the victims, begun to rebuild New York and the Pentagon. . . . For many Americans, these four months have brought sorrow and pain that will never completely go away." However, the "cause is just, and it continues." In some ways, the president was moving Americans from an emotional response to a "new ethic and new creed: 'Let's roll.'"

Just what this new ethic entailed is explained below. First, we will look at the continuation of the themes and frames advanced by the Bush administration, and then we will look at the adjustments made to those frames. Finally, we will see how the press responded to the State of the Union address.[2]

The President's Speech

One obvious point made by the president was that, for the foreseeable future, the budget and the prosecution of the War on Terror would be firmly linked: "Our first priority must always be the security of our nation, and that will be reflected in the budget I send to Congress. My budget supports three great goals for America: We will win this war; we'll protect our homeland; and we will revive our economy." The president then touched upon these three areas in his speech. Intertwined with his plans are the War on Terror themes he and his administration had developed over the previous few months; additionally, the framing of those themes was further refined. Two-thirds of the speech concerned the War on Terror, and it is with that portion of the speech the following paragraphs are concerned.

Good vs. Evil and Civilized vs. Barbaric

The president portrayed a "good" America who would "lead by defending liberty and justice because they are right and true and unchanging for all people everywhere." Leadership goes hand in hand with sacrifice, he said, and both capitalize on volunteerism; specifically, the president stated, through the USA Freedom Corps and the Peace Corps, the world would capitalize on the gathered "momentum of million of acts of service and decency and kindness [and] overcome evil with greater good." President Bush also pointed out that Americans, through common 9/11 experiences, have "come to know truths that we will never question: evil is real, and it must be opposed." He highlighted the importance of his view that the struggle was for civilization over barbarity with the opening words of his address: "As we gather tonight . . . the civilized world faces unprecedented dangers." Although not specifically calling America civilized, the message was clear: America is cut of a different cloth from the enemy; for example, he noted America's use of "expensive precision weapons [to] defeat the enemy and spare innocent lives." In deep contrast, "America's enemies . . . are evil," and indiscriminately murder men, women, and children.

Freedom vs. Tyranny

Freedom was linked with America's purpose and new course of action: "Steadfast in our purpose, we now press on. We have known freedom's price. We have shown freedoms' power. And in this great conflict . . . we will see freedom's victory." Moreover, the United States and its allies "will demonstrate that the forces of terror cannot stop the momentum of freedom." The president depicted the United States and its allies as agents of freedom: "History has called America and our allies to action, and it is both our responsibility and our privilege to fight freedom's fight."

Nature of the War

Little was said about the nature of the new war, although the president did state that America's "war on terror is only beginning." Moreover, this new war had the "entire world as a battlefield. . . . Thousands of dangerous killers, schooled in the methods of murder, often supported by outlaw regimes, are now spread throughout the world like ticking time bombs, set to go off without warning." Bush repeated that the War on Terror was something just begun: the "campaign may not be finished on our watch—yet it must be and it will be waged on our watch. We can't stop short. If we stop now . . . our sense of security would be false and temporary." And thus the war, as was seen in chapter 3, was one demanding patience: "Our nation will continue to be steadfast and patient and persistent in the pursuit [of this war]."

Nature of the New Enemy

The nature of the enemy was again made clear in strong, descriptive language: these "terrorist parasites . . . laugh about the loss of innocent life." The "depth of their hatred is equaled by the madness of the destruction they design." However, the framing of the enemy was expanded in an important manner in this speech; no longer simple terrorists, the enemy now *clearly* included the regimes that sponsor terrorists. For example, North Korea was portrayed as "arming with missiles and weapons of mass destruction, while starving its citizens. Iran aggressively pursues these weapons and exports terror. . . . Iraq continues to flaunt its hostility toward America and support terror. The Iraqi regime has plotted to develop anthrax, and nerve gas, and nuclear weapons for over a decade." Importantly, although the president mentioned only these three countries by name, he left open the possibility of others when he proclaimed:

> *States like these*, and their terrorist allies, constitute an axis of evil, arming to threaten the peace of the world. By seeking weapons of mass destruction, these regimes pose a grave and growing danger. They could provide these arms to terrorists, giving them the means to match their hatred. They could attack our allies or attempt to blackmail the United States. In any of these cases, the price of indifference would be catastrophic.[3]

Working with Other Nations: An International Coalition

In several places in the speech, the president touched upon the intended international scope of the War on Terror: "My hope is that all nations will heed our call. . . . Many nations are acting forcefully. We will work closely with our coalition." The president's most concentrated effort at describing the international nature of the coalition came toward the end of his speech:

> [A] common danger is erasing old rivalries. America is working with Russia and China and India, in ways we have never before, to achieve peace and prosperity. In every region, free markets and free trade and free societies are proving their power to lift lives. Together with

friends and allies from Europe to Asia, and Africa to Latin America [we will persevere].

The Press Response

The most frequently quoted line of the State of the Union address was its opening sentence: "As we gather tonight, our nation is at war, our economy is in recession, and the civilized world faces unprecedented dangers, yet the state of our union has never been stronger." *Nightline* paraphrased it like this:

NIGHTLINE HOST TED KOPPEL: A nation at war.

PRESIDENT GEORGE W. BUSH (clip from speech): Thousands of dangerous killers, schooled in the methods of murder, often supported by outlaw regimes are . . . now spread throughout the world liked ticking time bombs set to go off without warning.

KOPPEL: An economy in recession.

BUSH (clip): When America works, America prospers, so my economic security plan can be summed up in one word: jobs.

KOPPEL: And Democrats look for scant political openings.

FORMER CLINTON CAMPAIGN STRATEGIST PAUL BEGALA: George W. Bush stands up there tonight and calls for greater transparency by corporations? Whew! The Democrats are going to kill him.[4]

This *Nightline* excerpt foreshadows three of the four main themes advanced by the press: The nature of the War on Terror; the axis of evil; the economy; and the Enron debacle. Specific framing of these themes emerged, and to these we now turn.

The Nature of the War on Terror

When considering a War on Terror as a response to 9/11, the overall news media framing of the nature of the war was of acceptance, agreement, and rightness of the war. For instance, speaking of the president's statement that the state of the union has never been stronger, ABC's *Good Morning America* stated: "The thrust of the president's speech is that the union will need all of that strength to combat the very real dangers that still face the country in the war on terrorism."[5] A *CBS*

News Special Report commented, "So far, we're winning the war and spending our money on that."[6] In another *Special Report*, CBS News noted that, talking about the war against terrorists, President Bush had said that the country has "paid freedom's price, showed freedom's power and he vows we will see freedom's victory."[7]

The *Washington Post* stated that no "challenge falls more squarely within the purview of the executive branch, and none is more important to the state of the union, than the war, broadly defined."[8] Along the same lines, a *USA Today* article said that President Bush was "hoping to capitalize on Americans' desire to help win the war on terrorism."[9] The *New York Times* wrote that "the Bush administration would continue its war against terrorism with its allies or without them. . . . Whether the rest of the world wished it, the war against terrorism was not over."[10] Michael McFaul of the *Washington Post* observed: "The United States is at war. President Bush therefore has correctly asked Congress to approve additional resources to fight this war."[11]

The majority of comments concerning the War on Terror accurately relayed the president's frame. For example, *NBC Nightly News* stated that the president would "not mention Osama bin Laden to make the point that the war is bigger than one target."[12] Commentator Doris Kearns Goodwin stated that the president had "found the rhetoric for a new kind of war. . . . [We] used to talk about the Cold War being over, and we were in a period of drift. . . . [When the president tonight] talked about the birth for freedom and the continuing war, pledges for the future, I think he provided some of that rhetoric."[13] *CBS News Special Report* stated that "there is a war going on and it would stretch us as far as we can see in the future" and noted that the president's speech had contained statements similar to those "made at the beginning of the Cold War, that this is a new and dangerous world and that it's going to require an indefinite commitment."[14] *Nightline* reported in a similar fashion: "There are . . . an estimated 100,000 men who have gone through terrorist training camps. Finding and neutralizing those men will likely occupy this president for as long as he remains in the White House."[15]

Good Morning America stated that this was "a very different kind of war, a war on terrorism, a war with no end in sight."[16] Along these same lines, *NBC Nightly News* said that "President Bush made it clear the war on terrorism is not over, that there are clear and present dangers of another attack."[17] Showing particular support, *The Early Show* agreed that "what's been a remarkably successful war on terrorism so far is merely the beginning."[18] ABC's *World News Now* stated that President Bush "told Americans the war on terrorism is only just beginning." A *Washington Post* article remarked that the president had "laid out a justification for a longer and broader war against terrorism" and that the "country will long remain vulnerable to attack. . . . 'Our war on terrorism is well begun, but it is only begun,' Bush said. 'This campaign may not be finished on our watch, yet it must be and it will be waged on our watch.'"[19]

USA Today stated:

> Bush said that despite early victories in the war on terrorism, it has "only begun." "We cannot stop short," he said. "If we stopped now, our sense of security would be false and temporary." Pleading for patience and persistence, he vowed to shut down terrorist camps, bring terrorists to justice and prevent regimes from developing chemical, biological and nuclear weapons.[20]

Another *USA Today* story observed:

> Bush made it clear that the swift victory in Afghanistan against al-Qaeda terrorist and their Taliban protectors is the first front in a war that will be fought on other battlegrounds. He said tens of thousands of terrorists "are now spread throughout the world like ticking time bombs."[21]

The *New York Times* likened this to "Mr. Bush describ[ing] the world as his battlefield.,"[22] And the *Washington Post* stated: "Mr. Bush was right when he promised a sustained war, one that requires the United States to use all the tools available. Sufficient support of peace and development should be in the tool kit."[23]

Not all reports so closely matched the president's frame for the nature-of-the-war theme. At issue here was the nature of the War on Terror. No press outlet examined for this chapter suggested that there *should not* be a "war on terror," but in a continuation of what was discovered in chapter 3, most framed certain elements of the War on Terror in a negative light; in short, we see an increase in oppositional framing by the press following the president's speech. For instance, *USA Today* framed the issue as follows: "Bush's choice of guns over butter is a risky one. 'Guns vs. butter' refers to the strain on domestic spending and the economy when a nation's priority turns to armaments and war." Setting the president's performance up to be judged by the economy, the article continued:

> With his words in recent weeks, Bush has been careful to express concern about Americans who have lost their jobs. But his deeds— especially the $2 trillion federal budget . . . demonstrate that for him

the overriding priority now . . . will be waging the war on terrorism.
. . . Polls show American overwhelmingly support him. Even so, these
calculations have been risky for political leaders. . . . There already are
some small warning signs for the current president.[24]

The most noticeable opposition, however, was in response to the
phrase "axis of evil," which is discussed below.

Axis of Evil

Demonstrating the expanded nature of the War on Terror, ABC
News stated that the president was

going to, once again, try to brace the American people for what
he's going to call a long and dangerous struggle against terrorism. He's
going to offer a tough restatement of what's called the Bush doctrine,
a warning that any states that facilitate terrorism will be held as guilty
as terrorists by the United States.[25]

It was this portion of the nature of the war—what the president described as an "axis of evil"—that was the primary source of the development of oppositional framing by the press.

The president was careful to define the axis of evil as inclusive of
numerous states, and he provided examples of three such nations.
However, even before the speech was given, the press had narrowed
the axis down to only those three states. *NBC Nightly News*, for instance, stated that the president would "be firm in his commitment to
take the war on terror wherever it leads. But no specifics on just how
he will hold Iran, Iraq and North Korea accountable."[26] *NBC News Special Report* stated that a "number of countries will be watching this
speech very carefully. And some of them—Iran, Iraq and North Korea—will be busy throughout the night in communication with their
home offices, based on what the president has to say." The show later
reported that the president had given a "very stern warning to Iran,
Iraq and North Korea."[27] The White House had provided copies of the
address to the press before the president's formal delivery, but the
speech used the three *as examples*; it did not present them as the *only*
evil states in the axis. The press, however, zeroed in on the three, leaving them in possession of the field of evil.

The day after the address saw extremely few in the press define the
axis of evil using more inclusive terms and thus accurately relaying the

concept as advanced by the president. One of these, *Today*, noted that President Bush had "defined what he calls an . . . axis of evil, nations like North Korea, Iran and Iraq."[28] *The Early Show* mentioned "'the axis of evil,' a list of nations including Iran, Iraq and North Korea, that threaten peace worldwide with weapons of mass destruction."[29] *Good Morning America* stated that President Bush "put on warning, states like Iraq and Iran that support terrorism, calling them an axis of evil."[30] In its lead news article describing the State of the Union address, the *Washington Post* wrote that the president "said that hostile nations, including North Korea, Iraq and Iran, represent 'an axis of evil' that is attempting to develop nuclear, biological and chemical weapons."[31]

The overwhelming majority of press reports framed this theme quite differently than those above. When looking at the responses as a whole, one witnesses a rather deliberate narrowing of the definition of the axis of evil down to only the three states mentioned in the president's speech. For instance, *World News Now* stated that "Mr. Bush singled out Iraq, Iran and North Korea as potential threats, calling them an 'axis of evil.'"[32] Additionally, the interpretations of the president's statements began to narrow the range of possible meanings of the phrase. For example, *CBS Evening News* declared, "In the history books it likely will be known as the 'axis of evil' speech," and the reporter went on to explain both the meaning and implication of the phrase: "President Bush took the war against terrorism to a whole new level by vowing to prevent Iran, Iraq and North Korea from ever acquiring chemical, biological or nuclear weapons, and he did it with words that carried an unmistakable echo of World War II."[33] Similarly, *World News Tonight* reported: "Mr. Bush declared a new 'axis of evil.' Iraq, Iran and North Korea pose a deadly and unacceptable threat to the country."[34] *World News Now* stated that the president said that "the U.S. will specifically keep an eye on Iraq, Iran and North Korea."[35]

Nightline host Ted Koppel and his two guests, former Clinton campaign strategist Paul Begala and *US News & World Reports* editor David Gergen, made it clear that the president had expanded the war's focus and singled out only three nations:

> BEGALA: My only concern is that he broadened the focus, and he may have lost part of the focus. I think he's right to remind us . . . that al-Qaeda has tens of thousands of terrorists who are highly armed . . . trained . . . motivated . . . financed and in place already. . . . But then when he confuses that with Iran, Iraq, North Korea . . . [and] we start to wonder, "Are we going to have three or four wars going at a time?"

KOPPEL: [The president] was suggesting . . . that the great threat is that Iran, Iraq, North Korea will in some way join forces with these terrorists and will . . . make weapons of mass destruction available to them. So I'm not sure, David, that you can separate the two, if that is so.

GERGEN: You can't. I think most of us expected he would talk . . . about going on into the Philippines, Indonesia. . . . Instead, he threw down the gauntlet . . . in a very serious way with regard to Iraq, Iran and—and North Korea. He laid the foundations tonight for serious U.S. military action. . . . When he . . . essentially call[s] them evil, the axis of evil, that means he's going to act.[36]

Similarly, *World News Now* stated that the

most striking thing is how much the president still views himself as a wartime president, his mission as president very focused on how to fight this war against terror. Last night, probably the biggest thing he said was extending the war . . . against rogue states. He called them axis of evil, a pretty strong phrase to use speaking about countries like Iraq, Iran and—and North Korea. And that really does elevate this war.[37]

USA Today wrote that the "heart of" the president's speech was the "imperative to continue the campaign against terrorism. He expanded the list of targets to three rogue nations . . . that are trying to develop weapons of mass destruction."[38] An editorial in the *New York Times* commented that the president spoke about taking the "next step in the battle against terrorism overseas, and in this area he was appropriately forceful. He named Iraq, Iran and North Korea as part of 'an axis of evil' . . . and he put those countries on notice that [America] will not stand by and let them develop" weapons of mass destruction.[39]

A more forceful interpretation of President Bush's use of the term "axis of evil" was provided by Michael R. Gordon in the *New York Times*, who highlighted Iraq as the most likely future target: "President Bush . . . laid the basis for an ambitious campaign of diplomatic pressure and potential military action against Iraq and other hostile nations . . . seeking to develop weapons of mass destruction." According to Gordon, President Bush "significantly broadened" the scope of the war against terror,

expanding it to include states that might threaten the United States with weapons of mass destruction. . . . Mr. Bush described those dangers as so great that he seemed to be building an argument in some cases for potential, preemptive military action. This was the strongest oratory that the president has used to date to describe Iraq's pursuit of weapons of mass destruction and the United States' determination to neutralize that threat.[40]

Tom Shales wrote in the *Washington Post* that President Bush "may have set a record for the most uses of the word 'evil' in a single evening, referring at one point to North Korea, Iran and Iraq as 'an axis of evil' threatening goodness and decency everywhere, or at least here."[41] Another *Washington Post* article made it abundantly clear that President Bush had singled out only Iran, Iraq, and North Korea:

> By singling out Iran, Iraq and North Korea as an "axis of evil" whose efforts to acquire and export weapons of mass destruction could no longer be tolerated, President Bush last night appeared to sharply increase both the immediacy and the gravity of the threat they pose. . . . As described by Bush last night, the United States has a long-term commitment to rid the world of those states who give the terrorists "the means to match their hatred."[42]

CBS Morning News highlighted the nature of the threat of the axis of evil, which the press had by now limited to only Iraq, Iran, and North Korea:

> [President Bush vowed] to prevent Iran, Iraq and North Korea from ever acquiring chemical, biological or nuclear weapons, and he did it with words that carried an unmistakable echo of World War II. "States like these and their terrorist allies constitute an axis an evil, arming to threaten the peace of the world." The president said Iran, Iraq and North Korea pose a grave and growing danger and that America would do what is necessary to protect itself.[43]

Of note is that this same report focused narrowly upon Iraq, relaying the assertion that Saddam Hussein had had his weapons of mass destruction program set back by allied air strikes, but that "the CIA believes [Iraq, as well as Iran and North Korea, have] been trying to develop nuclear weapons and already have chemical and probably biological weapons."[44]

USA Today stated that in

> singling out North Korea, Iran and Iraq as an "axis of evil," President Bush appears to be extending the war on terrorism to countries that are developing arms of mass destruction. Foreign policy analysts say

... all three are believed to be seeking nuclear, chemical or biological weapons. Few experts disagree with Bush's description of Iraq's regime as "evil," but some say he erred by lumping in North Korea and Iran.[45]

Whereas *USA Today* critiqued the president by pointing out similarities and differences among the three countries, the *New York Times* focused on negative international reactions:

> In Japan and South Korea . . . people reacted nervously today after President Bush singled out North Korea as a new focus for America's war on terror. "It's very scary," said Choi Jin Wook, a senior researcher in Seoul. . . . "Some people think the chances of war have increased as a result." In Japan . . . many foreign policy analysts urged moderation with their isolated and often bellicose neighbor. "I don't think it is a wise thing to corner the North Koreans and cut any routes to talking with them," said Yukihiko Ikeda, a congressman and a former foreign minister.[46]

In a different article the *New York Times* pushed the negative reaction further: "The three countries pinpointed by President Bush as an 'axis of evil' . . . reacted angrily today while commentators in many other nations, including European allies, bristled at what they saw as the combative, go-it-alone tone of the State of the Union address."[47] The *Washington Post* used similar language:

> European security officials expressed alarm today about what they considered an aggressive, go-it-alone-stance staked out by President Bush in his State of the Union address. . . especially his warning that the United States was prepared to take preemptive action against Iraq or other countries that provide terrorists with nuclear, chemical or biological weapons.[48]

Editorially, the *New York Times* summed up the angle taken by its news reports well:

> The application of power and intimidation has returned to the forefront of American foreign policy. That was the unmistakable message delivered by President Bush . . . when he labeled Iran, Iraq and North Korea an "axis of evil" that he would not permit to threaten the United States with [weapons of mass destruction]. Not since America's humiliating withdrawal from Vietnam . . . has our foreign policy relied so heavily on non-nuclear military force, or the threat of it, to defend American interests around the world.[49]

USA Today was more circumspect in calling attention to the aspects of the "axis of evil" phrase: "Hours after he called North Korea, Iran and Iraq an 'axis of evil' . . . allies reacted strongly against what sounded to many like imminent, unilateral U.S. military action." Later, in the same editorial, the newspaper added: "If Bush's State of the Union threat overreached, it at least should provoke a more open and thoughtful debate exploring all the risks and rewards, costs and consequences of [American options]."[50]

The *Washington Post* relayed that the Bush administration "has charged that Iraq and Iran are well along in the production of chemical or biological weapons . . . and the acquisition of ballistic missile technology to deliver it, and warned that they may be tempted to pass them along to terrorist organizations."[51] *Today* interviewed Clinton administration secretary of state Madeleine Albright, stating that President Bush had "used the term 'axis of evil' in referring to North Korea, Iran and Iraq." The interviewer, cohost Matt Lauer, asked for her response.

> ALBRIGHT: Well . . . all of us certainly know that fighting terrorism is the major priority. I think it was a big mistake to lump those three countries together.
>
> LAUER: And does he run the risk of alienating some of our allies by making statements [such as] that?
>
> ALBRIGHT: Absolutely. And so I don't know what the value is.[52]

USA Today also took up this theme of lumping the three states together when it reported that the State of the Union "remarks, in which [the president] also labeled [North Korea,] Iraq and Iran as members of an 'axis of evil,' sparked criticism that he was lumping together different political systems."[53]

The *New York Times* focused heavily on negative international reaction to the president's use of the phrase:

> Moscow did not support an extension of the war on terrorism to include Iraq. China . . . warned the administration not to strike countries that have no clear tie to the Sept. 11 attack [and] emphasized that the American-led antiterrorism campaign should not be "arbitrarily" widened. Like China, Russia says it has no proof that those nations support terrorism. Washington says they do.[54]

Continuing with the negative international framing, the *Washington Post* quoted former Ford and Bush (Sr.) administration national security advisor Brent Scowcroft as being "critical of Bush's use of the phrase 'axis of evil' . . . to describe Iran, Iraq and North Korea. 'I really don't know what it was designed to do.'" The article went on to quote numerous officials: Sen. Chuck Hagel (R-Neb.) said, "I'd just as soon not have seen that in the speech." Another Nebraska Republican, Rep. Doug Bereuter, added, "I'm not sure it (the phrase) was necessary." The criticism from Congressional Democrats was especially highlighted. Rep. Tom Allen (D-Maine), for example, said Bush had muddied the waters by including North Korea in his list. . . . Said Rep. James P. Moran Jr. (D-Va.): "It was reckless rhetoric to lump all three countries together." All in all, between the "axis" phrase and the speech's general neglect of Europe, the State of the Union address "sent absolutely the wrong signal to the allies," said Robert Hunter, a former U.S. ambassador to NATO.[55] In an apologia for Iran, the *Post*'s Giandomenico Picco wrote, "If I had three enemies, instead of uniting them as an axis, it would seem useful to keep them apart."[56]

Economy

The economy received disproportionately intense coverage in relation to the weight given it in the president's speech. Additionally, whereas the president attempted to explain the economy in relation to the War on Terror, the press greatly minimized this interpretation; instead, it highlighted the economy as separate from the War on Terror and also as a topic that politically damages the president. The *Washington Post*, for instance, remarked that although President Bush is attempting to convert "a foreign military action into a domestic mobilization," the "Democrats are desperate to decouple the foreign from the domestic."[57] David Broder wrote:

> Bush sought to link his military-diplomatic strategy with his domestic agenda under the rubric of "security," but he gave far different weight to the two pieces. Democrats have to try to separate the domestic issues on which they disagree with Bush from the war on terrorism to have any hope of prevailing in the November elections. Strong as his support on the war undoubtedly is, he has left his political opponents an opening.[58]

Bush had put forth a rather striking proposal: that his budget, and thus the economy, was linked with the War on Terror and needed to be understood in that relationship. The press reported little on this link, instead casting proposals in such a way as to separate the War on Terror from domestic concerns, while simultaneously casting the domestic as the sphere of influence for the Democrats.

Even before the speech, *NBC News Special Report* stated that the president would

> talk a lot . . . about the American economy. . . . He'll talk about the importance of economic security, linking the strength of the economy to . . . homeland security. While the president has enjoyed support for his handling of the war, he knows the economy is an area where he is vulnerable to attack from Democrats.[59]

Nightline asserted that with "broad strokes . . . the president laid out his budget and the programs he wants Congress to fund. While support for war is nearly universal on Capital Hill, the parties do split over how to pay for it."[60] The *Washington Post* opined that the president "faces pressure to appear engaged on a broad range of issues, notably the economy, and that's legitimate; the long-term fiscal challenge facing the country demands his attention and his commitment to bipartisan solutions."[61]

World News Now reported that the "events of September 11th took their toll in immeasurable human terms, but they also eroded confidence in the economy." After a clip of President Bush saying, "When American works, America prospers. So my economic security plan can be summed up in one word: jobs," the report continued, "In the Democratic response [it was] made it clear that the president will get his way on a lot of things, but not everything." This was followed by a clip of Rep. Dick Gephardt's (D-MO) Democratic response to the State of the Union, with the sound bite of choice for both broadcast and print news: "I refuse to accept that while we stand shoulder to shoulder on the war, we should stand toe to toe on the economy."[62]

In one news story, *USA Today* stated that President Bush had noted that

> deficits are needed for now to fight the war on terrorism, protect the homeland and boost the economy. But, Bush promised, the return to deficit spending will be "small and short-term." Don't believe that for a moment. Even before the official numbers are released, one thing is clear: the deficits will be big and will last for nearly a decade. Only by resorting to accounting gimmicks that would make Enron blush can Bush claim otherwise.[63]

On *Today*, host Katie Couric asked reporter Tim Russert if he thought that President Bush paid "enough attention to the economy given the current economic conditions" in the United States.

> RUSSERT: I don't think that he has any choice considering his mindset. The last week he said that 50 percent of his day was spent on the war, but 90 percent of his concern. Clearly, he's fixated. . . . But when he did shift gears and talked about economic security, you could feel the entire dome lift off the Capitol. Both parties want to focus on that because it's very much on people's minds.
>
> COURIC: [He] seemed to equate getting the economy back on track with success overseas in fighting this war. . . . Do you think it was fair to equate those things, Tim?
> RUSSERT: I think it's probably very smart politics.
>
> COURIC: Democrats . . . still have to really walk a fine line, don't they? They can't be too critical of the president given his skyrocketing approval ratings.[64]

Picking up on this same line of reasoning, *CBS Morning News* stated that "Democrats backed the president's war on terrorism, but . . . Richard Gephardt . . . had tough words for the president's economic proposals, but offered cooperation." This was followed by the same Gephardt clip: "I refuse to accept that while we stand shoulder to shoulder on the war, we should stand toe to toe on the economy."[65] *World News This Morning* also picked up on the partisan theme, observing that the president's "vision for the second year of his presidency is a two-front war against terrorism . . . while at the same time recovering from the recession. Mr. Bush's guns and butter priorities will revive the federal deficit and some partisan battle lines."[66] Similarly, the *Washington Post* reported on the partisan edge:

> But for all the cheers that punctuated Bush's recitation of progress in the war on terrorism, and of the challenges yet to come, there also were signs that life on Capitol Hill—with all its partisan trappings— is returning to normal. Democrats' reactions to the president's proposals in several domestic areas might best be described as polite skepticism.[67]

The *New York Times* pushed a conciliatory interpretation to the Democratic opposition:

> Faced with a popular president rallying the nation for a long struggle against terrorism, Democrats sought tonight to stand united with

President Bush in the war effort and to showcase their own compet-
ing domestic agendas without appearing partisan or confrontational.
"I refuse to accept that while we stand shoulder to shoulder on the
war, we should stand toe to toe on the economy," Mr. Gephardt said,
suggesting that the president hold a bipartisan "economic growth
summit" at the White House.[68]

Editorially the *New York Times* put a partisan edge to its interpretation:

> Simply asking for a lot more money for military projects is a modest
> goal for a man with the ability to move the nation in a whole new di-
> rection. On the domestic front Mr. Bush asked mostly for easy victo-
> ries. He adopted the Democrats' calls for increased spending on
> domestic defense. In the economic sphere, Mr. Bush was disappoint-
> ing. He seemed intent on using his popularity to press the tired hard-
> right Republican agenda of accelerating and, in the name of
> "economic security," making permanent the tax cuts for the rich that
> were enacted last year.[69]

Perhaps these examples are enough, but the sheer weight of the
press framing in this area suggests that a few more are in order. For instance, E. J. Dionne Jr. narrowed President Bush's choices considerably
when he wrote in the *Washington Post*: "During the Vietnam era, President Lyndon B. Johnson thought he could have guns and butter—that
he could keep his domestic Great Society program and fight the war at
the same time. Now President Bush thinks he can have guns and tax
cuts. It's an unfortunate choice."[70] After the release of the president's
budget proposal on February 4, 2002, the *Post* declared that the president had

> issued a budget wrapped in the American flag. Just in case Congress
> didn't get the message from the stars and stripes on the cover . . . he
> flew to a military base to proclaim that lawmakers should show sup-
> port for the war on terrorism by fully funding his requests for a record
> increase in defense spending.[71]

Two days later, Robert Borosage added:

> The United States is a rich country. It can afford to waste money on
> the military if that makes it feel good. But military spending now con-
> sumes over half of all discretionary spending. The domestic side of
> the Bush budget is a tale of small cuts and large deferred hopes—no
> real prescription drug program, no drive for energy independence, no
> new investment in teachers and preschool, no new funding for
> worker training and corporate accountability.[72]

The Enron Situation

I do not believe the Enron scandal to be a theme within the War on Terror, but the economy was a theme, and the press made the scandal part of the overall coverage of the State of the Union address. Enron was mentioned in 40 of 110 articles and news reports examined in this chapter, and the press framed it as a Republican issue. In short, the issue was framed in such a way as to discredit both President Bush and Republicans, thereby casting doubt on the president's ability to handle the economy, which was the area of weakness identified by the press as being ripe for Democrat attacks.

Even before the president gave his speech, the press was asking about the Enron scandal. For example, *Today* stated that "a top advisor said the president won't talk specifically about Enron because the Justice Department is conducting a criminal investigation."[73] *Good Morning America* raised this issue during an interview with White House counselor Karen Hughes: After a piece in which reporter Terry Moran said that during the State of the Union Bush would make "an oblique and indirect reference to the one cloud on the horizon in this administration at this point, and that's Enron," the program turned to anchor Diane Sawyer's interview with Hughes:

SAWYER: Will he mention Enron?

HUGHES: I don't think specifically, Diane. As you know, our government is investigating Enron.

Sawyer concluded, "Again, no specific mention of Enron tonight."[74]

World News This Morning framed the Enron situation so that it became the problem child of the Bush administration: "The president who failed to win the popular vote is enjoying popularity seen by few of his predecessors, but as he heads into his first State of the Union address, the Enron debacle and the costs of the war on terrorism threaten to undermine President Bush's agenda."[75]

Nightline also specifically brought up Enron. Guest Paul Begala earlier on the show had suggested that the president should mention Enron.

KOPPEL: It sounds as though the president was listening to you and decided to ignore your advice.

BEGALA: He did. And I suspect the Secret Service was worried about that thunderbolt coming from above, when he actually stood there—

get this—he's lecturing corporate America that they should disclose more about their finances, when he, himself, is facing a lawsuit from the general Accounting Office because he refuses to disclose the meetings that this government has had with Enron. And for him to try to lecture American business, you know, he's going to basically say Wall Street should open up, but the White House is not going to, is untenable.

KOPPEL [turning to guest David Gergen]: The president . . . clearly does not believe that this is a political scandal. . . . Do you agree with him or with Paul?

GERGEN: At the moment, he's right. But I think . . . this is turning on the Republicans, and if the Democrats were clever, they could clearly take the offensive on it. I don't see the Democrats, at this point, who have taken a lot of money from these folks, too, I don't see that they're very gutsy on this issue, either. It's the media right now that's leading this charge.[76]

Approximately four and a half months after 9/11, Kevin Phillips wrote in the *New York Times* that the president's

talk of escalating America's war against terrorism to include new foes . . . stands in sharp contrast to *his abandonment of a domestic battlefront.* This is the area that many in Congress and the nation as a whole want to declare—the war on money politics and the big-contributor stranglehold on policy making that lets a rogue corporation [such as] Enron rise to influence and power. President Bush's ties with Enron are longstanding.[77]

USA Today noted that Bush

called for Congress to pass new protections for workers' pension plans. But he did not mention energy giant Enron by name, nor did he mention campaign-finance reform. . . . Many Enron workers lost their retirement savings as the company collapsed. Enron and its executives have been among Bush's most generous campaign donors and advised the administration on its energy policy.[78]

Although numerous other companies advised the administration, *USA Today* and the other press analyzed here failed to mention any others.

A *New York Times* article inserted a statement by a Democratic congressman who "called the president a practitioner of 'Enron economics: giving more money to rich people and large corporations and hoping it will trickle down to everyone else.'"[79] No rebuttal was provided. A different *New York Times* article said of the State of the Union address that the

> tableau was that of a celebration of a war hero, even as polls show that voters suspect his administration may be hiding something about Enron, and even as some Republicans question Vice President Dick Cheney's refusal to provide records to Congress about talks he held with Enron executives.[80]

The story fails to cite which polls were referenced or to mention that the citation of executive privilege concerning the meeting with Enron also applied to the other corporations advising the administration on its energy policy.

On *NBC Special Report*, Tom Brokaw asked reporter Lisa Myers, "What do they think on [Capitol] Hill? Do they think that Enron has political legs for the Democrats? Because the fact is, that as many on that side of the aisle have taken money from Enron as have on the Republican side." Myers's reply indicates the biased thinking of the press:

> The Democrats think the Republicans are most vulnerable on the issue in which the president attempted to inoculate himself tonight. That is the . . . belief among the American people that the Republicans are the party of corporate America and that they favor the rich over the little guy. [The Democrats] think they can use the Enron issue to press that case, Tom.[81]

Summary

Four and a half months after 9/11, the themes used by the Bush administration to describe the War on Terror had developed consistent and coherent frames that depict Americans in one light and the terrorists in another. However, these themes were no longer separate lines of thought but increasingly interanimated ideas that fueled the administration's framing of its master frame, the War on Terror. In short, we see something of a conflation of terms now, with America working within an international coalition for the Good, the Civilized, and the Free. In contrast, the terrorists were working within an axis of evil, embracing uncivilized and tyrannical actions and ideals. In the words of President Bush:

Our enemies send other people's children on missions of suicide and murder. They embrace tyranny and death as a cause and a creed. We stand for a different choice, made long ago, on the day of our founding. We affirm it again today. We choose freedom and the dignity of every life.

Freedom is never really defined, except in opposition to the nature of the terrorists: Freedom is to America what living under terrorists and the states that sponsor them is not.

During the weeks prior to this speech, the president hinted at something new, and it again emerged in this speech: the subtle laying of groundwork for the possibility of preemptive war. Although not using the term specifically until his speech at the 2002 graduation ceremony at West Point, the president here hints at the policy as an action for the country: "But some governments will be timid in the face of terror. And make no mistake about it: If they do not act, America will." It is this failure to act in the face of terror that is offered as justification for action; the United States simply cannot rely for its safety on the potential actions of other nations. Thus, Bush declared strongly that all "nations should know: America will do what is necessary to ensure our nation's security." Moreover, the president came close to saying that the best defense is a strong offense when he stated: "We are protected from attack only by vigorous action abroad."

The framing of the War on Terror allowed the president to advance a particular conception of action for the country: "Americans will take the side of brave men and women who advocate these values around the world, including the Islamic world, because we have a greater objective than eliminating threats and containing resentment. We seek a just and peaceful world beyond the war on terror." To achieve this, however, Americans were called upon to become involved in the war effort. Following 9/11, there was considerable speculation as to what this effort should look like; in this address, Bush offered a plan for action. Although he stressed that Americans must continue with their day-to-day lives, he expanded this into a larger vision. The president's call was

> for every American to commit at least two years—4,000 hours over the rest of your lifetime—to the service of your neighbors and your nation. If you aren't sure how to help, I've got a good place to start. I invite you to join the new USA Freedom Corps. And America needs its citizens to extend the compassion of our country to every part of

> the world. So we will renew the promise of the Peace Corps . . . and ask it to join a new effort to encourage development and education and opportunity in the Islamic world. And we have a great opportunity during this time of war to lead the world toward the values that will bring lasting peace . . .

namely, education, freedom from poverty, freedom from violence, and freedom from oppression.

The press, however, left a very different impression. In general, the press was supportive of the idea of a war on terror, but presented either a questioning of or hostility toward the president's notion of an axis of evil. In short, it was not reporting on the president's idea as news, but rather presenting its dislike of his idea as news. Additionally, the press reporting on the economic aspects of the State of the Union address was decidedly negative, with frequent attempts to separate the economy from the larger picture of the War on Terror—the very same tactic adopted by congressional Democrats. To these ideas we now turn.

In a definitive shift from the previous chapters, opinion essays and editorials examined in this chapter took a decidedly negative shape. There was much talk from critics that centered on the inappropriateness of the "axis of evil" metaphor, especially any thought of exercising the military as opposed to diplomatic option. Although the press raised the memories of World War II, nobody speaking out against the "axis of evil" metaphor mentioned *appeasement*, something with which anyone familiar with Neville Chamberlain and World War II should be familiar. In this manner, the press cherry-picked its World War II examples to strengthen its own interpretation of Bush's policies.

Unlike the other speech responses examined in chapters 2 and 3, the focus now was not on the nature of the war or the nature of the enemy (the latter something taken for granted now), but rather on *how* the war should be conducted: unilateral or multilateral; police action or military action? Additionally, the economic aspect added here acted to fracture the overall framing of the War on Terror by allowing the press to agree with the War on Terror *in principle* while arguing vociferously against both the administration's economic policies and its plan for conducting the war. *CBS News Special Report* exemplified this approach when it stated: "The . . . unanimity applies only to the war on terrorism. It certainly doesn't apply to his plans for homeland security, and it certainly doesn't apply to his plans for the economy."[82] In short, the press appears to have been saying, It is acceptable to have a War on Terror, but we will contest every idea you have concerning *how* that war is to be conducted. One area of action particularly stressed by the president was volunteerism, particularly with USA Freedom Corps and the Peace Corps. This idea, a *central piece* in the State of the Union, was mentioned only 9 times in the 110 articles and news stories covered in this chapter.

The press failed utterly to present a representative picture of the Enron situation, thus framing that aspect of the president's State of the Union in such a way that Democrat efforts to undermine Bush administration credibility found a ready ally in the press reports. The press failed to mention that from 1989 to 2002, 43 percent of Enron contributions to congressional representatives went to Democrats.[83] Additionally, the press reported that President Bush, Vice President Dick Cheney, and Republicans in general accepted donations from Enron. However, remaining unnamed were prominent Democrats who had taken Enron dollars—including Senate Majority Leader Tom Daschle (D-SD); Sen. Charles E. Schumer (D-NY); Sen. Jeff Bingaman (D-NM), former chair of the Committee on Energy and Natural Resources; Rep. Ken Bentsen (D-TX), Rep. Sheila Jackson Lee (D-TX), and Rep. John D. Dingell (D-MI), a member of the Committee on Energy and Commerce.[84] Perhaps most importantly, the press failed to mention that the overwhelming majority of Enron's then alleged wrongdoings occurred under the Clinton administration.[85] Plainly speaking, the press injected Enron into its coverage of the State of the Union address and *intentionally* framed that issue as the problem child of the Republicans.

5

Remarks by the President from the USS *Abraham Lincoln*, May 2003

> The war on terror is not over; yet it is not endless. We do not know the day of final victory, but we have seen the turning of the tide. No act of the terrorists will change our purpose, or weaken our resolve, or alter their fate. Their cause is lost. Free nations will press on to victory.
>
> —George W. Bush

> The president's made-for-TV arrival on the . . . *Lincoln* signals the opening of his 2004 campaign and his expected focus on national security. And with polls showing the struggling economy is by far the biggest concern of most Americans, Mr. Bush is also determined not to repeat his father's mistake of appearing unconcerned.
>
> —*CBS Evening News*

On 17 March 2003, President Bush delivered an ultimatum to Saddam Hussein: "All the decades of deceit and cruelty have now reached an end. Saddam Hussein and his sons must leave Iraq within forty-eight hours. Their refusal to do so will result in military conflict, commenced at a time of our choosing."[1] Forty-eight hours later, the president again addressed the nation:

> My fellow citizens, at this hour, American and coalition forces are in the early stages of military operations to disarm Iraq, to free its people and to defend the world from grave danger. On my orders,

coalition forces have begun striking selected targets of military importance to undermine Saddam Hussein's ability to wage war.[2]

Highlighting the importance of the international coalition his administration had built, the president stated that these

are opening stages of what will be a broad and concerted campaign. More than thirty-five countries are giving crucial support—from the use of naval and air bases, to help with intelligence and logistics, to the deployment of combat units. Every nation in this coalition has chosen to bear the duty and share the honor of serving in our common defense.[3]

Approximately six weeks later, on 1 May 2003, the crew of the USS *Abraham Lincoln* looked to the sky as they awaited the arrival of President Bush. When he arrived, it was not by helicopter but inside a Navy S-3B Viking jet making a tailhook landing. The president intended to thank U.S. troops and announce the ending of formal military operations in Iraq. The speed of the campaign had been remarkable, and the excitement of the presidential visit was in the air. Behind the president as he spoke was a banner made hastily by the crew of the *Lincoln*. It read, "Mission Accomplished."

The President's Speech

In his speech from the deck of the *Lincoln*, the president thanked the troops, announced the end of formal military operations in Iraq, spoke about the larger War on Terror, and rearticulated the Bush Doctrine. The president was quite clear that "mission accomplished" meant only the overthrow of Hussein, and that the second phase of the Iraq war was now under way: "In the battle of Iraq, the United States and our allies have prevailed. And now our coalition is engaged in securing and reconstructing that country."[4] Thanking the troops, the president called into remembrance the "character of our military through history—the daring of Normandy, the fierce courage of Iwo Jima, the decency and idealism that turned enemies into allies"—and stated that the character inherent in earlier days "is fully present in this generation. When I look at the members of the United States military, I see the best of our country, and I'm honored to be your Commander-in-Chief."

Additionally, as in his other major speeches concerning the War on Terror, the president touched on the themes inherent within that overall frame. For example, continuing the bipolar theme of the United States representing the good and civilized and terrorists representing the evil and barbaric, Bush clearly placed the United States within the realm of prudence in the manner in which it conducted the war: "Our actions have been focused and deliberate and proportionate to the offense. We have not forgotten the victims of September the 11th. . . . With those attacks, the terrorists and their supporters declared war on the United States. And war is what they got." Speaking directly to the civilized and humanitarian sides of America, the president stated:

> For hundred of years of war, culminating in the nuclear age, military technology was designed and deployed to inflict casualties on an ever-growing scale. In defeating Nazi Germany and Imperial Japan, Allied forces destroyed entire cities, while enemy leaders who started the conflict were safe until the final days. Military power was used to end a regime by breaking a nation.

In contrast, he said, the United States today has the

> power to free a nation by breaking a dangerous and aggressive regime. With new tactics and precision weapons, we can achieve military objectives without directing violence against civilians. No device of man can remove the tragedy from war; yet it is a great moral advance when the guilty have far more to fear from war than the innocent.

In stark contrast to the actions of the United States is the nature of the terrorists: "The battle of Iraq is one victory in a war on terror that began on September the 11th, 2001—and still goes on. That terrible morning, 19 evil men—the shock troops of a hateful ideology—gave America and the civilized world a glimpse of their ambitions." The nature of the war and the nature of the terrorists are two themes comprising the larger War on Terror master frame that had been well established by the president. With each presidential usage, the War on Terror frame was increasingly well established, so that those who have followed his words found it easy to comprehend when they heard him say:

> Our mission continues. Al Qaeda is wounded, not destroyed. The scattered cells of the terrorist network still operate in many nations, and we know from daily intelligence that they continue to plot against free people. The proliferation of deadly weapons remains a serious danger. The enemies of freedom are not idle, and neither are we.

Drawing upon the previously established theme concerning the nature of the war, the president again echoed words with which the general population was familiar:

> The war on terror is not over; yet it is not endless. We do not know the day of final victory, but we have seen the turning of the tide. No act of the terrorists will change our purpose, or weaken our resolve, or alter their fate. Their cause is lost. Free nations will press on to victory.

This last sentence brings to mind another theme resonating within the War on Terror frame, that of freedom versus tyranny. Speaking directly to those who joined the fight in Iraq, the president said, "This nation thanks all the members of our coalition who joined in a noble cause," and to the members of the U.S. military, he added: "Because of you, our nation is more secure. Because of you, the tyrant has fallen, and Iraq is free."

An additional component of the theme of freedom versus tyranny involved the interanimated ideas of liberty and peace. In his speech, the president brought specificity to these concepts that play such an important part of his administration's overall framing of the War on Terror: In the battle of Iraq, he said, Americans "have fought for the cause of liberty, and for the peace of the world." The human spirit craves freedom, the president noted, and as an example he touched upon the recently seen "images of celebrating Iraqis." In these images, people around the globe had seen more than happy Iraqis liberated from a tyrant—they had "also seen the ageless appeal of human freedom." President Bush expanded these themes, stating that decades "of lies and intimidation could not make the Iraqi people love their oppressors or desire their own enslavement. Men and women in every culture need liberty like they need food and water and air. Everywhere that freedom arrives, humanity rejoices; and everywhere that freedom stirs, let tyrants fear."

Liberty goes hand in hand with freedom, and Bush made this point in his speech; at the same time, he also demonstrated how the battle of Iraq was only part of the larger War on Terror. As such, the president stated:

> Our commitment to liberty is America's tradition. . . . We are committed to freedom in Afghanistan, in Iraq, and in a peaceful Palestine. The advance of freedom is the surest strategy to undermine the appeal of terror in the world. Where freedom takes hold, hatred gives way to hope. When freedom takes hold, men and women turn to the

peaceful pursuit of a better life. American values and American interests lead in the same direction: We stand for human liberty.

Be that as it may, the battle of Iraq was not the end of involvement, and
President Bush stressed that the battle of Iraq, along with its ideal of
freedom, had entered a second and more complicated stage:

> We have difficult work to do in Iraq. We're bringing order to parts of
> that country that remain dangerous. We're pursuing and finding lead-
> ers of the old regime, who will be held to account for their crimes.
> We've begun the search for hidden chemical and biological weapons
> and already know of hundreds of sites that will be investigated. We're
> helping to rebuild Iraq, where the dictator built palaces for himself, in-
> stead of hospitals and schools. And we will stand with the new leaders
> of Iraq as they establish a government of, by, and for the Iraqi people.

Drawing upon the larger theme of freedom inherent in the War on Terror frame, Bush declared that the "transition from dictatorship to democracy will take time, but it is worth every effort."

The president returned to a theme of patience in this speech. In this
new kind of war, Americans needed to be reminded about the duration
of action, and of the costs involved: "We are hunting down al Qaeda
killers. Nineteen months ago, I pledged that the terrorists would not es-
cape the patient justice of the United States." Additionally, the president stressed the progress that American patience would allow to
continue: "And as of tonight, nearly one-half of al Qaeda's senior op-
eratives have been captured or killed." Dovetailing into this was the
emphasis on the importance of the battle of Iraq to the War on Terror.
The president had already begun to come under criticism for Operation Iraqi Freedom, so from the deck of the *Lincoln*, surrounded by
cheering military personnel, Bush reiterated that the

> liberation of Iraq is a crucial advance in the campaign against terror.
> We've removed an ally of al Qaeda, and cut off a source of terrorist
> funding. And this much is certain: No terrorist network will gain
> weapons of mass destruction from the Iraqi regime, because the
> regime is no more.

The international aspect of the War on Terror was highlighted as well:

> We're working with a broad coalition of nations that understand the
> threat and our shared responsibility to meet it. The use of force has
> been [our] last resort. Yet all can know, friend and foe alike, that our

nation has a mission: We will answer threats to our security, and we will defend the peace.

This last point—self-security and defense of the peace—also allowed the president to further clarify the Bush Doctrine:

Our war against terror is proceeding according to principles that I have made clear to all: Any person involved in committing or planning terrorist attacks against the American people becomes an enemy of this country, and a target of American justice. Any person, organization, or government that supports, protects, or harbors terrorists is complicit in the murder of the innocent, and equally guilty of terrorist crimes. Any outlaw regime that has ties to terrorist groups and seeks or possesses weapons of mass destruction is a grave danger to the civilized world—and will be confronted. And anyone in the world, including the Arab world, who works and sacrifices for freedom has a loyal friend in the United States of America.

Of note in this speech is the weight given to a religious interpretation of America's actions: "Every name, every life is a loss to our military, to our nation, and to the loved ones who grieve. There's no homecoming for these families. Yet we pray, in God's time, their reunion will come." The theme of America the Good versus the evil terrorists allows for increased use of religious references to better understand the adversaries' evil: "By seeking to turn our cities into killing fields, terrorists and their allies believed that they could destroy this nation's resolve, and force our retreat from the world. They have failed." It also allows for a better understanding of the actions of Americans in the War on Terror:

Those we lost were last seen on duty. Their final act on this Earth was to fight a great evil and bring liberty to others. All of you—all in this generation of our military—have taken up the highest calling of history. You're defending your country, and protecting the innocent from harm. And wherever you go, you carry a message of hope—a message that is ancient and ever new. In the words of the prophet Isaiah, "To the captives, 'come out,'—and to those in darkness, 'be free.'"

The Press Response

Four key themes ran through the press framing of President Bush's speech:

1. the Iraq war as part of the larger War on Terror
2. domestic issues
3. the president's manner of arrival
4. the "real" purpose of the speech

Each theme was framed in a manner that acted to minimize the point of view stressed by the president.[5]

Iraq War and War on Terror

President Bush linked the Iraq war with a larger War on Terror frame. This linkage was relayed by the press. The *Washington Post*, for instance, stated that "Bush's remarks will carry substantial political and foreign-policy implications for a president who has made the dismantling of the Iraqi government part of a broader war on terrorism."[6] In a different article, the *Post* declared that "President Bush proclaimed victory in Iraq tonight . . . but he cautioned that much remains to be done in the broader war against terrorism. 'The battle of Iraq is one victory in a war on terror that began on September the 11th, 2001, and still goes on.'"[7] CBS News heralded the general theme in the president's speech well when it wrote of the president speaking on the "end of combat operations in Iraq. But President Bush will caution the American people tonight that there is still a lot of difficult work ahead to build the foundations of democracy there."[8]

The *New York Times* reported:

> Mr. Bush made it clear that he considered the Iraq conflict just one major moment of a broader fight that he would pursue against Al Qaeda and other terrorists. He spoke . . . not only about the troops who toppled Mr. Hussein but also about the Sept. 11 attacks, melding the battle against terrorism with the battle against Iraq.[9]

USA Today, too, reported that "President Bush joined cheering sailors and Marines on an aircraft carrier . . . and hailed America's triumph in Iraq but warned that the war against terrorism is far from over. [He cast] the war against Saddam Hussein's regime as a milestone in the campaign against terrorism."[10] In a different article, *USA Today* also saw the larger concern of the Bush administration and suggested that "the Bush administration's focus on Syria is an indication that it hopes to capitalize on its military victory in Iraq to broaden the war on terrorism."[11] *NBC Nightly News* stated: "When the first Gulf War was over, it was over. The troops returned and the issue was dead by the [1992] campaign. This time around, the White House has carefully sought to link Iraq with a permanent war on terror."[12]

Yet the press also added a bit of coloring to the framing of the president. Reports relayed Iraq's position in the War on Terror, but with more than the simple assertion that this was what the president had said. For example, *Nightline* conveyed a sense of incompleteness with the lead-in: "On a day the president sought to at least convey a sense of victory, ABC's Bill Blakemore found a country still drifting between war and peace." In the ensuing report, Blakemore, just hours after major operations were declared over, stated: "The war may be over for the most part but the peace hasn't exactly begun. And the waiting is getting on people's nerves."[13] The next evening, *Nightline* quoted the president saying that "the liberation of Iraq is a crucial advance in the campaign against terror," followed by a quote from an anonymous American intelligence analyst who remarked, "This is yet another instance of the Americans smashing Muslim people."[14] DeWayne Wickham wrote in *USA Today* that President Bush "is the commander in chief leading the assault on the forces that traumatized us on 9/11—a fight he has turned into a worldwide campaign against our evil enemies (as opposed to our evildoing friends)."[15]

Domestic Issues

The president's speech did touch upon domestic issues, but for the press, the main theme within a domestic concern was the economy. Specifically, the press framed this issue in an extremely negative light, and I have highlighted certain statements below to draw more attention to this deliberate counterframing.

The Early Show jumped to domestic issues almost before the president's jet landed, stating: "All right. Now that the major conflict in Iraq is over, all eyes on the economy. President Bush is wanting Congress to OK this $550 billion tax-cut plan."[16] *Today* asked White House communications director Dan Bartlett prior to the speech how much the country was "going to hear from the president tonight . . . on tax cuts, economic stimulus, domestic policy";[17] although not an inappropriate question to ask, the press knew in advance that the speech would focus on the military and the war on terror.

Nightline specifically turned the issue from the military and homeland security to the economy in a segment that presented a collage of responses from Americans:

ABC NEWS REPORTER CHRIS BURY: And here in the U.S.?

MALE RESPONDENT ONE: Time to do something about the economy.

MALE RESPONDENT TWO: The economy sucks right now.

FEMALE RESPONDENT ONE: You know, just the economy, *getting that back on board right now*, you know, really being focused on the American public.

Later in the broadcast, Bury stated: "In his speech tonight, the president wrapped his remarks on Iraq in the popular cloak of the war on terrorism. Certainly the public gives him high marks for that. . . . But [our survey] also suggests some *danger signs for the President on economic issues.*"

ABC NEWS REPORTER MICHEL MARTIN: And when Americans are asked about the most pressing concerns, as we did today in several cities, it is *the economy that emerges as the clear and present danger.* Even with many voters, like the woman in Atlanta, who supported the war.

FEMALE RESPONDENT TWO: There's so many older people that *don't have very much of an income.* And I know that the drugs, medicine and things are *so expensive* that a lot of them have to make choices. You know, *am I going to take my medicine or am I gonna eat today or pay my bills?*

FEMALE RESPONDENT THREE: I think *our attention needs to be focused on the economy.* And President Bush needs to help us come up with a plan.

To all of this, Betsy Stark of ABC News commented, "So, you put it all together and . . . *I think there's plenty of reason for people to feel anxious*, even though the numbers say *the economy continues to limp along."* Reporter Martin then put a damper on even this grudging display of optimism:

MARTIN: In an ABC News poll released this evening, *nearly half of those surveyed said most people have lost ground financially since the President took office.* Just 10 percent said most are better off. And *there is real doubt* about the President's plan for the economy.

MALE RESPONDENT TWO: Over two million Americans have lost their job since Bush took office. *The economy sucks right now.* Not, not solely because of him. But if he was a good president, he would be *trying to fix that instead of manufacturing a war* that everyone can rally behind him so he can get reelected.[18]

Note that the survey above, if reliable, actually reports what Americans think *about the situation for others*, not what they think about their own situation.

The *New York Times* reported that President Bush was paying attention to the economy, but inserted its point of view regarding the president's actions: The day after he declared formal military operations ended in Iraq, wrote David E. Sanger, the president

> confronted rising unemployment [and returned] to his tax-cut battles with Congress. . . . He called for the elimination of the tax on corporate dividends, *even though* members of his own party have backed away from that proposal, and *his own White House endorsed, tepidly*, a move in the House to lower the tax rate on dividends and capital gains rather than eliminate them.

The president, Sanger continued,

> equated tax cuts with job growth . . . *even though* many economists have suggested that there would be more direct and swifter ways to create employment. [Democrats stated] that *against the advice* of [Federal Reserve] Chairman [Alan] Greenspan and *the consensus of economists*, the Republicans leadership is pushing *another dose of a prescription that has already failed.*[19]

Karen DeYoung of the *Washington Post* wrote, "In a symbolic segue from military to economic policy, Bush will travel Friday to a factory manufacturing Bradley Fighting Vehicles, in the *depressed* Silicon Valley, to talk about the economy."[20] *NBC Nightly News* put it in more dramatic terms: "The day after President Bush declared combat over in Iraq, the economy fired back at him at home. This morning, the president took off from the USS *Abraham Lincoln*, only to be hit hard with *bad news on the domestic front*: that increase in unemployment to 6 percent."[21]

World News Tonight put this in a starker way. Pointing out the change from flight suit to "sober business suit," anchor Peter Jennings stated that the change symbolized the president's "shift of focus from the war to the *troubled economy*. Later . . . Mr. Bush argued the *grim new unemployment rate* confirms the need to pass his big tax cut."[22] *NBC Nightly News* stated the network's opinion clearly: "A war victory in the Persian Gulf, *a stumbling economy at home*."[23]

Maureen Dowd of the *New York Times* was more forceful yet:

Every time you cut taxes and raise deficits while you're roaring ahead with a pre-emptive military policy, *you're unsafe*. National unemployment goes up to 6 percent and you just hammer Congress to pass your tax cut. *The only guys sure about their jobs these days are defense contractors connected to Republicans. . . . You're dangerous.*[24]

DeWayne Wickham wrote in *USA Today*:

Bush's hold on the White House is indeed vulnerable to a concerted attack by a Democratic candidate who hammers away at the fact that the *huge* budget surplus he inherited from Bill Clinton has turned into a *whopping* deficit. He's also weakened by the *big jump* in joblessness.[25]

Another *USA Today* article, entitled "Jet Ride Was Smooth, But Tax Cuts Hit Turbulence," stated that the "*real worry, of course,* is the economy. Bush must also surmount the reality that 1.9 million jobs have disappeared since February 2001."[26]

Citing an anonymous "Republican leadership aide on Capitol Hill," the *Washington Post* suggested that the questions being raised by Democrats [about the president's carrier landing] were "uncomfortable," but noted that the discussion "*at least means they're not talking about Medicare or the economy.*"[27] Francis X. Clines of the *New York Times*, speaking of presidential advisor Karl Rove, wrote: "He made the Bush strategy clear: It's the terror, not the economy, Stupid, *even if the nation is suffering rolling deficits and relentless unemployment, and despite Mr. Bush's serial tax cuts for the captains of industry.*"[28]

Contextualizing in such a way to cast even positive developments in a negative light, Chris Matthews on his eponymous show stated:

First up: economic warrior. As the president turns his attention to the economy, there are major hurdles and some positive signs. On the downside, the Dow Jones stock average has dropped 2,000 points since he took office. The economy has lost two million jobs, and the federal budget deficit is now pushing $300 billion a year. But the gross domestic product grew some in the last quarter *despite high oil prices and the war anxiety. . . .* How much time does the president have to *turn this economy around?*[29]

In the same show, Matthews also asked: "The president says ousting Saddam is one victory in the war on terror, but can top gun Bush now score a victory for our economy?"[30]

Top Gun Arrival

The arrival of President Bush received an enormous amount of press commentary; 47 of 91 articles and broadcasts made mention of it. However, the reporting of the arrival fell short of straight description, instead entering into the realm of the glaringly interpretive. Although a handful of articles and newscasts related the president's arrival accurately, most of the rest put a very negative interpretation on it. In an example of more neutral reporting, *The Early Show* cohost Harry Smith said to Rear Adm. John Kelly: "We need to make it clear that . . . you're too far at sea for . . . the president's helicopter . . . to take him out there safely, so how is the president going to land there today?" Kelly replied: "The president is coming aboard on Navy One, which is an S-3B." Unlike the overwhelming majority of the press accounts, Smith focused on the pilot, not the president: "No small amount of pressure on that pilot today."[31]

The above is an exception to the rule of interpretive reporting on the president's arrival. I have broken down the level of interpretive commentary into three groups of low, medium, and high to reflect the amount of coloring the reports injected into the coverage.

Low

Whereas *NBC Nightly News* stated that President Bush "arrived on the carrier in style,"[32] *NBC News Special Report* stated that President Bush "arrived today in spectacular fashion on board a Navy jet that landed in classic style on the deck."[33] *Good Morning America* initially stated that Bush "became the first U.S. President ever to land on an aircraft carrier in a jet. He even took the controls for part of the flight." Then, moving from observation to interpretation, the reporter stated, "It was clearly intended for powerful political effect."[34]

Medium

USA Today stressed that the president had originally desired to fly to the carrier in an "F-18 fighter jet. . . . [Instead] he'll board a four-seat Navy S-3B. Previous presidents' visits to carriers have been by helicopter, but the *Lincoln* will be too far from shore. An airplane landing is more exciting."[35] *Today* called it a *"Top Gun* setting for a prime-time speech."[36] Later in the same broadcast, *Today* cohost Matt Lauer tried repeatedly to force his point:

LAUER: I've landed on the deck of carriers in fighter jets before. It's thrilling, but it's also very dangerous. Why take this risk with the commander in chief?

WHITE HOUSE DIRECTOR OF COMMUNICATIONS DAN BARTLETT: It's been about thirty years since he's climbed in the cockpit of . . . a jet. And . . . he's looking forward to it. In fact. . . .

LAUER: And looking forward to it, but you could land him in a helicopter. It'd be an awful lot safer.

BARTLETT: Well, actually. . . .

LAUER: . . . in real terms, is this symbolism overshadowing safety?

BARTLETT: Actually . . . the people who looked at this from a safety concern believe that flying into it in a jet is actually safer than a helicopter because you have the ability to eject.[37]

CBS Evening News reported that the arrival was

a first-of-a-kind photo op. Beginning with his dramatic flight onto this decorated carrier, the White House has sent a clear signal: It is pulling out all the stops choreographing this finale to the war. The president chose to fly in on a Navy jet because he wanted to experience landing on a carrier . . . and the adrenaline rush that comes with it.[38]

Nightline declared, "In terms of political showmanship, a picture of the president landing on the deck of an aircraft carrier is hard to beat. At the end of the day, that swashbuckling image may be just what the White House wanted television viewers . . . to remember above all else."[39]

The *Washington Post* reported that both the president's "arrival and stay [on the ship] provided the ultimate in presidential symbolism. For a president fresh from victory in battle, who has cultivated an aggressive, can-do image, it was a scene straight from 'Top Gun' that is sure to appear in future campaign ads."[40] Contradicting the declaration of military experts, the *New York Times* editorialized that the arrival set "a new standard for high-risk presidential travel."[41] The *Times*'s Clines called the president's landing a "cheeky performance in fighter pilot regalia at the carrier-deck victory tableau."[42]

On *Good Morning America*, reporter Charles Gibson stated: "An arrival Hollywood style. It was quite a setting for his speech, and quite an arrival onboard the aircraft carrier," to which host Diane Sawyer replied: "You're right. Even the Democrats said it was a John Wayne moment." Gibson agreed: "Yeah. Indeed it was."[43] *The Early Show* called the arrival a "made-for-TV-moment."[44]

Nightline's Chris Bury set the tone for the discussion to follow when he said of the landing:

> The President's performance aboard that . . . carrier . . . has stirred up a fuss among Democrats. His *Top Gun* landing, they complain, was over the top, a political stunt crafted for the cameras and his reelection campaign. But an incumbent President clearly enjoys an advantage. And the White House can always muster up a good reason for any event. In this case, that the commander in chief was thanking American troops in person for a job well done.[45]

High

Chris Matthews asked, "Can top gun Bush now score a victory for our economy? Lights, camera, action. The president bonds with troops in a war-ending spectacle. Was this a Reaganesque moment or what?" On the same show, guest Lou Dobbs of CNN called the arrival "a stunt."[46] *Today* stated that with the president's "dramatic landing in an S-3 . . . a presidential first, George Bush emerged with a swagger."[47]

The *Washington Post* stated:

> For Bush . . . the whole day was devoted to linking his presidency to the aura of the U.S. military. When the . . . S-3B carrying Bush made its tailhook landing on the aircraft carrier . . . Bush emerged from the cockpit in full olive flight suit and combat boots, his helmet tucked jauntily under his left arm. As he exchanged salutes with the sailors, his ejection harness, hugging him tightly between the legs, gave him the swagger of a top gun.[48]

The *New York Times*, too, described the president in unflattering terms: "Mr. Bush emerged for the kind of photographs that other politicians can only dream about. He hopped out of the plane with a helmet tucked under his arm and walked across the flight deck with a swagger that seemed to suggest that he had seen 'Top Gun.'"[49] Maureen Dowd of the *Times* wrote of the landing:

> out bounded the cocky, rule-breaking, daredevil flyboy, a man navigating the Highway to the Danger Zone, out along the edges where he was born to be, the further on the edge, the hotter the intensity. He flashed that famous all-American grin as he swaggered around the

deck. . . . Compared to Karl Rove's . . . myth-making cinematic style, Jerry Bruckheimer's movies look like 'Lizzie McGuire.' This time Maverick [President Bush] didn't just nail a few bogeys. . . . this time the Top Gun [President Bush] wasted a couple of nasty regimes. . . . He swaggered across the deck to high-five his old gang.

Putting words in the president's mouth, she had him uttering: "That's right. . . . I am dangerous."[50]

Also in the *New York Times*, Paul Krugman likened Bush to Georges Boulanger, a "French General, minister of war, and political figure who led a brief but influential authoritarian movement that threatened to topple [France's] Third Republic in the 1880s."[51] Krugman then compared "that history" with

George Bush's 'Top Gun' act . . . c'mon, guys, it wasn't about honoring the troops, it was about showing the president in a flight suit—[it] was as scary as it was funny. A U.S.-based British journalist told me that he and his colleagues had laughed through the whole scene. And nobody seemed bothered that Mr. Bush, who appears to have skipped more than a year of the National Guard service that kept him out of Vietnam, is now emphasizing his flying experience.[52]

World News Tonight led with the following line: "Bush Exploits War for Photo Op." Anchorman Jennings called the arrival a "powerful photo opportunity" and then explained how two Democrats were criticizing it, "asking government auditors to figure out how much the trip cost the taxpayers" and claiming that the landing was "an affront to the Americans killed or injured in Iraq for the President to exploit the trappings of war for the momentary spectacle of a speech."[53]

The above paraphrases came from Rep. Henry A. Waxman (D-CA) and Sen. Robert C. Byrd (D-WV), respectively, and were quoted extensively from May 6, 2003, on. For example, after the *Washington Post* wrote that President Bush had engaged in a "'Top Gun' style event," it quoted Senator Byrd extensively: "Byrd . . . delivered an impassioned speech on the Senate floor, saying he was 'deeply troubled' [by what he considered President Bush's] 'flamboyant showmanship.' 'To me, it is an affront to the Americans killed or injured in Iraq for the president to exploit the trappings of war for the momentary spectacle of a speech.'"[54]

This aspect of the press criticism resulted from a change—*minimally reported* by the press—in the location of the USS *Abraham Lincoln* as it was approaching the port. When the White House originally announced to the press that the carrier would be out of helicopter range, that statement reflected the conditions at that time. Between then and the president's arrival, the weather had changed, and the carrier had cruised closer to shore than originally planned. The *New York Times* failed to make this clear, though, when, in its first paragraph in an article on this issue, it suggested the White House had lied:

> The White House said today that President Bush traveled to the carrier *Abraham Lincoln* last week on a small plane because he wanted to experience a landing the way carrier pilots do, not because the ship would be too far out to sea . . . to arrive by helicopter, as [the White House] had originally maintained.[55]

It was not until the very last sentence of the article that Ari Fleischer, White House spokesman, was paraphrased as saying that weather had caused the change.

Dan Rather on *CBS Evening News* announced that not "all critics of the Halliburton deal are Democrats . . . but many of them are, and the contract is not all they're upset about tonight. They're also critical of President Bush's triumphant trip to the . . . *Lincoln* last week, a trip about which the White House now has changed some of its story." Reporter John Roberts followed up:

> It was a photo op to die for, a full tailhook landing . . . . But the adrenaline-pumping arrival is under attack tonight from Democrats as an unnecessary political stunt. Making matters worse, an evolving White House story. The jet was necessary, it first said, because the *Lincoln* was out of range for the president's helicopter. Then, with the skyline of San Diego in plain sight, the story changed. President Bush simply wanted to make a *Top Gun* landing.[56]

Neither Roberts nor Rather mentioned the reason for the changed story.

In another example of making it seem as if the White House had lied about the landing, the *Washington Post* led with a story entitled "Ship Carrying Bush Delayed Return; Carrier That Spent the Night off San Diego Could Have Gone Straight to Home Port." Although the *Post* did quote naval officials about not wanting to return to home port before the announced day for fear of "tricking [the families] and coming in sooner," it left out any mention of the bad weather, the *very* reason the carrier came into the area early. Instead, the *Post* stated:

The possibility of a taint emerged . . . when the White House acknowledged that Bush had not needed to arrive in the Navy jet . . . as first asserted, but instead could have used a helicopter. That would not have required that olive-green flight suit and helmet that Bush posed with.[57]

In a similar vein, *USA Today* wrote: "The White House initially said the carrier was too far out at sea to use a helicopter. [Ari] Fleischer acknowledged that the ship was close enough and said Bush took the jet because he wanted to experience a carrier landing."[58] Again, no mention of the weather, Navy docking procedures, or that the Navy had said that landing in a jet was safer than in a helicopter.

In another article, the *New York Times* continued to press an interpretation that left out both the weather and Navy assertions about proper docking procedures:

Democrats seized on the White House admission that Mr. Bush had landed on the carrier in a . . . jet because he wanted to, not, as White House officials had told reporters, because the ship was too far off shore for a helicopter. . . . In fact, the ship was only about 30 miles away from San Diego when Mr. Bush popped out of the plane. . . . [The White House today] spent much of the morning beating back accusations that Mr. Bush had delayed the arrival of the ship and added to the government's projected deficit of $246 billion this year. . . . Mr. Fleisher arrived at the White House . . . armed to answer the accusation that taxpayer dollars had been squandered so Mr. Bush could relive his youth.[59]

Frank Rich of the *Times*, utterly ignoring Navy protocol and weather reports, wrote: "The White House has absorbed the [Jerry] Bruckheimer aesthetic so fully that its 'Top Gun' was better, not to mention briefer, than the original [movie *Top Gun*]. [The] return of the *Lincoln* and its eagerly homeward bound troops was delayed by a day to accommodate the pageantry of Mr. Bush's tailhook landing."[60]

In the *Washington Post*, E. J. Dionne Jr. also disregarded information contrary to his beliefs when he wrote:

Bush and his White House say whatever is necessary, even if they have to admit later that what they said the first time wasn't exactly true. Consider this paragraph from the *New York Times* . . . about [the] Bush-in-a-flight-suit moment. "The White House said today that President Bush traveled to the carrier . . . on a small plane because he wanted to experience a landing the way carrier pilots do, not because the ship would be too far out to sea . . . to arrive by helicopter. . . ." Now that's very interesting. You can be absolutely sure that if an Al Gore White House had . . . misled citizens about the reason . . . Gore would have been pilloried. . . . Yet Bush's defenders have done a good job selling the idea that it's churlish to raise questions . . . even if the White House was not exactly honest about the circumstances of the flight.[61]

Reelection Speech

Very few articles or broadcasts focused on the speech as given by President Bush. Those that did mention the purpose of the speech negatively mixed both attention to the means of presidential arrival and the situation in Iraq with the president's message. Very few reports— less than ten—stated the purpose of the speech as the White House had announced that purpose: "to tell the American people the major combat in Iraq is now over, but still difficult challenges lie ahead."[62] The lion's share of reports on the purpose of the speech set it squarely into the realm of the president's forthcoming, yet unannounced, reelection campaign.

For example, *NBC Nightly News* quoted Democratic consultant Peter Fenn saying the entire event was "tailor-made for television. But to . . . assume . . . that this is a foreign policy event when it really is geared to domestic political concerns . . . you have to be a little skeptical."[63] Similarly *CBS Evening News* stated, "The images that the president will present tonight, with the splendor of the *Lincoln* all around him, is that of the commander in chief fully in charge, an image that the White House hopes will be etched in the minds of voters as Mr. Bush now turns his sights toward domestic concerns."[64]

The *Washington Post* quoted historian Douglas Brinkley, who said that the president would find the aircraft carrier visit in his biography. The *Post* then wrote, "Even before that biography is written, Bush's carrier visit may appear somewhere else: 2004 campaign footage. Brinkley called it 'the opening salvo for his presidential campaign.'"[65] Tom Shales wrote in the *Post* that the event was not so much a speech as a "patriotic spectacular, with the ship and crew serving as crucial backdrops for Bush's remarks. . . . It was a White House production and just as surely marked the president's reelection campaign as it did the end to" major combat operations in Iraq.[66] In a different *Washington Post* story, White House officials were described as acting with "an eye on the 2004 election. . . . But as last night's speech . . . demonstrated, the president's advisors are determined to draw maximum attention to, and take maximum advantage of, his role as commander in chief."[67]

In the *New York Times*, David Sanger wrote: "Earlier in the day, in a visit to the carrier that the White House arranged for maximum political effect. . . . The image of the president surrounded by beaming sailors was an image that White House officials clearly intend to use in the 2004 presidential campaign."[68] Editorially, the *New York Times* wrote that the "Top Gun" visit by the president "will undoubtedly make for a potent campaign commercial."[69]

Similarly, *USA Today* wrote that the administration "crafted the visit to highlight Bush's credentials as commander in chief and lay the political groundwork for the 2004 presidential campaign."[70] Another *USA Today* article a few days later commented that "President Bush effectively launched his re-election campaign last week with his made-for-TV speech."[71]

CBS Morning News cast the visit as "what was clearly designed to be one of the all-time great photo opportunities."[72] Along the same lines, *CBS Evening News* stated:

> The president's made-for-TV arrival on the . . . *Lincoln* signals the opening of his 2004 campaign and his expected focus on national security. And with polls showing the struggling economy is by far the biggest concern of most Americans, Mr. Bush is also determined not to repeat his father's mistake of appearing unconcerned.[73]

This press framing of the landing continued in the same vein throughout the period covered in this chapter. For example, Krugman of the *New York Times*, while on ABC's *Nightline*, said "What [the White House] is basically doing is turning the military victory in Iraq into a personal showpiece for the President." On the same show, *Washington Post* columnist Shales said that "it wasn't so much the end of the war as the start of his re-election campaign. This was the kickoff. And he was using the United States armed forces and a big aircraft carrier and all the money that that involves as his props."[74]

USA Today wrote: "A school of thought holds that the 2004 election was . . . decided the moment Airman-in-Chief George W. Bush landed on the flight deck of the . . . *Lincoln*."[75] In the *New York Times*, Clines complained that "the difficulty of the Democrats' task was exemplified after some party leaders tried to complain about political crassness in the president's cheeky performance in fighter pilot regalia," while Rich wrote, "George W. Bush delivered his prime-time address from the

U.S.S. *Abraham Lincoln* declaring that the war on terrorism will not end before he is re-elected."[76] The *Washington Post* opined that "Mr. Bush's visit to the . . . *Lincoln* may have been the real kickoff of his presidential campaign. If the Democrats' tone-deaf handling of his episode is any indication, he may well get his four more years."[77]

Summary

Questions of politics aside, the president's speech served three broad purposes. First, it served to announce the end of formal military operations and to publicly thank U.S. military personnel for their work in Iraq. "Mission Accomplished" meant only that the military had succeeded in overthrowing Saddam Hussein and that the second phase of the Iraq war was now under way. Second, the speech allowed the president to rearticulate the themes within the War on Terror, especially placing them within the context of the Iraq war. Finally, the speech allowed the president to rearticulate the Bush Doctrine.

As in his other major speeches concerning the War on Terror, Bush here restated the basic themes inherent within the master frame for the War on Terror. Patience was again called for, and the president also returned to the theme of international cooperation in fighting terrorism. He again carefully used the bipolar themes of the United States representing the good and civilized and terrorists representing the evil and barbaric. Additionally, the themes of the nature of the war and the nature of the terrorists were again hammered home in this speech. The president's frame for the War on Terror was now well established. Iraq was clearly depicted as only part of the larger War on Terror. As such, Bush could state: "Our commitment to liberty is America's tradition. . . . We are committed to freedom in Afghanistan, in Iraq, and in a peaceful Palestine. The advance of freedom is the surest strategy to undermine the appeal of terror in the world."

Finally, what had come to be called the Bush Doctrine was further articulated in this speech. The president made clear that "any person involved in committing or planning terrorist attacks against the American people becomes an enemy of this country. . . . Any person, organization, or government that supports, protects, or harbors terrorists is . . . equally guilty of terrorist crimes." All "will be confronted," he promised. The president was careful, however, to point out that any country that works and sacrifices for freedom, "including the Arab world . . .

has a loyal friend in the United States of America." Importantly for the Bush Doctrine, the president left open the nature of the confrontation.

Overall, the press gave supportive lip service to the War on Terror, but acted in opposition to most of what the president said. Although it was a considerable focus of the Bush speech, the press offered no real discussion about the nature of war or of the nature of the terrorists. Moreover, the content of the president's speech was overshadowed by the press obsession with the means of his arrival and the economy. The president's arrival was cast in a mocking light: Top Gun Bush delayed docking for a day in order to dramatically land by jet on an aircraft carrier and swagger in front of the camera's for reelection campaign promotions. The press failed to draw attention to alternate reasons for the trip or to the pragmatic reasons that the carrier was so close to shore. The landing was framed as a publicity stunt. In terms of the economy, the press simply asserted that it *was* bad; no explanation or justification for *why it was bad* was ever provided, nor were alternate economic indicators mentioned by the press. Fueled by cherry-picked examples and ignored evidence, the press placed the yoke of a bad economy squarely on the shoulders of President Bush.

The negative focus on the economy came from the press assumptions that Bush was beginning his reelection campaign with this speech and that, to avoid the mistake his father made, he would have to face the economy now, since the economy was so bad. For example, the *Washington Post* compared father and son when it wrote:

> Bush has benefited far less from the successful outcome in Iraq than his father . . . did from the U.S. victory in the 1991 Persian Gulf War, largely because the country remains polarized over the younger Bush's presidency. . . . That means Bush does not have as far to fall to find himself in the same kind of jeopardy over the economy that helped defeat his father in 1992.[78]

NBC Nightly News highlighted the press focus on analogies with father and son: "The parallels are striking. Then and now, they both had successful Gulf wars and high approval ratings. Then as now, the economy was weak at home. So it's becoming a nagging question, an obsession really, among journalists. By election day 2004, will it be like father, like son?"[79] *USA Today* wrote that "Bush now is experiencing much the same euphoric high that lofted his father's job ratings after he ejected the Iraqis from Kuwait in 1991. The laws of political gravity caught up with the senior Bush, but his son is exerting great effort to demonstrate that he is not inattentive to U.S. economic problems. Is this enough?"[80]

Attentive or not, the press presented an extremely negative focus on the economy, and this included bias concerning the reporting of economic conditions and the president's plans. For instance, the White House called President Bush's plan for stimulating the economy a "jobs and growth package"; Democrats called it "tax cuts for the rich." The majority of the press reported it simply as a "tax cut." The *Washington Post*, for example, actually put "jobs and growth" in quotation marks, followed by, "Democrats have said the *tax cut* would primarily benefit rich corporate interests." Later in the same article, the *Post* again referenced "jobs growth" in quotation marks, but then wrote that the "While House has signaled it would be prepared to accept a [smaller] *tax cut package*."[81] *NBC Nightly News* also pushed the tax cut angle: "Many believe a new round of *tax cuts* helps the rich more than the economy."[82] Like most in the press, Wickham of *USA Today* placed the economy in the context of the upcoming 2004 election: "While I think almost any one of the nation's leading Democrats would be a better president than George W. Bush, I don't believe just any Democrat can beat him next year." Ignoring the historical context of the economy, he continued, asserting that president Bush had turned "the huge budget surplus he inherited from Bill Clinton . . . into a whopping deficit."[83]

Of note is the volume of information then available that either contradicts or questions the press interpretation of the economy. For example, it was known even in 2003 that the recession began under the Clinton administration; in particular, gross domestic product (GDP) growth dropped dramatically in the third quarter of 2000, but by late 2001 was well on the way to recovery. The National Bureau of Economic Research has said that the recession ended in November 2001.[84] Total job figures pushed by the press are also contested. For example, by 1 May 2003, job losses since 9/11 had been replaced.[85] Even the claims the press made about retirement can be disputed. For instance, one study found that those retiring between 1998 and 2002 had an average household income of $49,000 and only one in five were "struggling financially." Incredibly, 84 percent said they were "'satisfied' with their new life status."[86]

As for the stock market, it was not until the mid-1990s that the Dow Jones average broke 10,000 for the first time in its history. With the recession and 9/11 it fell, and by mid-2003 it was at 8,500; however, by the end of 2003, seven months after the president's speech, and amid general wailing by the press about the economy, the Dow was up almost to 10,500. Additionally, the economy was steadily climbing during the time of the speech, and this was reflected in "GDP growth of 8.2% in the third quarter 2003. This represents the best quarterly growth since December 1983."[87] The press failed to explore these figures, and instead pushed the same negative interpretation of the economy that it had since before 9/11.

Press responses to this speech also highlighted that the press had defined the Bush Doctrine as an aggressive military policy of preemption, even though the president had left all options open. Although there were exceptions, generally speaking the press framed the Bush Doctrine in such a way that the use of military force was highlighted. For example, the *Washington Post* stated that the president portrayed "the anti-terrorist battles in the tradition of the Normandy invasion and Iwo Jima," and in so doing, he "placed his own doctrine of overwhelming American strength and the use of preemptive force alongside . . . Roosevelt's Four Freedoms, the Truman Doctrine of containment, and Ronald Reagan's challenge to the Soviet Union's 'Evil Empire.'"[88]

Demonstrating concern over the acceptability of the Bush Doctrine, *USA Today* wrote that it was "critical" to

> avoid overselling the applicability of this military victory to other foreign crises. After 9/11, Bush outlined the doctrine of preemption—which he repeated [on the *Lincoln*]—to rally the world behind the war against Afghanistan and the global hunt for al-Qaeda. . . . Without more details about Saddam's banned weapons and ties to al-Qaeda, questions remain about whether Iraq posed the immediate threat to U.S. security that White House officials claimed in the buildup to war. Prematurely embracing the doctrine as a successful model could undermine global support for the war on terrorism.[89]

6

President Bush Addresses the United Nations General Assembly, September 2003

> The Security Council was right to be alarmed. The Security Council was right to demand that Iraq destroy its illegal weapons and prove that it had done so. The Security Council was right to vow serious consequences if Iraq refused to comply.
>
> —George W. Bush

> Bush offered no apology for ordering the invasion of Iraq in March after the U.N. balked at endorsing it.
>
> —*USA Today*

> Most diplomats and scholars focused on Mr. Bush's unapologetic tone on the subject of the war in Iraq.
>
> —*New York Times*

The President's Speech

President Bush's speech before the United Nations on September 23, 2003, is no exception to the rule that each speech is unique. Given the ongoing nature of the War on Terror and the Bush administration's remarkable consistency in framing the war, it is not surprising that the president again carried forward the same themes and frames as the previous speeches covered in this book; however, this was done with the specific situation and moment in time well reflected in the speech. This is to say, the speech is indicative of its connection to a difficult past and an uncertain future. This link is shown in the president's use of New York City as a "symbol of an unfinished war."[1]The war, of course, is against terrorists, and the president stated that by "the victims they choose, and by the means they use, the terrorists have clarified the struggle we are in." It is not the United States, he said, but the terrorists who "have set themselves against all humanity. Those who incite murder and celebrate suicide reveal their contempt for life, itself."

We see again the discordance of the civilized and the barbaric, readily apparent after so many speeches consistently hammering home the opposition of U.S. actions and those of the terrorists. The president pushed these poles even farther apart when he stated: "Between these alternatives there is no neutral ground. All governments that support terror are complicit in a war against civilization." For the Bush administration, the terrorists presented the civilized world with

> the clearest of divides: between those who seek order, and those who spread chaos; between those who work for peaceful change, and those who adopt the methods of gangsters; between those who honor the rights of man, and those who deliberately take the lives of men and women and children without mercy or shame.

As example of this dichotomy, Bush highlighted the Iraqi people now experiencing "dignity and freedom" instead of a "squalid, vicious tyranny." In this sense, then, their "life is being improved by liberty," a core American value.

The Bush administration used two primary justifications for going to war with Iraq:

1. that Iraq possessed, and was in the process of producing, weapons of mass destruction (WMD) that could be used by terrorists
2. Saddam Hussein's depraved treatment of his own people

In short, the Bush administration used both WMD and humanitarian justifications for going to war. It is not surprising, given that stockpiles of WMDs were not found in Iraq, that the administration would of necessity clarify its position.

Concerning the humanitarian aspect, little doubt existed but that Hussein was a butcher: "The torture chambers, and the rape rooms, and the prison cells for innocent children—are closed. And as we discover the killing fields and mass graves of Iraq, the true scale of Saddam's cruelty is being revealed." It is not so much that Hussein was a terrorist, or was directly behind the 9/11 attacks, but rather that Hussein was an "ally of terror." Thus, for example, President Bush stated that the

> regime of Saddam Hussein cultivated ties to terror while it built weapons of mass destruction. It used those weapons in acts of mass murder, and refused to account for them when confronted by the world. The Security Council was right to be alarmed. The Security Council was right to demand that Iraq destroy its illegal weapons and prove that it had done so. The Security Council was right to vow serious consequences if Iraq refused to comply.

Note above the linking of the administration's interpretation of intelligence reports about the WMDs to the past actions of the United Nations. Not only is the interpretation linked, but all of the actions of the United States are linked to the international sanction of the United Nations, as well as to the larger philosophical concerns of the UN. The United States did not act alone, rather it was the leader of a coalition whose "actions in Afghanistan and Iraq were supported by many governments." Additionally, the president declared,

> [as] an original signer of the U.N. Charter, the United States of America is committed to the United Nations. And we show that commitment by working to fulfill the U.N.'s stated purposes, and give meaning to its ideals. The founding documents of the United Nations and the founding documents of America stand in the same tradition.

Importantly, both "require—both recognize a moral law that stands above men and nations, which must be defended and enforced by men and nations."

When linking the past actions of the United States to the United Nations, Bush also linked the principles of the United Nations with future concrete actions of the United States. For instance, the broad overlapping principles of the United States and the United Nations demonstrated that

> there was, and there remains, unity among us on the fundamental principles and objectives of the United Nations. We are dedicated to the defense of our collective security, and to the advance of human

rights. These permanent commitments call us to great work in the world, work we must do together.

Moving into the realm of an uncertain future, the president specified concrete actions that showed Iraq as just one battle in the War on Terror. The new actions for America and the world included three distinct areas: First, the president insisted "we must stand with the people of Afghanistan and Iraq as they build free and stable countries. The terrorists and their allies fear and fight this progress above all, because free people embrace hope over resentment, and choose peace over violence." Moreover, it is the United Nations that "has been a friend of the Afghanistan people." It has been the "United Nations [that is] carrying out vital and effective work every day." Specifically, and importantly in terms of responding to criticisms of his policies, the president saw a role for the United Nations in rebuilding Iraq and invited UN participation:

> And the United Nations can contribute greatly to the cause of Iraq self-government. America is working with friends and allies on a new Security Council resolution, which will expand the U.N.'s role in Iraq. As in the aftermath of other conflicts, the United Nations should assist in developing a constitution, in training civil servants, and conducting free and fair elections.

The United States, as part of the international coalition and a member of the United Nations, has been "meeting it[s] responsibilities." Moreover, the "coalition is helping to improve the daily lives of the Iraqi people." This included, importantly, the consideration that "Iraq now has a Governing Council, the first truly representative institution in that country." Additionally, the "success of a free Iraq will be watched and noted throughout the region. Millions will see that freedom, equality, and material progress are possible at the heart of the Middle East."

The second new area involved WMDs. By this time, it was apparent that Iraq was not yielding the cache of weapons that the Bush administration, many Americans, and so many around the world had thought it would. The president sought to redirect the focus from Iraq and onto a larger issue:

> A second challenge we must confront together is the proliferation of weapons of mass destruction. Outlaw regimes that possess nuclear, chemical and biological weapons—and the means to deliver them— would be able to use blackmail and create chaos in entire regions. These weapons could be used by terrorists to bring sudden disaster

and suffering on a scale we can scarcely imagine. The deadly combination of outlaw regimes and terror networks and weapons of mass murder is a peril that cannot be ignored or wished away. If such a danger is allowed to fully materialize, all words, all protests, will come too late.

Thus it was no longer a question of whether or not Iraq *actually possessed* weapons at the start of the war, but that *the intentions* of the Bush administration and the United Nations were correct: weapons of mass destruction cannot be allowed into terrorists' hands. Bush pushed this line of thought in asking the UN Security Council to "adopt a new antiproliferation resolution" that would criminalize the proliferation of weapons.

The third, and seemingly unrelated, action promoted by President Bush consisted of a "challenge to our conscience." In this area, he spoke for the approximately one million persons sold into slavery each year; additionally, he spoke directly to the sex trade associated with this slavery. Although not directly linked with the War on Terror, this area possesses strong humanitarian dimensions, and one of the reasons cited for the war in Iraq was humanitarian in nature. Thus, this call was meant to strengthen the humanitarian standing of the Bush administration.

In summing up, Bush sought to link the concerns of the United States and the United Nations, implying that future American actions would anticipate the approval of the United Nations:

> All the challenges I have spoken of this morning require urgent attention and moral clarity. Helping Afghanistan and Iraq to succeed as free nations in a transformed region, cutting off the avenues of proliferation, abolishing modern forms of slavery—these are the kinds of great tasks for which the United Nations was founded. In each case, careful discussion is needed, and also decisive action.

Moreover, the president specifically called for expanding the role of the UN in Iraq; he also spoke about a new UN resolution in Iraq and having the UN directly involved in supervising elections and in helping Iraq develop its constitution.

The Press Response

There existed a distinct disjunction between the themes and frames used by President Bush and those reported by the press.[2] The press focused not on the War on Terror, nor even directly on President Bush's speech. Instead, it focused on the overall situation surrounding the president's speech and framed that as "dire straits." By this I mean that the press framed Iraq as being in chaos, thus putting the Bush administration in dire straits and forcing it to beg the United Nations—especially France, Germany, and Russia—for help. However, a defiant Bush offered no apology for unilaterally invading Iraq without United Nations approval and also offered no concessions or compromises. Because of this, Americans were not to expect any help from the United Nations (which represented a united world community against the United States). This is a full-bodied frame, yet it represents the press coverage of President Bush's speech to the United Nations.

Iraq in Chaos

The press presented the situation in Iraq in the most negative of terms and shared only examples that would support this frame. *The Early Show*, for example, quoted Sen. Edward Kennedy (D-MA) saying that he "called the situation in Iraq out of control." After quoting Kennedy, reporter Bill Plante emphasized Kennedy's interpretation when he ended his report by stating: "With the chaos in Iraq and his popularity dropping, Mr. Bush simply wanted to make the point that he has a policy."[3] *USA Today* wrote: "Fallout from Iraq is triggering many Republicans' concerns. The continuing deaths of U.S. troops are raising qualms about the wisdom of the war. The pace of reconstruction is prompting questions about the administration's competence." Later in the same news article, it added: "Rebuilding Iraq has become a bloody, expensive struggle. Saddam and al-Qaeda leader Osama bin Laden are still at large."[4] Another *USA Today* reporter wrote that the administration was "stuck in a worse-than-expected struggle" and quoted a Democratic advisor saying that the United States "could well wind up locked into this conflict as we were in Vietnam."[5]

The *New York Times* relayed France's call for early transfer of sovereignty to Iraq as a way of "calm[ing] the anti-American violence there"[6]; no explanation was given concerning who was committing this violence. In a news summary, the *New York Times* reiterated its position that Iraq had erupted into "anti-American violence."[7] An editorial in the same edition implied that Iraq's transition to self-rule might "founder on the considerable anti-American bias within the country. The United States clearly fears that if the United Nations takes over the job, it will make a mess of things. We are in a mess already." The edi-

torial added that Bush "desperately needs" UN assistance.[8] In a more
cautionary tone, the *Washington Post* called the U.S. efforts in Iraq a
"struggle to stabilize" that nation.[9] The *Post*'s Richard Cohen wrote
that the "facts on the ground are so awful" and referred to the "sloppy
and incredibly expensive occupation of Iraq."[10]

The above examples represent the majority of press responses.
There were a few reports less inflammatory, but even these imparted a
sense of urgency to the situation. For instance, *CBS Evening News* reported that "President Bush urgently needs the world to chip in to help
pay the bills and marshal more troops."[11] *NBC Nightly News* called the
situation in Iraq "a critical time for the administration and American
foreign policy," going on to say that UN support "is so desperately
needed now."[12] *Today* relayed a quote from the president of the Council on Foreign Relations, Richard Haass: "The United States is in serious need."[13] ABC News *Special Report* stated that the president was "up
against a lot of challenges both abroad and domestically. He's also
coming in . . . a very weakened political state."[14]

Appeals for Help

Within this urgent setting, the press depicted a White House appealing for aid due to its mishandling of the war and its impudence for
acting without the blessing of the United Nations. *CBS Evening News*,
for example, reported that "President Bush appealed today for international help."[15] *The Early Show* commented that Bush went to the
United Nations "looking for help after going to war in Iraq without UN
sanction."[16] *Today* noted that after "challenging the UN's relevance, the
president now wants UN members to send money and troops." The
show then quoted a former U.S. deputy United Nations ambassador:
"Having run rough-shod over the UN . . . the U.S. now realizes it needs
its allies."[17] On the same show, another comment mentioned that "the
president will appeal for help."[18]

World News Tonight with Peter Jennings stated that President Bush
was "asking for support [for] rebuilding Iraq from the same organization he was willing to work without when the U.S. went after" Iraq.[19]
Good Morning America reported that the president was "there to try to
convince world leaders to help out in Iraq."[20] Later on the same program, criticism of the president was relayed: "some say his hat is in his
hand" as he went to speak to the United Nations.[21] Moreover, it was
said to be a "high-stakes speech . . . asking a skeptical world for help in
Iraq."[22] *USA Today* wrote that the president's "appeal to the United

Nations . . . to help reconstruct Iraq is a tacit admission that his administration has reached a foreign policy turning point."[23]

A Defiant Bush Defends Actions

According to the press, it was with a defiant attitude that the president held his hat in his hand asking for help, and this acted against U.S. ability to attract aid. In short, the president had the gall to defend U.S. actions when they were clearly wrong. *CBS Evening News* reported that the president "defended his decision to go to war."[24] *NBC Nightly News* observed that the president's reception would not "be a love fest for his Iraq policy," and that in "defend[ing] those policies" he was "defiant in the face of critics."[25] Talking between themselves, Charles Gibson of *Good Morning America* asked, "Is he on . . . the defensive to some extent?" to which George Stephanopoulos replied, "I think he is."[26] The *Washington Post* wrote that the president would be "in an unfamiliar position: on the defensive."[27] *CBS Morning News* stated that delegates to the United Nations "heard the president defend his policy."[28] The *New York Times* wrote that the president was "vigorous in his defense of the war."[29]

Defense, though, turned increasingly to defiance. For example, Noah Feldman wrote in the *New York Times* that the president had given a "defiant speech" at the United Nations.[30] Dana Milbank of the *Washington Post* wrote that President Bush was "defending the invasion of Iraq" in his speech; he went on to say that Bush "suggested that his actions were in support of U.N. wishes, not defiance."[31] Editorially, the *Post* described Bush's comments concerning "his decision to proceed with and invasion . . . without [UN] support" as a "defense."[32] In the same edition, Jim Hoagland wrote that "he seemed unnecessarily unrepentant, and a trifle defensive."[33] In a *New York Times* article, the point was driven home: the president's "tone was not that of a supplicant. He coupled his appeal for help . . . with defiance about the war itself. . . . Mr. Bush was defiant."[34]

No Apology?

I believe the press interpretation of defensiveness and defiance developed because journalists thought the White House actions to be wrong and also thought the president owed the United Nations and the world an apology. *Today* reported that the "president is offering no apologies for his Iraq policy today to a tough audience" at the United Nations.[35] The *New York Times* wrote that Bush spoke as the "unapologetic commander in chief [but] behind the proud words will be a president in a less potent political position than a year ago."[36] Before the speech, *The Early Show* said that "the president is unapologetic,"[37] and afterward made a point of stating that the president received a "very cool reception" at the General Assembly, implying that it was because "he made no apology for going to war . . . without UN backing."[38] *CBS Morning News* iterated that same point of view: the president "was unapologetic, and the response was cool."[39]

On *Today*, cohost Matt Lauer remarked to Democratic presidential candidate Gen. Wesley Clark that the president "walked into the general Assembly, lot of opposition in that room. He was unbending, he was unapologetic, basically saying, 'We were right in Iraq. . . .' What did he accomplish, in your mind?" Clark responded, "I think he . . . laid down a marker of the kinds of tragic arrogance that this administration's represented in its conduct in the international community."[40] *USA Today* reported that "Bush offered no apology for ordering the invasion of Iraq . . . after the U.N. balked at endorsing it."[41] The *New York Times* stressed that "most diplomats and scholars focused on Mr. Bush's unapologetic tone on the subject of the war in Iraq."[42] And in another *New York times* story, the president was described as addressing the UN "without apology."[43]

Going in Alone

Although President Bush made mention of the international coalition supporting the invasion of Iraq, the press continued to push a frame of unilateral White House actions. *CBS Evening News* repeatedly stressed, for instance, that the United States had gone in alone, without world support: "He went to war without [the UN]. But the world, it seems, isn't ready to move on. . . . The rest of the world fundamentally believes that how we have handled Iraq has been wrong from the [start]."[44] *Today*'s coverage included this clip: "Having run rough-shod over the UN . . . the U.S. now realizes it needs its allies, the United Nations, and, yes, even France and Russia and Germany, in trying to get it right in Iraq."[45] While interviewing the Council on Foreign Relations's Haass, *Today* asked: "So you're basically saying this is too little too late in terms of trying to create an atmosphere of multilateralism?"[46] *CBS Morning News* implied that it was the "U.S.'s decision to go to war unilaterally" that was the root of President Bush's UN difficulties.[47] *USA Today* quoted French president Jacques Chirac: "The U.S.-led invasion 'has undermined the multilateral system. . . . No one can act alone in the name of all.'" Later in the same article, the invasion was characterized as a "unilateral action."[48]

The *New York Times* relayed UN secretary-general Kofi Annan's use of the term *unilateral action* to assert that it was "a clear reference to the Bush administration's policy of using pre-emptive force."[49] In a different article, the *New York Times* highlighted statements from several interviews in order to emphasize the administration's alleged unilateralism. For example: it contextualized a remark by Igor S. Ivanov, Moscow's foreign minister, to a Russian television reporter by saying he "chose not to criticize Mr. Bush directly, falling back instead on a general endorsement of multilateralism." Later in the same article President Megawati of Indonesia was quoted as commenting "I do believe that a great many lessons can be learned from the Iraq war," to which the *Times* added, "in particular, that unilateralism carries heavy costs." And it chose to quote Annan—in a "sharp rebuke" of the U.S. war without UN approval—later in the article saying that it "could set precedent that resulted in a proliferation of the unilateral and lawless use of force."[50] The *Times* also described the world as thinking: "The invasion of Iraq, to them, remained a dangerous act of unilateralism now beset by intractable problems."[51]

The *Washington Post* suggested that President Bush "endured a torrent of criticism from world leaders who warned that his policy of unilateral action to confront emerging threats" to the U.S. was dangerous to the United Nations. Later the article carried the same quote by French president Chirac: "No one can act alone in the name of all."[52] Richard Cohen described the Iraq invasion as the "pugnacious arrogance of a year ago—a bristling unilateralism."[53] The *Post* also relayed anonymous quotations to relate its point of view. For example, describing the Bush administration's overall approach to the Iraq war and international affairs, the *Post* wrote, "'It's unilateral by design,' said the former official, who described a White House and Pentagon that do not reach out or listen very well."[54]

An Uncompromising Bush

In terms of the role the United Nations could play in a postwar Iraq, the press made it seem as if the president had offered nothing at all, except to allow the UN to provide money and troops. Implying that the administration was unwilling to compromise, the *Washington Post* wrote that the White House,

> after deciding a month ago to seek U.N. help in getting more foreign troops and funds for Iraq, quickly concluded that it would not be possible to get the help it needed on the terms it wanted. Thus, instead of hailing a new agreement to cooperate, Bush will defend his actions in Iraq.[55]

World News Tonight reported that "many leaders [at the UN] were listening closely for some sign of compromise on the issue of who controls postwar Iraq. And on that . . . Mr. Bush did not budge."[56] Although *Good Morning America* mentioned Bush's suggestion that "the UN might also play a bigger role," it added, "he's not willing to relinquish control over postwar Iraq."[57] Interviewing Democratic presidential contender Wesley Clark, Matt Lauer of *Today* stated that President Bush "was unbending" and asked, "What did he accomplish?" Clark replied, "Well, I think he really laid down . . . a marker that he was going to be standing firm and everybody else was going to have to come to us."[58]

USA Today wrote that President Bush "showed no give on allowing the United Nations a more central role in Iraq, which critics of the [White House] resolution also want."[59] A different *USA Today* article quoted Senator Kennedy: "Our policy can't be all take and no give."[60] And on the very issue of concessions, the *New York Times* quoted a German foreign policy professor, who said: "The situation in Iraq is likely to deteriorate further, with more guerrilla fighting and U.S. casualties. If this happens, Bush will be forced to make some concessions."[61] The *Washington Post* wrote: "The Bush administration wanted control and it wanted international help on U.S. terms. [The UN] confirmed that President Bush cannot have both, so he has settled for control."[62]

Summary

President Bush's UN speech sought to accomplish several goals, including continuation of the framing of the War on Terror, rebuilding strained alliances, and inviting the United Nations to help rebuild Iraq. The themes involved in the War on Terror were included in his speech, although some were not as prominently displayed as in past speeches.

Certainly the president highlighted civilized versus barbaric actions, but other themes were less obvious, such as the nature of the war. There was no major digression from the established framing of these or the other themes that comprised the War on Terror master frame. Bush did, however, further push the dichotomy between (barbaric) terrorists and (civilized) America and its allies. In this way the nature of the terrorists was further clarified, but the president was also able subtly to advance understanding of the Bush Doctrine: civilization will defend itself against the barbarians, and also those who enable barbarian actions. These extremes in behavior allowed for no neutral ground; as the president stated, it presented "the clearest of divides."

Additionally, the president reasserted his administration's justifications for going to war: Hussein's WMD threat and humanitarian reasons. The humanitarian concerns proved to be all too true; the expected cache of superdestructive weapons did not. According to the president, neither after-invasion fact mattered, given that the *expectations* of both the United Nations and the Bush administration were the same. Both of these reasons were linked with numerous past UN resolutions against the Hussein regime. Since the White House used these same UN beliefs as justification for war, Bush was attempting to say that his actions were an extension of the UN's past will in the matter. Perhaps there was a disagreement on the timing of the war, or with the very necessity, but essentially the UN believed the same things about Hussein that the United States had used to justify its invasion. In this way, all of the actions of the United States were linked to the international sanction of the United Nations, as well as to the larger philosophical concerns of the UN.

Importantly in this speech, the president made the effort to acknowledge the strain on the alliances with America's strategic partners by offering the United Nations a larger role in rebuilding Iraq; these concessions were concrete and represented a distinct change in policy for the administration. This was presented as a natural decision, given that the basic values of the United Nations matched those of the United States. In the future, American actions in the War on Terror would anticipate the sanction of the UN.

The press could easily have framed these issues in a manner different than it did. For example, it could have suggested that President Bush was asking the United Nations to shoulder its share of the burden. It could have said that a conciliatory Bush, after being denied UN approval for the war, still offered a role for the UN in rebuilding Iraq. It could have said that the president, even in the face of UN hostility, asserted America's right to defend itself from terrorists. These examples may well be contested, but they do offer alternative frames for consideration. The press made a decision to frame the president's speech in a particular manner—one that ran counter to both the administration's frames and the themes President Bush touched upon in his speech.

To begin with, the press relayed an Iraq spiraling out of control and devolving into chaos. The press deliberately chose to offer only negative examples and assertions concerning the situation in Iraq and laid these at the feet of President Bush. As an example of an assertion, and one clearly dripping with argumentative satire, the *New York Times* editorially stated that President Bush's UN speech "seemed a Panglossian report on how well things are going in Iraq."[63] Implying that the president is blindly or naively optimistic in claiming that rebuilding operations in Iraq were going well is easy to do when the mainstream press focused almost exclusively on the negative occurrences.

We also see here the distinct beginnings of criticism of the administration's rationale for war: no WMDs and no direct al-Qaeda link were found in Iraq. Although true, this reporting deliberately ignored evidence that suggested *capability and desire* to build WMDs, and terrorist links other than with al-Qaeda. The press also pointedly ignored the past actions of the United Nations and also ignored many in America who agreed with the administration's rationale for going to war.

The United States had invaded Iraq without UN approval—specifically over the objections of France, Germany, and Russia. Without the imprimatur of the United Nations, the press refused to legitimate the actions of the Bush administration or to accurately relay its rationale for war. It was of little consequence to the press that there was a coalition of international states supporting the United States; without the UN seal of approval, the action was illegitimate and was described by the press as unilateral. Understanding this, it is easy to see how the press could have expected and desired an apology from the Bush administration; it also explains why the press provided such negative coverage of the speech after an apology did not appear: The president was depicted as both defiant and unapologetic. Additionally, the press hammered home the theme that Bush made no concessions, yet in his speech the president clearly spoke about expanding the role of the UN in Iraq. Moreover, he also spoke about a new UN resolution in Iraq, having the United Nations directly involved in helping Iraq develop its constitution, and having the UN supervise upcoming Iraqi elections. All of this represented a significant concession, yet the press pointedly ignored these points.[64]

Taking the previous chapters into consideration, we see increasing press opposition both to how the president framed certain themes and also to the information Bush wished to emphasize. If one were to assign a name to the press framing of the president's speech, it would be a frame of failure. The press imposed its goals on the speech, ignoring the goals of the White House, and then reported that Bush had failed to meet those goals. Thus we see that the goals the president failed to obtain matched well with the goals the press offered *as the administration's goals*: more troops and money. For example, *CBS Evening News*, even *after Germany offered to help in Iraq*, reported: "Mr. Bush's pitch at the United Nations fell flat, no offers of troops or money."[65]

Other, more general instances of bias occurred when members of the press made damaging assertions but allowed no reply from those of whom they spoke. For instance, *Today* cohost Katie Couric stated: "Obviously, a lot of Democratic candidates . . . are sort of seizing the moment and saying that the Bush appearance before the United Nations is simply too little too late."[66] The *New York Times* remarked that the president "might have drawn a little inspiration from the Dalai Lama's warning that war—in general, not specifically the combat in Iraq— amounted to 'legalized violence.'"[67] A different *New York Times* article flat out speculated that "what struck people [who] watched Mr. Bush in action last week was how readily he treated the United Nations like the Texas Legislature, or as a group of politicians he could try to charm, lobby and outsmart," asserting that the president tried to "schmooze the United Nations."[68]

During the week prior to the president's speech, Senator Kennedy intemperately attacked the Bush administration, calling the reasons to go to war "fraud" and accusing the administration of "bribing" other nations to contribute troops to Iraq. Yet in another example of damaging assertions that are allowed to go unchallenged, the *Washington Post* described the Republican *response* to Kennedy's remarks this way: "Yesterday's *Republican attack* and Democratic *counterattack*. . . . To bolster the Senator's assertion that the administration could not account for billions of dollars and was 'bribing' nations to send troops to Iraq, his office this week released a list of approved loans, expenditures and spending proposals."[69] Following this, five such loans were detailed, but no direct quote from an administration official to explain the White House's position on the issue.

7

President Bush Commemorates Veterans Day and Discusses the War on Terror, 11 November 2005

> We didn't ask for this global struggle, but we're answering history's call with confidence, and with a comprehensive strategy. Defeating a broad and adaptive network requires patience, constant pressure, and strong partners. . . . [Together,] we're disrupting militant conspiracies, we're destroying their ability to make war, and we're working to give millions in a troubled region a hopeful alternative to resentment and violence.
>
> —George W. Bush

> "Stay the course" doesn't play as a strategy when the course seems to lead nowhere. What is victory in Iraq? When will we know we've won? . . . The saying goes that when you're in a hole, the first thing to do is to stop digging. But the president . . . just keeps burrowing deeper into that pile of manure.
>
> —Eugene Robinson, *Washington Post*

The President's Speech

As mentioned in previous chapters, every speech is unique. President Bush's Veterans Day address began with commemoration of military veterans' service, with that service woven into the situation in Iraq.

However, this speech in many ways echoed a speech delivered by the president on October 28, 2005, in Norfolk, Virginia. That speech was designed to counter increasing criticism of the Bush administration's handling of the Iraq war; additionally, it was designed to answer criticism about the gathering and use of prewar intelligence. In short, Bush had begun a concerted offensive against the critics of his administration. The references to the veterans aside, what most differentiated the Veterans Day speech from the October 28 one was that the president specifically mentioned some "Democrats and anti-war critics" who were claiming that he deliberately manipulated prewar intelligence.[1] By specifically responding to these charges, he brought the abstract nature of the War on Terror down to the level of specific political utterances made by those seeking to undermine his political capital.

In this speech, then, Bush sought to counter the unchecked criticism of his administration and to lay out in some detail the underlying strategy of continued U.S. involvement in both Iraq and the larger War on Terror. Even more strongly than in his other speeches in this book, President Bush here sought to convey the very real nature of the terrorists threatening the United States and the world. There is a distinct sense of urgency conveyed in this speech, one that arose in part in response to an ever increasing press focus on the U.S. commitment to the Iraq war and to a diminishing focus on the nature of the terrorist threat. Thus in this speech, the president moved from thanking veterans to again framing for America the War on Terror as a prolonged battle with evil. Specifically, he described in concrete terms the nature of terrorists and then shifted to actions the United States would take in continuation of the War on Terror.

Rooted firmly in public memory, 9/11 evokes words, images, and actions linked to that horrific day. Drawing upon that memory, the president mentioned that Americans "saw the destruction that terrorists intend for our nation. We know that they want to strike again." Bush declared that during the previous four years the "evil that reached our shores has reappeared on other days, in other places." He listed fourteen specific locations around the world and mentioned in passing that there were even more. Knowing public memory regarding specific acts tends to fade, he noted that these "separate images of destruction and suffering . . . can seem like random, isolated acts of madness. . . . Yet, while the killers choose their victims indiscriminately, their attacks serve a clear and focused ideology—a set of beliefs and goals that are evil, but not insane."

The president worked to demonstrate that al-Qaeda is not the only terrorist organization with which America must be familiar; there exist

instead numerous terrorist organizations and splinter groups, all unified worldwide through their ideology and vision. Specifically, terrorist ideology "exploits Islam to serve a violent, political vision: the
establishment, by terrorism, subversion and insurgency, of a totalitarian empire that denies all political and religious freedom." Moreover,
the terrorists conditioned by such an ideology engage in "terrorist
murder against Christians and Hindus and Jews—and against Muslims . . . who do not share their radical vision."

Although Americans recognized the name al-Qaeda and had experienced the touch of terrorism, the war in Iraq had supplanted the
larger problem of terrorism in the minds of many Americans; the president used his speech to demonstrate to Americans that the War on Terror was not only with al-Qaeda but with a larger evil. He demonstrated
that many of those embracing terrorist ideologies

> are part of a global, borderless terrorist organization *like* al-Qaeda—
> which spreads propaganda, and provides financing and technical as-
> sistance to local extremists, and conducts dramatic and brutal
> operations *like* the attacks of September 11th. Other militants are
> found in regional groups, often associated with al-Qaeda. . . . Still oth-
> ers spring up in local cells—inspired by Islamic radicalism, but not
> centrally directed. Islamic radicalism is more like a loose network
> with many branches than an army under a single command.[2]

Important, however, is the point that all of the terrorists have in common both a similar ideology and a shared vision for the world.

Bush's speech served to make the abstract nature of terrorism a
concrete reality. He accomplished this using the words of the terrorists
themselves to describe their vision for the world: "First, these extremists want to end American and Western influence in the broader Middle East, because we stand for democracy and peace, and stand in the
way of their ambitions." Specifically, he mentioned a letter written by
al-Qaeda's second in command, Ayman Zawahiri, who believes that
the "Vietnam War [should be] a model for al-Qaeda." The president
stated that the letter mentioned Americans running away from Vietnam, as well as from "Beirut in 1983 and Mogadishu in 1993." Bush
hammered home the consequences of these actions: the terrorists "believe that America can be made to run again—only this time on a larger
scale, with greater consequences."

The second aspect of the terrorist vision involves "the militant network [wanting] to use the vacuum created by an American retreat to
gain control of a country—a base from which to launch attacks and

conduct their war against non-radical Muslim governments." In the past, countries such as Saudi Arabia, Jordan, Egypt, and Pakistan were targeted. Afghanistan was taken over with bloody results; the terrorists had now targeted Iraq, which, in Zawahiri's words, is "the place for the greatest battle." Thus it was not only the Bush administration that believed Iraq to be the center of the War on Terror at that time; "the terrorists regard Iraq as the central front in their war against humanity." The president urged all Americans to "recognize Iraq as the central front in our war against the terrorists."

The third aspect of the terrorist vision is that "these militants believe that controlling one country will rally the Muslim masses, enabling them to overthrow all moderate governments in the region, and establish a radical Islamic empire that spans from Spain to Indonesia." Bush pointed out that Zawahiri also wrote that the terrorists must first expel the "Americans from Iraq. . . . Establish an Islamic authority over as much territory as you can . . . into Iraq. Extend the jihad wave to the secular countries neighboring Iraq."

The terrorist vision involves distinct goals as well, and the president reiterated these in this speech: to "develop weapons of mass destruction; to destroy Israel; to intimidate Europe; to assault the American people; and to blackmail our government into isolation." Although both the vision and the goals are extreme, Bush stated forcefully that "they should not be dismissed" for the "enemy is utterly committed." He noted that the leader of al-Qaeda in Iraq, Abu Musab al-Zarqawi, "has vowed, 'We will either achieve victory over the human race or we will pass to the eternal life.'"

In making the vision and goals of the terrorists easier for Americans to understand, President Bush also reiterated the nature of the terrorists. He accomplished this by linking his characterization to existing public knowledge: "The civilized world knows very well that other fanatics in history, from Hitler to Stalin to Pol Pot, consumed whole nations in war and genocide before leaving the stage of history. Evil men, obsessed with ambition and unburdened by conscience, must be taken very seriously." Although the terrorists themselves, and also some in America, have said that it was the invasion of Iraq that began this War on Terror, the president pointed out that the terrorists themselves had used numerous excuses for murder, even "the Crusades of a thousand years ago." Accordingly, it was no "act of ours that invited the rage of killers." Importantly for this speech, Bush stated that America and the world are "not facing a set of grievances that can be soothed and addressed. We're facing a radical ideology with inalterable objectives: to enslave whole nations and intimidate the world."

For the Bush administration, the "murderous ideology of the Islamic radicals is the great challenge of our new century—and no concession, bribe, or act of appeasement would change or limit their plans
for murder." This position is linked with what I called in chapters 1 and
2 the Cold War metanarrative. The president stated that like "the ideology of communism, Islamic radicalism is elitist, led by a self-ap-
pointed vanguard that presumes to speak for the Muslim masses."
Drawing from American public knowledge about the Cold War, Bush
continued with the comparisons: "Like the ideology of communism,
our new enemy pursues totalitarian aims" and

> is dismissive of free peoples. And like the ideology of communism, Is-
> lamic radicalism contains inherent contradictions that doom it to fail-
> ure. By fearing freedom . . . this ideology undermines the very qualities
> that make human progress possible. . . . Like the ideology of commu-
> nism, our new enemy teaches that innocent individuals can be sacri-
> ficed to serve a political vision. And this explains their cold-blooded
> contempt for human life.

Examples of this contempt were provided: the beheadings, the terrorist attacks in Iraq targeting Muslims who were ending their Ramadan
fast, the murder of 25 Iraqi children, the murder of schoolteachers in
their schools. "This is murder, pure and simple—the total rejection of
justice and honor and morality and religion." The president stated that
it is "cowardice that seeks to kill children and the elderly with car
bombs, and cuts the throat of a bound captive, and targets worshipers
leaving a mosque."

A Comprehensive U.S. Strategy

In well-focused contrast to the terrorists, President Bush relayed to
the world that it is "courage that liberated more than 50 million people
from tyranny. It is courage that keeps an untiring vigil against the enemies of rising democracies. And it is courage in the cause of freedom
that will once again destroy the enemies of freedom." Explaining the
comprehensive U.S. strategy in the War on Terror, Bush stated, "First,
we're determined to prevent attacks of the terrorist network before
they occur." Along with this, he gave information that the United
States had already "disrupted a number of serious al-Qaeda terrorist
plots since September 11th—including several plots to attack inside the
United States. Our coalition against terror has killed or captured nearly
all those directly responsible for the September the 11th attacks."

Second, Bush said his administration was "determined to deny weapons of mass destruction to outlaw regimes, and to their terrorist allies who would use them without hesitation." Libya, which had abandoned its chemical and nuclear weapons program, was mentioned as a specific success, and others were mentioned as well.

Third, the administration was "determined to deny radical groups the support and sanctuary of outlaw regimes." Financial and other sanctions were said to be working and helping to keep funds and other forms of support out of the hands of terrorists.

Fourth, the administration was "determined to deny the militants control of any nation, which they would use as a home base and a launching pad for terror." The press here mentioned work in Afghanistan, Pakistan, and Iraq. In light of recent and mounting criticism, Bush specifically mentioned military operations in Iraq. However, he also heralded the "inspiring progress toward building democracy" being made by the Iraqi people:

> Iraqis are gearing up for December 15th [2005] elections, when they will go to the polls to choose a government under the new constitution. With two successful elections completed, and a third coming up next month, the Iraqi people are proving their determination to build a democracy united against extremism and violence.

Fifth, Bush declared that the administration would

> deny the militants future recruits by replacing hatred and resentment with democracy and hope across the broader Middle East. If the peoples of that region are permitted to choose their own destiny, and advance by their own energy and participation of free men and women, then the extremists will be marginalized, and the flow of radicalism to the rest of the world will slow and eventually end.

Taken together, this five-part strategy was not presented as an easy road to victory. Instead the president stressed the very real nature of the struggle in which Americans and the world were involved: "With the rise of a deadly enemy and the unfolding of a global ideological struggle, our time in history will be remembered for new challenges and unprecedented dangers." As he had since the first days after 9/11, the president also stressed the unknown nature of the war, its trials, and its course:

> We don't know the course of our own struggle will take, or the sacrifices that might lie ahead. We do know, however, that the defense of

freedom is worth our sacrifice, we do know the love of freedom is the mightiest force in history, and we do know the cause of freedom will once again prevail.

Comments to Critics

In this speech, President Bush responded specifically to critics of the Iraq war. He prefaced this response with a reiteration of the nature of the terrorist threat: they "are as brutal an enemy as we've ever faced, unconstrained by any notion of our common humanity or by the rules of warfare. No one should underestimate the difficulties ahead, nor should they overlook the advantages we bring to the fight." Importantly, the response to critics of the war was placed next to comments about terrorists wanting to obtain control over a nation, and the administration's strategy to deny this. Central to this is the war in Iraq, about which the president stated: "Some observers look at the job ahead and adopt a self-defeating pessimism. In contrast, the elected leaders of Iraq are proving to be strong and steadfast." Following this, the president relayed the positive aspects of the situation in Iraq: "I have said, as Iraqis stand up, Americans will stand down. And with our help, the Iraqi military is gaining new capabilities and new confidence with each passing month. And no fair-minded person should ignore, deny, or dismiss the achievements of the Iraqi people." And then came the Sunday punch: "And our debate at home must also be fair-minded." With these words, the president launched a brief but direct attack on those critics of the war who have removed criticism from policy disagreement and placed it instead in the realm of obtaining political advantage. Because of the extreme press focus on these few lines, I provide them in their entirety here:

> One of the hallmarks of a free society and what makes our country strong is that our political leaders can discuss their differences openly, even in times of war. When I made the decision to remove Saddam Hussein from power, Congress approved it with strong bipartisan support. I also recognize that some of our fellow citizens and elected officials didn't support the liberation of Iraq. And that is their right, and I respect it. As President and Commander-in-Chief, I accept the responsibilities, and the criticisms, and the consequences that come with such a solemn decision.
>
> While it's perfectly legitimate to criticize my decision or the conduct of the war, it is deeply irresponsible to rewrite the history of how that war began.

Some Democrats and anti-war critics are *now* claiming we manipulated the intelligence and misled the American people about why we went to war. These critics are fully aware that a bipartisan Senate investigation found no evidence of political pressure to change the intelligence community's judgments related to Iraq's weapons programs.

They also know that intelligence agencies from around the world agreed with our assessment of Saddam Hussein. They know the United Nations passed more than a dozen resolutions citing his development and possession of weapons of mass destruction. And many of these critics supported my opponent during the last election, who explained his position to support the resolution in the Congress this way: "When I vote to give the president of the United States the authority to use force, if necessary, to disarm Saddam Hussein, it is because I believe that a deadly arsenal of weapons of mass destruction in his hands is a threat, and a grave threat, to our security." That's why more than a hundred Democrats in the House and the Senate—who had access to the same intelligence—voted to support removing Saddam Hussein from power.

The stakes in the global war on terror are too high, and the national interest is too important, for politicians to throw out false charges. These baseless attacks send the wrong signal to our troops and to an enemy that is questioning America's will. As our troops fight a ruthless enemy determined to destroy our way of life, they deserve to know that their elected leaders who voted to send them to war continue to stand behind them. Our troops deserve to know that this support will remain firm when the going gets tough. And our troops deserve to know that whatever our differences in Washington, our will is strong, our nation is united, and we will settle for nothing less than victory.[3]

The Press Response

The press response to President Bush's Veterans Day address exemplified and extended upon the oppositional framing seen growing in the previous chapters.[4] The number of negatively framed themes inserted into coverage of the president's speech multiplied, as did the strength of opposition to his message. Specifically, the press focused upon only a narrow portion of Bush's overall message: the few paragraphs of the whole where the president unambiguously mentioned antiwar critics' charges (quoted above). The remainder of the speech was ignored. Putting it bluntly, the press *chose* to focus on only five paragraphs of a sixty-six-paragraph speech, thus making it seems as if the president had only "lashed out" in anger instead of having given a major policy speech concerning the War on Terror. The press framing of the speech essentially cast Bush as lashing out at critics of the War on Terror who were saying they did not have the same prewar intelligence as the administration and who were also saying that the administration had no strategy in Iraq.

Throughout coverage of the president's address, the overall focus was on the purpose of the speech. The press here simplified so greatly that the speech was presented as attempting only one goal: to deflect criticism about the war from the administration. Two general areas of criticism emerged here. The first concerned assertions about inappropriate use of prewar intelligence, the second, assertions that the administration lacked a comprehensive Iraq war policy.

Prewar Intelligence: False Pretenses

The main argument made by President Bush was that Democrats in Congress had had access to the same intelligence as did he when they voted for the war, but that they were now saying that they had been misled and thus were now against the war. This was a key focus of those few paragraphs that he devoted to the topic, but very few press accounts carried this argument. The *Washington Post* was one exception, writing:

> [Some] critics, he complained, "are now claiming we manipulated the intelligence and misled the American people about why we went to war." The president said that "it's legitimate to criticize my decision or the conduct of the war" but added that "the stakes are too high and the national interest is too important for politicians to throw out false charges."[5]

Even before the speech was given, *The Early Show* stated that "Mr. Bush will go on the offensive and accuse his critics of trying to rewrite history."[6] A different *Washington Post* article said that the president had "accused war critics of trying to reconstruct history. 'The stakes in the global war on terror are too high and the national interest is too important for politicians to throw out false charges.'"[7]

These few examples were made invisible given the overall framing of this issue by the press. Instead of accurately conveying the statements of the president, the press instead *chose* to frame the speech in a completely different manner. For example, *Today*, reporting before the speech was delivered, commented that the president would try "to counter critics who accuse his administration of twisting intelligence to justify going to war."[8] In a similar manner, the *New York Times* reported prior to the speech:

> Faced with a bleak public mood about Iraq and stung by Democratic accusations that he led the nation into war on false pretenses, President Bush is beginning a new effort to shore up his credibility and cast his critics as hypocrites. Mr. Bush will take on a new round of accusations by Democrats that he exaggerated the threat posed by [Iraq's] weapons programs.[9]

After the speech, *CBS Evening News* stated that an "embattled President Bush chooses Veterans Day to strike back at the critics of his war policy." Later in that same show, the assertion was expanded:

> The way that President Bush told it today, critics of his war policy are trying to rewrite history and the result, he said, is undercutting American troops in Iraq. The president also had harsh words for Democrats and their renewed charges that he misled the nation to war by manipulating intelligence.[10]

NBC Nightly News also reported on exactly what it had decided the president would say: "Fighting words. President Bush accuses his critics of rewriting history about how the Iraq war began, and say they are hurting American forces in battle." Later in the broadcast *NBC Nightly News* stated that Bush had "taunted antiwar Democrats" such as John Kerry by saying that these "critics are fully aware that a bipartisan Senate investigation found no evidence of political pressure to change the intelligence community's judgments. . . . These baseless attacks send the wrong signal to our troops and to an enemy that is questioning America's will."[11]

In an opening paragraph, a front-page *New York Times* article summarized well the overall frame used by the press: President Bush, it said, "sharply criticized Democrats who have accused him of misleading the nation about the threat from Iraq's weapons programs, calling their criticism 'deeply irresponsible' and suggesting that they are undermining the war effort." In its very next sentence, the story reiterated the point: "Mr. Bush made his most aggressive effort to date to counter the charge that he had justified taking the United States to war by twisting or exaggerating prewar intelligence."[12]

The above are circumspect descriptions when compared to others that described the situation. Some in the press made a deliberate attempt to characterize the Bush administration as lying, while at the same time couching their comments in the guise of objective reporting. For example, *CBS Evening News* ended one of its reports with this statement: "The Senate Intelligence Committee concluded there was little useful intelligence collected that helped determine Iraq's possible links to al-Qaeda, but you would never have known that from listening to the president and his aides."[13] Frank Rich of the *New York Times* called the White House's assertions prior to the Iraq war a "set of lies in the administration's prewar propaganda blitzkrieg" and then wrote that those who agree with the Senate Intelligence Committee report (exonerating the White House) were exhibiting "brazenness" if they publicly stated that.[14] In a later column, Rich continued his harangue against the administration:

> The web of half-truths and falsehoods used to sell the war did not happen by accident; it was woven by design and the foisted on the public by a P.R. operation built expressly for that purpose. . . . [It's] a losing game to ask what lies the White House told along the way. A simpler question might be: What was not a lie?[15]

The majority of press reports conveyed the idea that the president was speaking out against all critics of the war, as opposed to only those accusing him of lying. For instance, *Good Morning America* stated that Bush had "launched a counterattack against critics of his Iraq war policy."[16] This made it seem that it was the conduct of the war at issue, and not, as clearly stated by the president, the charge of lying about prewar intelligence. Further, it allowed the press to frame the issue in such a way that the president was seen as being wrong for stifling criticism, even though he specifically said in his speech that criticizing U.S. policy was an acceptable action. *Saturday Today* stated: "War of words. President Bush answers his critics about the war in Iraq in his strongest comments since last year's campaign."[17] *USA Today* wrote that with "support for the Iraq war eroding and the president's popularity crumbling with it, the White House spin machine is abruptly switching gears. It's going on the offensive."[18]

NBC Nightly News described the speech as a "counterattack on critics" and stated that he had "lashed out at his critics."[19] In similar vein, the *Washington Post* wrote that the president "used Veterans Day . . . to lash out at critics [and] the sharp tenor . . . resembled an election-year campaign more than a policy disagreement."[20] The *Post* also described the president's response by saying "he lashed out at critics of his Iraq war policy."[21] *The Saturday Early Show* declared that President Bush was "lashing back at critics of his Iraq War policy."[22] In addition to "lashing out," the president's replies to critics were cast in a negative campaign light: on the *CBS Evening News*, the president was said to have "pulled a page out of the Karl Rove campaign playbook. . . . [When] somebody says something bad about you, you hit them with as much as you've got."[23]

The tone set in this initial reporting carried itself beyond the immediate aftermath of Bush's speech and into a general commentary about the nature of his remarks. For example, *World News Tonight* reported that the president said "that people who question his rationale for going to war in Iraq, are not only wrong but irresponsible and unpatriotic," and this was interpreted as meaning that the "White House was trying to silence critics of the war."[24] *USA Today* quoted Republican senator and potential presidential hopeful Chuck Hagel of Nebraska, who, it said, "also objects to the White House description of war critics as reprehensible, irresponsible people playing politics. 'For the administration to penalize or demonize those who question is not who we are as Americans.'"[25]

Prewar Intelligence: But We Didn't Have It All

The press presented a mixed interpretation of the president's criticisms. As just seen, Bush was depicted as responding to criticisms about prewar use of intelligence. However, as noted in the section about the speech, the president had attacked only those who had characterized him as manipulating intelligence in order to lead the country into war.

One of the main assertions made by the president was that Congress had had access to the same intelligence as did he. The press, however, made a point of contradicting that fact, except for one report, with which we will begin.

Today, during an interview with counselor to the president Dan Bartlett, provided the only example of the press relaying to the public the evidence backing up the president's statements. Matt Lauer, cohost of the show, stated: "Critics are after the . . . president over the prewar intelligence in Iraq . . . saying it was manipulated . . . and the White House is firing back . . . saying . . . Democrats saw very same prewar intelligence that the administration saw. Is that technically accurate?" Bartlett answered that open dissent is a "strength" of U.S. democracy, but added, "What's deeply irresponsible is when Democrats put forward this charge that President Bush deliberately misled [Americans about the war]. . . . That is absolutely false. And there's been no evidence . . . to suggest [otherwise]." Lauer replied with the main argument used by the Democrats attacking President Bush: "But doesn't the president see different information in that very sensitive daily briefing that he gets that members of Congress don't get?" Bartlett noted that Democrats have tried to "raise that point and what the bipartisan Silverman-Robb Commission . . . said was that the PDB [Presidential Daily Briefing] did not have any more nuanced complex position. . . . [They] said it may have been even more one-sided than the type of intelligence that . . . Congress had access to."[26]

Frames act to enhance a certain interpretation of material, while at the same time *lowering* the salience of that information that runs counter to the established frame. In this instance, the information provided above was simply invisible in the overall frame. Essentially, when prewar intelligence was mentioned, the press presented only assertions. For example, the *Washington Post* offered the rare example of the president directly stating that the military had a right to know that those in Congress "'who voted to send them to war continue to stand behind them.' He added that . . . 'Democrats who had access to the same intelligence' voted for the resolution."[27] The article quoted three senior Democratic senators immediately thereafter, each contradicting the president with only an assertion:

- Senate Minority Leader Harry Reid (D-NV): Bush is "attacking those patriotic Americans who have raised serious questions about the case the Bush administration made to take our country to war."
- John Kerry (D-MA): "This administration misled a nation into war by cherry-picking intelligence and stretching the truth beyond recognition."
- Ted Kennedy (D-MA): The president is "tearing down those who seek the truth about the clear manipulation of intelligence in the run-up to the Iraq war."[28]

NBC Nightly News presented the issue as a question: "But did Senate Democrats really have as much intelligence as the president? Today, Democrats said no, that's just plain wrong." The report continued with claims from Democrats; for example, Sen. Richard Durbin (D-IL) was quoted as saying, "Certainly, the president, as commander in chief, has the most information." As support for this statement, the reporter asked: "So what did the Democrats know? . . . [The] CIA reported to Congress in [a] top-secret report that Saddam Hussein was trying to reconstitute his nuclear weapons program. The State Department called that conclusion highly dubious. But its dissent was buried on page 84."[29]

Exacerbating the tension, *The Early Show* boiled the entire issue down into two sharp assertions: First, President Bush was shown in a clip: "It is irresponsible to say that I deliberately misled the American people when it came to the very same intelligence they looked at and . . . many of them came to the same conclusion I did." The reporter then noted, "But Democrats, growing increasingly vocal, shot back." Senator Kennedy was shown in another clip: "The suggestion that . . . Congress has access to the same classified material as the president is preposterous." Instead of examining the charges, the reporter asked the show's anchor this question: "We sat here . . . four weeks ago [and] said we'd never seen the vitriol, the anger, the power of words going back and forth. It's worse [now]. What do you think all of this means?"[30]

CBS Morning News reported the situation in similar fashion, observing that President Bush had stated that "Democrats saw the same intelligence that he did." Many of these Democrats had agreed with the administration's assessment and voted to authorize the war. The reporter commented: "Democrats claim Congress did not see the same intelligence as the president. They did not get the raw reports, cables and underlying sources. They also claim some dissenting views were ignored and that the intelligence was politicized."[31] Lost here was that Bush would also not receive raw reports and cables, but summaries of information, and that this information *was* made available to members of Congress, both Democrats and Republicans. However, the press failed to mention this or to examine in detail any of the claims.[32]

No Plan, No Progress

Aside from five sentences buried at the end of a *New York Times* article, no substantial mention was made of the progress in Iraq or the president's overall strategy for the war.[33] Instead, the press presented critics of the war as demanding the very information Bush had presented in his speech. Given that the press failed to convey the president's plan for progress that he had provided in his address, the charges made by Democrats carried considerable weight, whereas had the press accurately relayed President Bush's plans, the charges would have seemed ridiculous.

For example, *NBC Nightly News* quoted Democratic senator Carl Levin of Michigan stating, "That's normal for this administration, not accepting responsibility, not addressing the issues which are raised, trying to change the subject, and frequently just trying to attack their critics instead of answering questions."[34] In a different broadcast, *NBC Nightly News* quoted a former press secretary to President Clinton, Joe Lockhart, who said the White House thinks "they have a PR problem; they don't. They have a policy problem. He's got to come clean, talk about how difficult this issue is and lay out some sort of strategy that the American public can get behind for success in bringing the troops home."[35] In an editorial, *USA Today* wrote:

> The best chance of salvaging an acceptable outcome is for the United States to stay long enough to see a stable government and strong Iraqi military force in place. There's no guarantee this will happen. For Bush, the challenge is not so much to stay the course as to define it— with the candor the American people deserve and the complexity this mission demands.[36]

Eugene Robinson in the *Washington Post* asked more directly:

> "Stay the course" doesn't play as a strategy when the course seems to lead nowhere. What is victory in Iraq? When will we know we've won? When the simmering, low-level civil war we've ignited sparks into full flame and somebody takes over the country? The mess that George Bush and Co. have created . . . doesn't have an unmessy solution. [Congressman John] Murtha's plan—just get out—isn't really attractive, but at least it's a plan. The saying goes that when you're in a hole, the first thing to do is to stop digging. But the president . . . just keeps burrowing deeper into that pile of manure.[37]

Writing of both President Bush and Vice President Dick Cheney, Frank Rich stated in the *New York Times* that "neither man engaged the national debate ignited by John Murtha about how our troops might be best redeployed in a recalibrated battle against Islamic radicalism. Neither offered a plan for 'victory.'"[38]

Mad for Murtha

When Democratic congressman John Murtha of Pennsylvania spoke out on the war just days after President Bush charged some Democrats with reckless political behavior, the press seemingly jumped at the opportunity to switch the coverage from Bush's charges to Murtha's new attack. Yet, more than Representative Murtha's call for troop withdrawal was related to the public. The press specifically advanced Murtha in a manner calculated to *enhance* his credibility and thus the weight of his *assertions*. For example, *ABC News Tonight* reported, "An influential member of Congress, a decorated war veteran, who had supported the war, called it a flawed policy, wrapped in illusion." Later in the same report, the reporter felt it necessary to say that many on Capitol Hill were "outraged" by the president's charges, "including powerful representative John Murtha, a decorated Marine who served in Vietnam."[39]

The Early Show reported that "the White House has been on the defensive lately, and now a highly respected Democrat on military matters has joined the debate on troop withdrawal." The reporter called Murtha's comments "strong words" and described the congressman as "a hawkish ex-Marine Democrat who voted for the war." Later in the same account, the reporter noted Murtha's "two Purple Hearts and a Bronze Star" and that he "actually went back into the military to fight the war in Vietnam."[40] A separate piece on the same *Early Show* episode reported that the "war of words" began "when Democrat and former Marine Jack Murtha called for the withdrawal."[41]

CBS Morning News called Murtha "a retired Marine, a veteran of two wars, and one of the Democrats' leading supporters of the military."[42] *NBC Nightly News* called Murtha a "conservative Democrat . . . and a decorated veteran who wants U.S. forces out of Iraq."[43] *The Osgood File* reported that Representative Murtha was an "ex-Marine Congressman" and then stated that "Murtha has always been a very strong supporter of the Pentagon, definitely on the right side of his party, . . . [is] pro-military . . . [and] looks out for the interests . . . of veterans."[44]

USA Today also stressed that Murtha was "one of Congress' most hawkish members" and that he was the "top Democrat on the House panel that pays for Pentagon programs [and] a former Marine who was the first Vietnam veteran to serve in Congress."[45] In a different article, *USA Today* called Murtha a "leading Democrat hawk," a "retired Marine colonel," and a "staunch supporter of the armed forces [who had] voted in 2002 to [support going to war. He also] spent 37 years in the Marines and is the recipient of two Purple Hearts. . . . He is also an influential House Democrat on defense spending."[46] The *New York Times* called Murtha a "Marine hero who wants the troops out."[47]

More than just Representative Murtha's credentials were pushed during this time. The press also pushed an interpretation of the White

House's response to the comment made by the congressman. *Today*, for example, stated that the White House was "lashing out at a pro-war Democratic congressman who says it's time for the troops to come home. . . . One of Congress' most hawkish Democrats, John Murtha . . . [is] a Vietnam veteran who voted for the war."[48] *USA Today* wrote that "Democrats have long assailed President Bush's Iraq policy. But [Murtha] is the top Democrat on the House panel that pays for Pentagon programs, a former Marine who was the first Vietnam veteran to serve in Congress and one of the most influential members of his party on military matters."[49]

By the time the press had finished fleshing out Murtha's credibility, the man was a demigod. Additionally, the Republican-led call for a vote on immediate troop withdrawal, which Republicans stated was designed to show support for the troops and the insanity of Murtha's call for immediate withdrawal, was ignored by all but one press outlet covered in this chapter. And of that vote, *NBC Nightly News* was able to report: "Last night's house vote rejecting an immediate troop withdrawal from Iraq was engineered by Republicans to fail in order to send a message of support to U.S. troops. Democrats called it a stunt." Rep. Nita Lowey (D-NY) was then shown calling it "a pathetic, partisan ploy," after which the reporter added, "The vote followed a call earlier this week by Democratic hawk Congressman John Murtha for troops withdrawal within six months."[50]

Summary

President Bush's speech was part of a coordinated White House campaign to relay to Americans the strategies involved in the War on Terror. First, he related in detail the strategy followed by the terrorists in Iraq; the president provided details from an intercepted letter from a high-ranking terrorist leader. Second, he explained in detail his administration's overall strategy for obtaining victory in Iraq, presenting both a plan for victory in Iraq and a blueprint for the continuation of the War on Terror. From both the point of view of the terrorists and the administration, Iraq was considered the central front of the War on Terror. Additionally, the president reserved a section of this speech to specifically address Democratic charges that he had misled the nation into war. It was not criticism of the situation in Iraq to which the president responded; rather it was to charges by some congressional Democrats who had voted for the war but now said they had been misled.

The overall themes used in the president's speech were the same ones we have seen in previous chapters: the nature of the enemy, the nature of the war, good versus evil, and so forth. The framing of these themes was also a continuation of past framing used by the administration. In this sense, the administration was quite consistent in its vision of the War on Terror.

There is much in the press response to this speech that bears examination. The press chose to focus on a thin slice of the president's overall message: the few comments where Bush had addressed those congressional Democrats who had supported the war but now charged him with misleading the nation. The press failed to comment on the remainder of the president's speech, thus denying Americans access to that important information. What little it did report about the speech, the press cast in an extremely negative light; the reports made it seems as if the president had angrily "lashed out" at those who dared to question him. Not relayed at all was that the president had actually given a major policy speech concerning the War on Terror; one that presented the very information—an overall strategy for victory in Iraq—for which the press and other critics had called. In this way the press framing of the speech took it out of the realm of the War on Terror and instead placed it as part of a partisan battle in which the administration was on the defensive because it had been caught in a lie about the war in Iraq.

The critics of the administration were portrayed as saying they did not have access to the same intelligence the White House possessed prior to the war in Iraq. Additionally, after the president's speech, these same critics were depicted as saying that the administration had no strategy in Iraq. Given that the press ignored those portions of the president's speech that responded to these charges, congressional Democrats were aided in their criticism of the administration. Although President Bush made it clear in his speech that he was responding to recent Democrat attempts as revisionism, the press made it seem as if he was responding to criticism of war itself, thus attacking free speech and veterans such as Rep. John Murtha. In this way, the press not only ignored the lion's share of the speech but also failed to properly contextualize the remarks of the small section it did cover. Because of this, two minor mentions aside, throughout all the reporting following Bush's speech, the full rationale for staying in Iraq went unreported. The president used the terrorists' own words to explain the situation in Iraq; the press completely ignored this, as they ignored all else in his speech except for the small portion given in reply to critics of prewar intelligence.

The press cast Bush as aggressively attacking his critics and pushed Congressman Murtha onto center stage as an example of someone standing up to the president, yet taking a beating. Murtha was portrayed in the most credible terms possible, while Republican respondents to the congressman's statements were cast in a negative light. Murtha's criticisms were added to the negative characterizations of the situation in Iraq that the press relayed to the public. Contrast this with the press reports on Democratic senator Joseph Lieberman, who returned from a visit to Iraq about two weeks after Representative Murtha first spoke out. Lieberman was cautiously optimistic about the Iraq situation; however, a Lexis-Nexis search of the print news covered in this chapter found this trip mentioned only three times. Broadcast news did report this trip; however, the reports cast Senator Lieberman in a negative light, as a Democrat "siding" with Republicans and putting a strain on his party. In short, the press gave different treatment to different points of views on the war. The person that supported their point of view received positive press; the person who did not support their point of view was ignored or cast in a negative light.

In another example of the press ignoring information that contradicted its point of view, only a small minority of reports mentioned that two Senate intelligence committees and a presidential commission had exonerated the Bush administration of blame for inflating intelligence on Iraq. Incredibly, this admission was qualified in such a manner that doubt was cast on the Bush administration nonetheless. For example, note carefully this passage in the *New York Times*:

> The Senate review described repeated, unsuccessful efforts by the White House . . . to persuade the Central Intelligence Agency to embrace the view that Iraq had provided support to Al Qaeda. According to former administration officials, [both George Tenet, then director of the CIA, and Colin Powell, then secretary of state] rejected elements of a speech drafted by aides to Vice President Dick Cheney that was intended to present the administration's case for war, calling them exaggerated and unsubstantiated by intelligence.[51]

We have here an instance of "aides" to the vice president having their draft speeches reviewed for accuracy by the director of the CIA and the secretary of state. Instead of offering this as evidence of the correct and proper working of a carefully reviewed draft and redrafting process, the press offered it as an example of an attempt by the vice president to deliberately mislead the American public.

After reviewing the press reports, I am inclined to believe that the White House was placed in a no-win situation. If it continued to ignore its critics, it would continue to be subjected to partisan attacks seeking to charge it with misrepresentation, incompetence, and outright lying. However, when the White House defended itself, the press suggested that it was reacting too strongly, lashing out at critics, and denying free speech. For example, the *New York Times* wrote that Bush's comments "only intensified the partisan battle" and that by "responding so strongly to the criticism, the White House seems to be throwing fuel on a political fire that it may not be able to control."[52]

Pushing the Polls

In addition to the above, the press was particularly adept at pushing its own poll data as evidence to support its interpretation of the president's speech. Of special note here is that the press discounted its own role in the falling poll numbers of the president. In short, the press used falling poll numbers to assert that the war, and not negative reporting about the war, was causing the president poll problems. Thirty percent of the reports covered in this chapter used poll data in this manner. Only three reported margin-of-error figures, and only one provided means to obtain poll questions and the raw data from the polls. Of note is that the poll stressed the very two issues the press focused on in their reports: prewar intelligence and the day-to-day course of the war. Both of these, as seen in this chapter, had been framed in a negative manner, and this for months prior to the reporting on the president's Veterans Day speech.

Some examples of this included an *NBC Nightly News* report which stressed that the president's speech illustrated

> how much the war has damaged his political standing. . . . The latest NBC News/*Wall Street Journal* poll found that 57 percent of Americans think the president misled the country about the case for the war. And nearly two-thirds disapprove of Mr. Bush's handling of the war.[53]

Saturday Today repeated this same information.[54] The *Washington Post* reported similarly that the "latest *Washington Post*–ABC News poll found that 64 percent of Americans disapprove of how Bush is handling the war and 60 percent believe it was not worth fighting . . . nearly 3 in 5 voters . . . do not consider Bush honest."[55] The *New York Times* reported "Mr. Bush's poll numbers crumbling. . . . [An] Associated Press–Ipsos Poll released Friday [November 11, 2005] found that

42 percent of Americans viewed Mr. Bush as honest, down from 53 percent at the beginning of the year."[56]

Many of these polls suggested *an immediacy to the effects of public speeches* by Democrats and Republicans. However, only efforts by Democrats were presented as successful, whereas Republican efforts were depicted as failures. For example, the *New York Times* wrote:

> Democrats are drawing blood with new attacks on how the nation got into the war. . . . A poll released Tuesday [November 8, 2005] by the Pew Research Center . . . found that 43 percent of Americans believe that the American and British governments lied about Iraq's weapons to justify the invasion, up from 31 percent early last year. An ABC News/*Washington Post* poll conducted last week [early November 2005] found that 40 percent of Americans believe Mr. Bush is honest and trustworthy, down from 53 percent 18 months ago and 70 percent 3 years ago.[57]

Contrast that with *NBC Nightly News*, whose anchor stated, "On the day after President Bush lashed out at his critics, a new poll out tonight shows a growing number of Americans are dissatisfied with his performance on the job. In fact, the president's approval rating, according to the *Newsweek* poll, has fallen to a record low." Stressing the timing, the reporter continued:

> One day after President Bush launched his counterattack on critics of the war . . . more evidence the public still don't approve of the Bush administration's course. . . . 36 percent say they approve of the president's job performance—a new low; while 58 percent disapprove. And when it comes to the phrase, "honest and ethical," a majority [50 percent] says it doesn't describe . . . the president.[58]

E. J. Dionne Jr. wrote in the *Washington Post*:

> Mr. President, it won't work this time. With a *Wall Street Journal*/NBC News Poll finding 57 percent of Americans agreeing that George W. Bush "deliberately misled people to make the case for war with Iraq," the president clearly needs to tend to his credibility problems. But his partisan attacks on the administration's critics . . . will only add to his troubles.[59]

Other examples include *The Saturday Early Show,* which reported that "an Associated Press poll found nearly six in ten Americans don't think he's honest."[60] *USA Today* simply stated, "Polls show most Americans believe the war was a mistake."[61] A *World News Tonight* reporter simply asserted: "A recent ABC News poll shows that 60 percent of Americans now believe the war was not worth fighting. And . . . that's a record high."[62]

On a different day, one reporter on *The Early Show* stated that "the support for this war on the Hill is evaporating." Another responded: "Is it because people are looking at the poll numbers? We look at President Bush's poll numbers and they have just continued to drop, drop, drop. I saw a Harris Poll that actually had him down at 32 percent. I mean, it's almost unimaginable. It can't really, realistically, go any lower than it is right now."[63]

The *New York Times*'s Rich interpreted results of a then-recent poll to support his belief that those senators speaking out against the war

> know the voters have decided the war is over. . . . A *USA Today*/CNN/Gallup survey last week found that the percentage (52) of Americans who want to get out of Iraq fast, in 12 months or less, is even larger than the percentage (48) that favored a quick withdrawal from Vietnam.[64]

Presented in this manner, the poll numbers allowed the press to suggest that the president's attempt to counter his critics was ineffectual. Poll numbers are not, however, a snapshot of public opinion about current information so much as they represent public opinion about news received during the weeks or months prior to the poll. In a sense, poll data usually reflect several months' worth of lag time or exposure to certain information. Polls here, though, were used to suggest that Bush's speech was unsuccessful, when the polls were actually measuring attitudes formed in the absence of knowledge about the president's speech. If we want to gauge in part how President Bush fared in his campaign to respond to his critics, we can look at the polls on this issue taken approximately a month after the speech covered in this chapter. Here we see Bush's numbers had improved dramatically, up to 47 percent from a low of 36 percent.[65]

Of note is that polling data can be framed to favor a specific interpretation and also that the polls may be framed to elicit specific answers from those polled. Recall the studies on framing mentioned in chapter 1. In one example, depending on how the issue was framed, Americans either supported or did not support mandatory testing for HIV. It is not a stretch of the imgination to concevie of polling questions framed in such a way that the majority of Americans, instead of thinking of the Iraq was as "not worth it," would consider the Iraq war "worth it."

8

News Media Reporting
of the War on Terror

It is virtually impossible to distinguish between our political
system and the media as separate entities.[1]

—Robert E. Denton

Tens of millions of Americans look to mainstream news to provide the
information they need to make informed political choices. Does the
Fourth Estate live up to its responsibility to provide this information?
This is an important question, since reportorial practices have a direct
impact on how Americans think about and act upon the public decisions that confront them. On general political issues, I have found the
answer to the above question to be a resounding no.[2] What about the
War on Terror, though? Fortunately, the practices of the press are easily
discerned when one looks for the frames it uses when it tells a story.
Having read this far, you know that the themes and frames used to describe the War on Terror differ considerably depending on whether the
source is the president or the press. It is my contention that the press
failed to objectively provide Americans with the information they
needed to make informed decisions concerning the War on Terror. The
details of this are explained in this final chapter.

Overview of News Media Functions

In chapter 1, we saw that agenda-setting theory asserts that the news
media tell us *what to think about* but not *what to think*; furthermore, the

theory explains how news audiences learn about an issue in direct proportion to press coverage of that issue. If we move beyond this perspective, we come to agenda extension: the identification of evaluative components to news media coverage of issues and events. Thus, the news media tell us not only what to think about but also *how to think about the information we receive*. This evaluative component comes with various names—for example, *priming* and *framing*. *Priming* is a specific term used to describe the contextual cues embedded within a news story that are used to evaluate the subject matter at hand. Applied to the speeches of President George W. Bush, this means that Americans are *primed* to evaluate him by how well he manages an issue in relation to the evaluative cues provided by the news media. In short, out of all the possible ways to understand an event, the press will highlight one or two attributes and thus prime their audiences to evaluate the performance of the president by how well he handles only those press-highlighted criteria.

My primary concern in this book has been to discover the War on Terror themes used by the president and the press and then to see how those themes were framed. I use the term *theme* in a very common manner in this book. Simply put, I treat it as the subject of discussion, that which is the subject of thought. Within any single news story or broadcast, there is at least one theme, the subject of the report; usually there are several themes. When looking at news reports over a period of time, certain themes recur, each being framed in a particular manner. As discussed in chapter 1, frames are central organizing ideas within a narrative account of an issue or event; they provide the interpretive cues used by news audiences to make sense of neutral facts. We have also been concerned with discussion of a master frame, which some researchers have defined as similar to paradigms in science.[3] Others have said that a master frame structures "the way in which its adherents process information coming from the environment and the manner in which they disseminate information to others."[4] I consider the War on Terror a master frame—one that is composed of numerous themes, each of which is framed in a particular manner.

When examining President Bush's speeches and the press response, I was particularly interested in determining if the press injected bias into its coverage of the War on Terror; that is to say, Did the press depart from neutral reportorial practices in favor of advancing its own agenda and beliefs? I found, as have others, that it did. Concerning this very issue, Thomas Patterson wrote that the news media cannot provide the guidance that citizens need. The function of news . . . is to signalize events. In carrying out this function properly, the press contributes to informed public opinion. However, politics is more a question of values than of information. To act on their interests, citizens must arrive at an understanding of the relationship of their values and those at stake in public policy. Political institutions are designed to help citizens make this connection. The press is not.[5]

Certainly when concerning issues such as the War on Terror, the practice of advancing a partisan interpretation of events over a neutral presentation of facts is especially dangerous.

The case studies in this book have demonstrated that the press knowingly acted in opposition to the president of the United States, omitting important information necessary for understanding his comments and actions. Unless the reader had firsthand access to transcripts of Bush's speeches, all information about those speeches was filtered through the frames of the press. These press frames supported a narrow interpretation of events, one that was often divorced from the president's speech and from other available information about the particular issue at hand.

Code of Ethics for the News Media

When I judge the performance of the mainstream news media, I do so using their own published standards for ethical reporting. Major news outlets publicly profess to adhere both to strict standards of objectivity and codes of ethical conduct. Looking at these codes, we can determine by what standard to judge the mainstream news reporting practices concerning the War on Terror. The American Society of Newspaper Editors Statement of Principles has been in existence since 1922. Several articles are particularly relevant to this study:

> ARTICLE I: The primary purpose of gathering and distributing news and opinion is to serve the general welfare by informing the people and enabling them to make judgments on the issues of the time. . . .
> ARTICLE IV: Every effort must be made to assure that the news content is accurate, free from bias and in context, and that all sides are presented fairly. Editorials, analytical articles and commentary should be held to the same standards of accuracy with respect to facts as news reports.

ARTICLE V: To be impartial does not require the press to be un-questioning or to refrain from editorial expression. Sound practice, however, demands a clear distinction for the reader between news reports and opinion.

ARTICLE VI: Journalists should respect the rights of people involved in the news, observe the common standards of decency and stand accountable to the public for the fairness and accuracy of their news reports.[6]

Those journalists who are members of the Society of Professional Journalists also have a well thought-out code of ethics:

Members of the Society of Professional Journalists believe that public enlightenment is the forerunner of justice and the foundation of democracy. The duty of the journalist is to further those ends by seeking truth and providing a fair and comprehensive account of events and issues. Conscientious journalists from all media and specialties strive to serve the public with thoroughness and honesty. Journalists should be honest, fair and courageous in gathering, reporting and interpreting information.

Journalists should: Test the accuracy of information from all sources and exercise care to avoid inadvertent error. Deliberate distortion is never permissible. Tell the story of the diversity and magnitude of the human experience boldly, even when it is unpopular to do so. Examine their own cultural values and avoid imposing those values on others.[7]

The Associated Press Managing Editors Code of Ethics is quite clear in describing sound reportorial practices. It states in part that:

1. The good newspaper is fair, accurate, honest, responsible, independent and decent.
2. Truth is its guiding principle.
3. It avoids practices that would conflict with the ability to report and present news in a fair, accurate and unbiased manner.
4. The newspaper should serve as a constructive critic of all segments of society. It should reasonably reflect, in staffing and coverage, its diverse constituencies.
5. The newspaper should guard against inaccuracies, carelessness, bias or distortion through emphasis, omission or technological manipulation.
6. The newspaper should strive for impartial treatment of issues and dispassionate handling of controversial subjects.[8]

The Radio-Television News Directors Association's Code of Ethics and Professional Conduct lists specific standards for ethical reporting:

1. Recognize that service in the public interest creates an obligation to reflect the diversity of the community and guard against oversimplification of issues or events.
2. Provide a full range of information to enable the public to make enlightened decisions.
3. Professional electronic journalists should pursue truth aggressively and present the news accurately, in context, and as completely as possible.
4. Continuously seek the truth.
5. Resist distortions that obscure the importance of events.
6. Report anything known to be false.
7. Professional electronic journalists should present the news fairly and impartially, placing primary value on significance and relevance.
8. Present a diversity of expressions, opinions, and ideas in context.
9. Present analytical reporting based on professional perspective, not personal bias.[9]

Additionally, individual newspapers have their own codes of ethics: the *Washington Post* asserts it still adheres to the 1935 principles penned by then publisher Eugene Meyer, a selection of which is provided here:

> The first mission of a newspaper is to tell the truth as nearly as the truth can be ascertained. The newspaper shall tell ALL the truth so far as it can learn it, concerning the important affairs of America and the World. The newspaper's duty is to its readers and to the public at large, and not to the private interests of its owners. The newspaper shall not be the ally of any special interest, but shall be fair and free and wholesome in its outlook on public affairs and public men.[10]

The *New York Times* states that its goal "is to cover the news as impartially as possible—'without fear or favor,' . . . and to treat readers, news sources, advertisers and others fairly and openly, and to be seen to be doing so."[11]

The central, undeniable point here is that the mainstream news media *voluntarily* commit to providing the American public with the *full details* of important issues within an *unbiased context*. The news media profess to act in such a way that all Americans are provided the news they need to make informed decisions.[12] In short, *they purport to being unbiased and objective in their reportorial practice.* This is why any biased news coverage is so deceitful coming from these news sources; they appear perched on a dais of objectivity, all the while injecting their own partisan beliefs into the very information they give to the public as objective news. As Gary C. Woodward has written, "Political journalism is—against its own high standards—a flawed enterprise," because it cannot live up to its stated goal of objectivity.[13] Clearly the press has disregarded numerous aspects of the above codes in the case studies presented in this book. In the sections that follow, we look specifically at how this was accomplished.

Framing analysis can help us determine if journalists are living up to their published standards of objectivity or if they are framing the news to impart a meaning in keeping with their own view of the world. In reviewing the differences in framing provided below, keep in mind that framing is the process whereby news stories and editorials act to shape our understanding, awareness, and evaluations of issues and events in a particular direction. During the earliest days of reporting about 9/11, the press was conscientious in presenting dissenting points of view; some of this coverage was highlighted in chapter 2.[14]

Presenting information that contradicts the president or that presents a different point of view is not necessarily an instance of negative or oppositional framing. It is, rather, a necessary part of providing full context for understanding complex issues and events. However, intentionally framing an issue or event so that important information is omitted or improperly contextualized is an instance of oppositional framing. In the sections that follow, we see that the press is well aware of this and that it intentionally framed much of its post-9/11 coverage in a way designed to damage the Bush administration.

Awareness of Framing

The press does not often admit its ability to manipulate interpretation of the news it offers, yet at times these admissions do surface. In the present case, press coverage of the president's speeches provided evidence that the press was aware that the way it reported an issue would have certain ramifications for the Bush administration. Additionally, some press utterances provide us with examples that demonstrate that the press was reporting in a particular fashion in order to politically damage the administration. For example, the *Washington*

Post wrote: "Iraq remains the most significant long-term threat to the president's political fortunes. Without more tangible signs of progress in the coming months, [White House advisors believe] Bush could find it enormously difficult to reassert his leadership."[15] Another *Post* reporter wrote that only "clear evidence of success in Iraq is likely to alleviate widespread unease about the central project of this presidency."[16] *The Early Show* passed along its interpretation of the mood of the nation: "We've got to see some progress in Iraq or [we're] going to have to leave."[17]

Today actually highlighted the negative reporting of the press when its cohost asked: "I often wonder how much of the president's problem with Iraq is a perception problem. Is it wrong to . . . measure the progress of this war by every insurgent attack, every U.S. soldier killed?" To this, Howard Fineman of *Newsweek* replied:

> I think the critics have a point on that. I think we do very little reporting about what's happening with a peaceful day at the schools or some hospital that's been rebuilt or other really amazing signs of progress in a country that was run by a dictator until three years ago. But that isn't front page news. And the insurgents are fully aware of the fact that they can affect the psychology of politics back [in the United States].[18]

These admissions are striking given the manner in which the press reported about the war. *The Early Show*, for example, began one show with these words: "Three more U.S. troops have been killed in the latest fighting in Iraq."[19] The *New York Times* reported that the "rising death toll and the difficulty American and Iraqi forces have had in containing the insurgency have depressed public support for the war."[20] *The Saturday Early Show* ended its report with these words: "The question of prewar intelligence would not be that much of an issue if the U.S. death toll in Iraq were still not on the rise two and a half years after the war began."[21]

More damaging is that many in the press were advancing the belief that the war was lost. For instance, Frank Rich wrote in the *New York Times*: "The war is lost both as a political matter at home and a practical matter in Iraq."[22] In the *Washington Post*, Eugene Robinson wrote that the United States is "trapped in the dark with no exit in sight."[23] Add to the above the fact that the press advanced an interpretation of the Iraq war that contradicted the president's assertion of it being the center of the War on Terror. For instance, Robinson wrote that the Bush administration "is losing the public debate [in part] because of its insistence on conflating the war in Iraq with the larger 'war on terror.'"[24] Rich stated that it was a "set of lies" to suggest that Iraq was the central front of the War on Terror: "To get the country to redirect its finite resources to wage war against Saddam Hussein rather than keep its focus on the war against radical Islamic terrorists, the White House had to cook up [lies]."[25]

The press knew that the White House needed the positive news in Iraq to be reported, it knew that a great deal of positive news existed, and it knew that it reported almost exclusively negative news. In short, it knew the focus on negative news was politically damaging to the White House. This focus was, in my opinion, a conscious decision, and one that certainly departed from any notion of objective news reporting.

News Bias: Summary of the War on Terror Master Frame

The tables and comments below are limited to those biased practices most observable from the press coverage of the War on Terror. Specifically, I summarize the differences in framing observed in the War on Terror coverage and then briefly discuss how this relates to the concepts of master frame and metanarrative.

9/11 to Afghanistan

Although it appears that during the period right after 9/11 the press adopted the themes used by the president and framed those themes in similar manner, the press did present oppositional and critical points of view; thus, the "rally 'round the president" effect mentioned by many researchers about this time period simply did not manifest itself.[26] The press reported what Bush said but also the comments of those critical of the president's plan—most notably, comments concerning the potential loss of civil liberties in the wake of policy changes to fight domestic terrorists. This was the only period covered in which the press did not actively push its own agenda, although it did begin to contest the president's assertion about the War on Terror being a war instead of a police matter.

Table 8.1.   9/11 to Afghanistan

Themes	President's Frame	Press Frame
Safety	Reassurance	Reassurance
	Safety at hand	Safety at hand
Emotional Catharsis	Time for sadness	Time for sadness
Nature of Enemy	Evil, barbaric	Evil, barbaric
Nature of War	War	War/police action

United Nations Address, November 2001

In only a few short weeks, the press had moved from essentially neutral reporting of information surrounding the events of 9/11 to actively countering the themes and framing of those themes by Bush. In a glaring omission of important information, the press rarely relayed the moral dimensions advanced by the president. By not reporting

Table 8.2.   President Bush Speaks to the United Nations, November 2001

Themes	President's Frame	Press Frame
Good vs. Evil	Struggle of good and evil	—
Civilization vs. Barbarism	Struggle of civilization and barbarism	—
Freedom vs. Tyranny	Struggle of freedom and tyranny	—
Nature of the War	Domestic/global/ long-standing	Domestic/global/ long-standing
	War	War/police action
Nature of the Enemy	Evil, implacable, murderers	Deadly, indiscriminant (Bush Administration)
World War II or Vietnam	—	World War II or Vietnam
Patience	—	For now, but running out
International Effort	Assumed	Weakly reported

accurately on how the president characterized the War on Terror—morally—the press failed to allow the larger American public the opportunity to accept or reject that claim.

For the White House, the War on Terror had established themes and frames by this time; it had evolved into a master frame. However, the press was not relaying this to the American people, thus again failing to allow them the opportunity to accept or reject. Instead, we see active press opposition to the framing of the nature-of-the-war theme and also the reframing of the theme of the nature of the enemy. In the latter case, instead of presenting civil liberties concerns in a neutral manner as before, the press implied that the enemy was no longer limited to terrorists but was beginning to include the Bush administration as well.

State of the Union, January 2002

The Enron scandal is not a theme within the War on Terror. That having been said, the economy was a separate theme stressed by the press, and the press made the Enron situation part of the overall coverage of the State of the Union address. By this time—four months after 9/11—the themes used by the White House were no longer separate lines of thought but increasingly interanimated ideas that fueled the administration's framing of its master frame, the War on Terror. In a sense, we see something of a conflation of terms now, with America working within an international coalition for the Good, the Civilized, and the Free. In contrast, the terrorists were working within an axis of evil, embracing uncivilized and tyrannical actions and ideals. In general, the press was supportive of the *idea* of a War on Terror, but presented either a questioning of, or hostility toward, the president's notion of an "axis of evil." In short, they were not reporting the president's idea as news but rather presenting their *dislike* of his idea as news. Additionally, press reporting on the economic aspects of the State of the Union address was decidedly negative, with frequent attempts to separate the economy from the larger picture of the War on Terror—the very same tactic adopted by congressional Democrats during this period.

Although the press raised the memories of World War II, none who spoke out against the axis of evil metaphor mentioned appeasement, an issue with which anyone familiar with World War II should be familiar. Unlike the other speech responses examined in chapters 2 and 3, the focus now was not on the nature of the war or the nature of the

Table 8.3.　State of the Union, January 2002

Themes	President's Frame	Press Frame
Good vs. Evil	Struggle of good and evil	—
Civilization vs. Barbarism	Struggle of civilization and barbarism	—
Freedom vs. Tyranny	Struggle of freedom and tyranny	—
Nature of the War	Domestic/global/ long-standing war	Response to 9/11 necessary
	—	President's actions questionable
	War linked with economy	Bush can't do both economy and war
Nature of the Enemy	Evil, implacable, murderers	—
	Parasites	—
	Terrorist sponsors: axis of evil	—
International Effort	Building international coalition	—
Axis of Evil	—	Only three
	—	Wrong to describe this way
	—	Bush using power and intimidation
Economy	Linked with War on Terror	Separate from War on Terror
	—	Bush has ruined
Enron	—	Republican scandal
	—	Demonstrates mishandling of economy

enemy but rather on *how* the war should be conducted: unilaterally or multilaterally, police action or military action? Additionally, the economic aspect added by the press acted to fracture the overall framing of the War on Terror by allowing the press to agree with the War on Terror *in principle* while arguing vociferously against both the administration's economic policies and its plan for conducting the war.

The press failed utterly to present a representative picture of the Enron situation, thus framing that aspect of the president's State of the Union in such a way that Democratic efforts to undermine Bush administration credibility found a ready ally in press reports. It was depicted exclusively as a Republican scandal, even though evidence existed showing that Democrats, too, had close ties with Enron.

Remarks aboard the USS *Abraham Lincoln*, March 2003

As in his other major speeches, aboard the *Lincoln*, the president restated the basic themes inherent within the master frame for the War on Terror. Patience was again called for, and Bush returned to the theme of international cooperation in fighting terrorism. Additionally, the themes of the nature of the war and the nature of the terrorists were hammered home in this speech. The president's master frame for the War on Terror is now well established, with Iraq clearly depicted as only part of the larger war.

Overall, the press again gave supportive lip service to the War on Terror, but acted in opposition to most of what the president said. Although it was a considerable focus of the Bush speech, the press offered no real discussion about the nature of war or of the nature of the terrorists. Moreover, the content of the president's speech was overshadowed by the press obsession with the means of his arrival and the economy. His arrival was cast in a derisive, mocking light: "Top Gun Bush." In terms of the economy, the press simply asserted that it was bad; no explanation or justification for *why* was provided, nor were the numerous positive economic indicators mentioned by the press. Fueled by cherry-picked examples and ignored evidence, the press placed the yoke of a bad economy squarely on Bush's shoulders. The negative focus on the economy was linked to the assumption that President Bush was beginning his reelection campaign with this speech; specifically, to avoid the mistake his father made, he would have to face the economy now, since the economy was so bad.

United Nations Address, September 2003

The Bush administration used two primary justifications for going to war with Iraq:

1. Iraq possessed, and was in the process of producing, weapons of mass destruction (WMD), which could be used by terrorists
2. Hussein's depraved and inhumane treatment of his own people

Table 8.4. Remarks by the President from the USS *Abraham Lincoln*, March 2003

Themes	President's Frame	Press Frame
Good vs. Evil	Struggle of good and evil	—
Civilization vs. Barbarism	Struggle of civilization and barbarism	—
Freedom vs. Tyranny	Struggle of freedom and tyranny	—
	Sharing liberty and eventual peace	—
Nature of the War	Domestic/global/ long-standing,	Response to 9/11 necessary
	not endless war prudently conducted	President's actions questionable
		Bush can't do both economy and war
Nature of the Enemy	Evil, implacable, murderers	—
	Parasites	—
	Terrorist sponsors: axis of evil	—
International Effort	Building international coalition	Acting unilaterally
	Acting within international coalition	—
Iraq War	Military operations over	Iraq a mess
	Central front in larger War on Terror	President misleading
	—	Drifting between war and peace
Economy	—	Separate from War on Terror
	—	Bush has ruined
	—	In terrible shape
Patience	Necessary for success	—
Means of arrival	Arrival necessary	Top Gun Bush
	Scheduling a Navy matter	Arrogant Swagger
	—	Lied about arrival
Purpose of speech	Thank Troops	Reelection ploy
	Signal end to military campaign	—

Table 8.5. President Bush Addresses the United Nations General Assembly, September 2003

Themes	President's Frame	Press Frame
Civilization v. Barbarism	Struggle of civilization and barbarism	—
	No neutral ground	—
Nature of the War	Iraq one battle	Must appeal for UN help
	Ongoing	—
Nature of the Enemy	Evil, implacable, murderers	—
Reasons for Iraq War	Belief in WMDs	Misled about WMDs; no WMDs found
	Humanitarian	—
	Acted in spirit of UN	Acted unilaterally; ignored UN
Iraq War	Presently central front in War on Terror	Iraq in utter chaos
	One battle in larger War on Terror	President misleading world
	On road to recovery	—
UN Role	Assist in rebuilding Afghanistan	Offered nothing
	Assist in rebuilding Iraq	Unapologetic for invasion
	—	Defiant attitude
Purpose of speech	Iraq update	Should apologize
	Invite UN participation	Bush failed: must beg UN for assistance
	Rebuild strained alliances	—

President Bush was careful in his speech to link his administration's interpretation of intelligence reports about WMDs in Iraq to the *past* actions of the United Nations against Iraq; he also linked the principles of the United Nations with *future* concrete actions of the United States. The president called for expanding the role of the United Nations in Iraq; specifically, he asked for a new UN resolution on Iraq and for having the UN directly involved in supervising elections and in helping Iraq develop its constitution. There existed a distinct disjunction between the themes and frames used by Bush and those used by the press; so great was this difference that the press seemed to be reporting on a completely different speech. Instead of reporting on what the president said, the press focused on the overall situation surrounding the speech and framed that situation as "dire straits." The press framed Iraq as being in chaos, thus forcing Bush to beg the United Nations for help. With this backdrop, the press then described a defiant Bush offering no apology or concessions for "unilaterally" invading Iraq without UN approval.

The press depicted an Iraq spiraling out of control and devolving into chaos. It deliberately chose to offer only negative examples and assertions concerning the situation in Iraq and laid this at the feet of President Bush. Although the press loudly asserted that the president made no concessions, in his speech the president clearly spoke about expanding the role of the UN in Iraq, but the press pointedly ignored these conciliatory gestures. Thus, at this point in time, we see both increasing press opposition to how the president framed certain themes and also the deliberate omission of information the president wished to emphasize. If one were to assign a name to the press framing of the president's speech, it would be a "frame of failure."

Veterans Day Address, November 2005

With this most recent speech, Bush sought to counter the unchecked criticism of his administration and to lay out in considerable detail the underlying strategy of continued U.S. involvement in both Iraq and the larger War on Terror. Even more strongly than in his other speeches concerning the War on Terror, the president here sought to convey the very real nature of the terrorists threatening the United States and the world. Most striking to me is that, to an even greater degree than with his other speeches, the press intentionally ignored or reframed the themes used by the president. The press chose to focus on only five paragraphs of a sixty-six-paragraph speech. Instead of presenting a nuanced policy speech, the press intentionally made it seem as if the president had only "lashed out" in anger against those who criticized him. Although the main argument asserted by President Bush in those five paragraphs was that Democrats in Congress had access to the same intelligence as he did when they voted for the war, this was lost in the press reporting of the speech.

No substantial mention was made of the progress in Iraq or the president's overall strategy for the war. Instead, the press presented critics of the war as demanding the very information Bush had presented

Table 8.6.   President Bush Commemorates Veterans Day and Discusses the War on Terror, November 2005

Themes	President's Frame	Press Frame
Civilization vs. Barbarism	Struggle of civilization and barbarism	—
Nature of the War	Iraq one battle	—
	Ongoing	—
	Global	—
Nature of the Enemy	Evil	—
	United by murderous ideology	—
	Brutal	—
Comprehensive U.S. strategy	Strategy for Iraq	—
	Strategy for larger war	—
Iraq War	Central front in larger War on Terror	Total mess
	One battle in larger War on Terror	Rep. Murtha's call for withdrawal
	On road to recovery	—
Comments to Critics	Iraq making real progress	Critics only complaining about misleading statements on prewar intelligence
	Defeatism plays into terrorism	—
	Critics had access to same intelligence	Democrats did not have same access to information
	Acceptable to criticize Bush	—
	Hypocrisy for critics to now change story	—
Purpose of Speech	Presents detailed strategy for victory	—
	Confront hypocrisy of some critics	Lashing out at critics
	—	Deflect criticism of failed war
	—	President has no plan
	—	President made no progress
	—	Polls show President unsuccessful

in his speech. Given that the press failed to convey the president's plan for progress, the charges made by Democrats—no plan, no progress—carried considerable weight. When Democratic congressman John Murtha of Pennsylvania spoke out on the war just days after President Bush charged some Democrats with reckless political behavior, the press specifically advanced Murtha in a manner calculated to enhance his credibility and thus the weight of his assertions.

The War on Terror: Master Frame or Metanarrative

Tellingly, in the words of Karen Callaghan and Frauke Schnell,

> The media are not simply intermediaries between political actors and the mass public. Journalists can actively limit the public's right to access and evaluate different policy platforms and thus diminish the quality of political dialogue. Such actions have the potential to inhibit pluralism by blocking out the preferred themes of interest groups and politicians.[27]

Looking back at how the press reported each of President Bush's speeches, we see that for the press there existed no master frame—just themes to describe opposition to whatever the president was advocating in his speeches. This presented a disjointed image to Americans; just what is the War on Terror?

Recall from chapter 1 that together, president and press act as providers of preknowledge (knowledge as yet unassimilated into the public consciousness and not yet formally part of public knowledge). Over time, some portions of this preknowledge will evolve into public knowledge. The public knowledge of Americans, the "accumulated wisdom of the people . . . serves as the authoritative ground for political discourse"; particularly in an atmosphere of crisis such as 9/11, the public would rely upon this "accumulated knowledge to define the situation."[28] Additionally, the public and its knowledge act to authorize policy decisions from those who are acting as representatives for the public—in our present case, President Bush. Yet how was President Bush to respond to 9/11? The Cold War metanarrative existed only in the past and so could not be used to guide future actions. So to what common knowledge could President Bush turn to invent (ground) his arguments concerning American action after 9/11?

The Bush Administration's response to 9/11 certainly needed justification on some level. Americans needed the attacks explained, but also needed the administration's continuing response explained. 9/11 was an event that allowed Bush the opportunity to begin to develop a new metanarrative: the War on Terror. However, considering the president and press framing over time, it is clear that no metanarrative on the War on Terror evolved. Certain recurring themes and frames must present themselves in both presidential and press utterances over time for the master frame of the War on Terror to take on the larger form of a metanarrative. Given the reportorial practices of the press described above, even the master frame existed only for the White House. In this sense, the press contributed to a fractured and confused perception concerning the meaning of the War on Terror. Those Americans with firsthand exposure to the framing of the Bush administration had a much clearer understanding of the country's actions than did those whose only exposure to information came from the mainstream news media.

Common Types of Bias

There are numerous ways other than framing in which the mainstream news media injects its bias into its reports, and following each of President Bush's speeches we see many examples of reporting that moved from a neutral act toward outright bias. In addition to bias introduced by framing, six other general examples of biased reporting emerged during the post-9/11 press coverage: agenda setting, priming, sandwiching, leading with a negative, pushing polls and partisan positions, and general bias. Given the large number of examples of each of these in chapters 2 through 7, I provide only a limited number of examples for each category below.

Agenda Setting

Agenda setting involves the press telling its audience what to think about. Although many studies focus on news coverage of a particular issue over time, the press can also keep a particular topic on the public agenda by inserting it into coverage of another issue. For instance, the *Washington Post*, instead of telling its readers what President Bush actually said on the flight deck of the *Lincoln*, injected thoughts of WMDs into its coverage:

In his address from the flight deck [Bush] made no claim that Iraq has or had biological and chemical weapons, though this accusation was the central argument the administration used in justifying the war to the international community. Instead of discussing the earlier mission of disarming Iraq, Bush emphasized other, less central and less widely supported, reasons for the war.[29]

CBS Morning News provides another example of the press pushing an agenda. A week after the president's speech, in a broadcast focusing on the United States asking the United Nations to lift sanctions from Iraq, reporter Bill Plante suddenly interjected: "The president is also still under fire from Democrats over his made-for-TV landing and victory speech aboard the carrier . . . *Lincoln*. His critics are calling it expensive and showy. They charge it will be used in his campaign. Mr. Bush called it an honor to thank the troops in person."[30]

Priming

The press can also prime its audience to evaluate the performance of the president by how it covers a particular issue. During its War on Terror coverage, the press often set Bush up to be judged on economic performance by making allusions to the first President Bush. For example, the *New York Times* wrote that Bush

was mindful of the fate of his father, a president who was as popular after the 1991 Persian Gulf war as the son is now, but who lost re-election the next year because of a failure to tend to the economy. Though [George W. Bush] made clear that fighting terrorism remained the focus of his presidency, he showed that the war he was most worried about winning was the one against the recession.[31]

Thus, President Bush was to be judged on how well the economy recovers.

In another example, the *Washington Post* wrote:

As with much of what Bush does, the effort to couple the domestic with the foreign is an attempt to avoid the mistakes of his one-term father. The elder Bush calculated, incorrectly it turns out, that the extraordinary popularity he earned for his handling of the Persian Gulf War would improve his standing on domestic matters. Instead, his support fell precipitously when the economy sagged and Americans felt their president was slow to react.[32]

At no time during the period covered did the press consider that the candidacy of Ross Perot could have played a part in the elder President Bush's reelection loss.

Following the president's 2003 address to the United Nations, *NBC Nightly News* asked, "Did the president get what he wanted at the United Nations, namely, a commitment from allies to contribute money and troops to the U.S. occupation? . . . No, not yet. And top officials conceded today it could take months."[33] Thus, even though Bush was asking for a different form of assistance, the press was priming its audience to judge his performance only upon the acquisition of money and troops.

In another clear instance of priming after the 2003 UN speech, *Today* host Katie Couric asked reporter Tim Russert, "What's got to happen that will keep President Bush in office?" Russert replied:

> There's a perfect cloud that has gathered now which is hurting the president and helping the Democrats. There are no weapons of mass destruction, Saddam Hussein is still on the loose, and . . . there are body bags coming home. . . . If all of those factors remain a year from now . . . that cloud will still linger against the president's political fortunes.[34]

In what I consider to be a typical press example of priming, George Stephanopoulos, on an ABC News *Special Report*, primed viewers to evaluate the performance of the president prior to his 2003 UN speech: The president, Stephanopoulos said,

> has to . . . say remember the speech he gave last year, [when] he challenged the UN to come together on the issue of Iraq. At first they did, [unanimously passing a Security Council resolution,] saying Iraq had to [allow full] weapons inspections. He has to . . . tell them they did the right thing. . . . What to watch for in the second half of the speech is any kind of notes of conciliation.[35]

Stephanopoulos went on to list certain items to look for; for example, will the president ask the UN for help administering the upcoming Iraqi elections? Or, will he specifically address other issues of importance to the UN, such as the global AIDS epidemic? Stephanopoulos also made reference to the UN speech given by Secretary-General Kofi Annan, who "gave a speech yesterday where he talked about you have to give people hope, you have to convince people that the world is gonna be a better place. That's how you fight terrorism. Does the president have the rhetoric that matches that rhetoric of Kofi Annan?"[36]

Sandwiching

This practice refers to the placement of one point of view between two other points of view of very different character; in a sense, the points of view are layered in a story line.[37] The press maintains that it is fair because it reports both sides of an issue. However, although it is true that an "other side" is often presented, the manner in which it is presented can detract from its potential impact, making it appear wrong or the minority point of view. The press can, if it so desires, place whatever side of the issue it *does not support* in between points of view complementary to its own. This *USA Today* article concerning the speech aboard the *Lincoln* provides an example of the technique of sandwiching:

> [Layer one, negative assertion] Congressional Democrats say Bush's rendezvous with troops returning home from Iraq was little more than a costly stunt designed to produce footage for his re-election campaign. [Layer two, administration reply] The president defended the decision to make the flight, telling reporters . . . that visiting the carrier was an unbelievably positive experience "and an opportunity to thank the troops." [Layer three, negative assertion and quotes] Staff members for Rep. David Obey of Wisconsin, the top Democrat on the House Appropriations Committee, calculated that the visit delayed the ship's arrival . . . and cost as much as $1 million in extra fuel costs, plus $100,000 in additional sea duty pay for the crew.[38]

The *Washington Post* provided another example of the technique of sandwiching in this article about the 2003 UN speech:

> [Layer one, negative assertion] In the view of many in attendance here, Iraq is largely a problem of Bush's making. [Layer two, administration reply] Bush, in defending the war, argued, "Events during the past two years have set before us the clearest of divides: between those who seek order, and those who spread chaos. . . ." [Layer three, negative assertion and quotes] But in two speeches that bracketed the president's address, Annan and French President Jacques Chirac suggested that it is the administration's doctrine of "preemption" . . . that threatens to spread chaos around the globe.[39]

Quotes from both men were provided, followed by, "The enthusiastic response to those speeches . . . compared to the tepid, almost perfunctory applause for Bush's presentation, underscored the difficult task" facing the Bush administration.[40]

These layers are not always in such neat order. For example, the press may well present its own point of view, then present supporting quotes for that point of view, and finally present the opposing point of view. The *Washington Post* provides us with an example of this in its coverage of the 2003 UN speech:

> [Layer one, negative assertion] President Bush, defending the invasion of Iraq before the United Nations . . . endured a torrent of criticism from world leaders who warned that his policy of unilateral action to confront emerging threats to U.S. security could destroy the 58-year-old organization. [Layer two, negative assertion and quotes] U.N. Secretary General Kofi Annan, in an unusually impassioned condemnation of U.S. policy, said unilateralism is an assault on the cooperative principles of . . . those who founded the United Nations that could spread the "lawless use of force. We have come to a fork in the road . . . . This may be a moment no less decisive than 1945 itself. . . ." [Layer three, administration reply] Bush, who did not sit in the chamber for Annan's address, emphasized the humanitarian work of the United Nations rather than his decision to go to war in Iraq without explicit U.N. backing. He suggested that his actions were in support of U.N. wishes, not defiance. "Because a coalition of nations acted to defend the peace and the credibility of the United Nations, Iraq is free."[41]

Leading with a Negative

One notable tactic of broadcast news media was to begin with a negative statement followed by a question. In this sense, the press placed the Bush administration on the defensive by contextualizing a topic in such a manner that the administration looked to be under fire. Below are several examples taken from the coverage of President Bush's speech aboard the USS *Lincoln*. An *Early Show* piece began:

> In his speech tonight, the president will say the war has been a success, but will not say that it has been won. Earlier, René asked the White House communications director [Dan Bartlett] if this week's shootings of Iraqis in . . . Fallujah have made Mr. Bush cautious about saying the war is over.

Bartlett was shown responding, "There are still dangerous elements throughout the nation of Iraq."[42]

The *CBS Evening News* reported:

> Not all the critics of the Halliburton deal are Democrats in Congress, but many of them are, and the contract is not all they're upset about. They're also critical of President Bush's triumphant trip to the USS *Abraham Lincoln* . . . a trip about which the White House has changed some of its story. CBS News chief White House correspondent has a Reality Check.[43]

Of particular note is the tactic of leading with a negative assertion while interviewing, thus placing the administration's representative immediately in the role of defending the administration. On *Today*, host Katie Couric began one interview with this:

> Senator Byrd really blasted President Bush for his appearance on the USS *Abraham Lincoln*, saying, "To me it is an affront to the Americans killed or injured in Iraq for the president to exploit the trappings of war for the momentary spectacle of a speech." He also added, "It should not be a made-for-TV back drop for a campaign commercial" and—and called the president's use of it "flamboyant showmanship." Do you agree with Senator Byrd about this?[44]

Although this may well put supporters of the administration at a disadvantage, opponents of the administration are often found in the enviable position of being able to respond to a negative assertion. For example, *Good Morning America* aired an interview with 2004 presidential hopeful Howard Dean.

> COHOST CHARLES GIBSON: Do you agree with Senator [Ted] Kennedy that the, that the reasons for going to war were a fraud made up in Texas?
>
> DEAN: I think, well, I'm not sure where it was made up. Obviously nobody has any way of knowing that, but I do think that the president was not truthful with the American People.
>
> GIBSON: And do you think . . . this administration, I'm using your words, shows contempt for democracy?
>
> DEAN: I do. I do. I think they truly do not believe that the rest of us have a voice and this is our country, 'cause it doesn't belong to the extreme right wing.[45]

Through all of the above examples, the reporter would direct the interpretation by negatively contextualizing the initial topic.

Pushing Polls and Press Positions

The press also generates its own news by reporting on its own poll results. ABC, CBS, and NBC, as well as the print press, commission polls, develop questions, and then report the results as news. In this manner, not only does the press have the opportunity to develop specific questions—sometimes close to push polling—but it is also able to interpret the responses, and in a sense, write its own press release, highlighting those aspects of the polls that support its frame.[46] In one sense, the press is here *making* news by setting the agenda. They also talk to each other, thus reinforcing their interpretation of events: We saw in chapters 5, 6, and 7 the heavy focus on negative economic comments.

Here is an example of the media talking to each other about the 2003 economy, pushing a partisan interpretation, from *Face the Nation*:

> HOST BOB SCHIEFFER: These states are really in a mess, aren't they, Karen [Tumulty of *Time*]? You wrote about that in the magazine this week. I was just in California where they're telling me that not only are they facing these huge deficits [but that one out of five jobs lost in America is in California].
>
> TUMULTY: That's right. And—and while these—these arguments we're having here in Washington over tax cuts may look sort of abstract to most people in America, it is not abstract when your kid's teacher gets laid off.
>
> SCHIEFFER: And . . . and that's what happening . . . in state after state.
>
> TUMULTY: Oh, libraries are closing, teachers are getting laid off. Gray Davis is in the position of having to decide whether he should . . . deny prosthetic limbs to poor people.[47]

General Bias

Usually when one thinks of bias, one thinks of overt examples, such as reporters attacking a politician or a policy overtly in news coverage. Coverage surrounding President Bush's speeches revealed numerous instances of noticeable bias against the president or the policies he advocated. There were no examples of positive bias, although numerous examples of negative bias exist, including the following.

USA Today, for one example, ran an editorial entitled "Skewed Intelligence Or Not, War Was A Mistake."[48] *The Osgood File* called a statement by Sen. Joe Biden (D-DE)—"All we have heard from the administration is misleading number after misleading number after misleading number after misleading number"—an example of "legitimate disagreement and discussion."[49] The *Washington Post*, reporting on Vice President Dick Cheney's 2005 comments at the American Enterprise Institute, wrote that he protested that

> he had been misunderstood when he said . . . that critics of the White House over Iraq were "dishonest and reprehensible." What he meant to say . . . was that those who question the White House's use of prewar intelligence were not only "dishonest and reprehensible" but also "corrupt and shameless." It was about as close as the vice president gets to a retraction.[50]

One expects points of view to emerge from opinion essays, and the ones in this study did convey opinion: decidedly negative toward President Bush. For example, the *Washington Post*'s Robinson wrote: "George Bush will inevitably get out of the mess he has made—he leaves office in three years and two months, not that anyone's counting."[51] In the *New York Times*, Rich called those Republicans defending the Bush administration the "White House's talking-point monkeys" and those who associate with the president, his "cronies."[52]

Special Consideration:
Exclusion of Oppositional Information

The most consistent and also the strongest way in which the press advanced a biased interpretation was through the exclusion of information that would contradict its preferred framing of an event or issue. The news media, who are supposed to protect and advance the *public interest*, ignore large portions of the public when they advance certain *personal and political interests* over the public's right to know all pertinent information about a given subject. In the sections above, we have seen examples of the numerous ways the press introduced its bias into the reportorial process.

One part of framing that is commonly ignored involves how frames are often supported by information that the press leaves out of its reporting. This failure to report information that would contradict the press's own point of view or that would harm the standing of those with whom the press sympathizes is yet another way in which the press introduces its bias.[53] As some communication researchers believe, the

> media's inadvertent reinforcement of existing attitudes through omission is far from the trivial effect that many scholars imply. Holding support under adverse new conditions is a crucial goal in politics, not just winning over new supporters. So one way the media wield influence is by omitting or de-emphasizing information, by excluding data about an altered reality that might otherwise disrupt existing support.[54]

I agree with the above position; the power of established frames can trap journalists as well as others. However, given what we have seen in the press response to the War on Terror, I am inclined to believe that the omission of information is often intentional. One can easily say that the press possesses neither the time nor the space to report everything and must make decisions about what to include in its news coverage. Although true, it is also true that the press strategically excludes information that would run contrary to its established frames for understanding the War on Terror.

For example, when President Bush spoke to the United Nations in September 2003, he clearly laid out the joint UN, NATO, and U.S. actions in Afghanistan, as well as plans for expanding the role of the United Nations in Iraq. He also spoke about a new UN resolution on Iraq and having the UN involved in helping Iraq develop its constitution and supervising its upcoming elections. The press had full access to this information. Yet these crucial details were conveniently ignored. For instance, following the president's 2003 UN speech, the *Washington Post* left out important information when it reviewed a

> new book by Wesley K. Clark, the retired Army general running for president. . . . In a searing critique, Clark accuses the Bush administration of carrying out a wrenching turn in U.S. foreign policy. Clark argues for adoption of "a more collaborative, collegiate" U.S. strategy marked by renewed cooperation with such international organizations as the United Nations and NATO and backed by substantial economic and political development aid.[55]

Incredibly, the very conduct Clark called for in his "searing critique" is exactly what President Bush had done in his UN speech, the very information the *Washington Post* left out of its story. Either the reporter intentionally excluded that information (deliberate framing to hurt the president) or he (as well as the entire mainstream media covered in this study) was unaware of the White House initiative (incompetence).

In another instance of omission of information, the press failed to mention the Bush administration's contributions to foreign aid to help other nations in the War on Terror. I find it particularly noteworthy that the one time the Bush administration's contributions to foreign aid were mentioned, it was to convey and support Democratic senator Ted Kennedy's accusations that the Bush administration was, with foreign aid loans, trying to "bribe" nations into helping the United States.[56]

Additionally, we saw that Bush took great pains to detail the nature of the terrorists in his 2001 UN speech. The press all but ignored that aspect of the speech. Also, we saw the president lay out a detailed strategy for Iraq in his 2005 Veterans Day speech. The press again all but ignored this and actually demanded the very information that the president had provided in that speech, thus implying that he had not addressed the issue.

Of course, other examples abound throughout the period covered in this book. The press omitted positive economic indicators, positive news about Iraq, the important information about Navy docking protocol, that Democrats had ties to Enron, and so forth. On and on it goes, and of course, the press failed repeatedly to provide important information contained in the speeches of the president.

Loose Ends

There are some final comments that flow from this study, but do not necessarily lend themselves to placement in any specific category. I place them here along with my final thoughts on the behavior of the press.

Hearsay

The use of hearsay and unnamed and anonymous sources was rampant throughout the news reports covered in this book. One article in the *Washington Post*, for example, quoted or paraphrased ten different officials and politicians to support its assertions about the Bush administration—but only one was named. The remainder were described in various ways: "a U.N. official," "a senior diplomat," "a European diplomat," or "one foreign official."[57] Without the proper citations of sources, the press is passing along little more than gossip at best and fictitious creations at worst.

Talk Shows versus Print

Although some studies find differences between how print and broadcast news frame issues, here I found no significant disparity concerning the themes advanced or the framing of those themes.[58] There were, however, some differences between how print news was able to maintain its favored frame and how talk shows were less able to do so. Simply put, print news was better able to cherry-pick quotes to use in supporting its constructed story line and ultimate framing. In contrast, talk shows, when they interviewed representatives of the Bush administration, had to allow these representatives to actually respond, thereby allowing them to say more to provide both ideas and context. *Meet the Press* provides one such example following the president's 2001 UN speech:

> HOST TIM RUSSERT: Many question whether Saudi behavior is that of an ally, with the hijackers, with the lack of cooperation in the investigation, with the funneling of money to Osama bin Laden. Why do you think the Saudis are such good allies in light of that kind of behavior?
>
> SECRETARY OF STATE COLIN POWELL: Because there are a lot of other "withs." With Saudi elimination of diplomatic relations with the Taliban. With Saudi dismissing Osama bin Laden, taking away his citizenship. And all of the things we have asked the Saudis to do, they have responded favorably. And there will be more we'll be asking them to do. *As the president said in his speech yesterday, we're off to a good start, but we need to do more.*[59]

Furthermore, administration representatives can occasionally inject their own ideas, thereby correcting the press or contesting the press's framing. For example, Gloria Borger on *Face the Nation* asked Secretary of Defense Donald Rumsfeld, "Mr. Secretary . . . if we have just been through stage one of the war [in Afghanistan], what can we expect in the next stage?" Rumsfeld responded: "We have not been through phase one. First of all, it's not clear to me there are phases to this war."[60] Unfortunately, the overwhelming majority of news about the War on Terror came not in the form of the interview, but rather in the form of news constructed solely by the mainstream media without other interaction.

Editorial Opinion and Hard News

Some researchers have found a strong relationship between editorial positions and the content of "objective" political news coverage.[61] I found this relationship to be extremely strong as well. In all cases, the general framing of news stories echoed the frames used by both editorial and opinion pages. Although news stories tended to be subtler in their denunciations and endorsements, they did support editorial positions. Editorials and opinion essays would assert their opinions forcefully. News stories would relay these same opinions by relying on the quotations of like-minded sources. What was readily apparent in news articles, opinion essays, and editorials was a willingness of the press to advance its own ideas over those being expressed by the administration.[62]

Negative on Iraq

Intentionally ignoring progress or intentionally highlighting negative aspects is putting a negative frame on information. Michael Kelly wrote an opinion piece in the *Washington Post* satirizing the news media's (primarily PBS's and the BBC's) handling of the war coverage as "all-negative, all the time."[63] Chapter 7 showed evidence that the press knew the administration needed positive reporting. As seen throughout this study, however, the press provided negative aspects almost exclusively. This finding is in concert with other studies looking into press coverage of the Iraq war. For example, one national-level study found the following concerning mainstream media news reporting on American involvement in Iraq during 2005:

- Network coverage has been overwhelmingly pessimistic. More than half of all stories (848, or 61%) focused on negative topics or presented a pessimistic analysis of the situation, four times as many as featured U.S. or Iraqi achievements or offered an optimistic assessment (just 211 stories, or 15%).
- News about the war has grown increasingly negative. In January and February, about a fifth of all network stories (21%) struck a hopeful note, while just over half presented a negative slant on the situation. By August and September, positive stories had fallen to a measly seven percent and the percentage of bad news stories swelled to 73 percent of all Iraq news, a ten-to-one disparity.
- Terrorist attacks are the centerpiece of TV's war news. Two out of every five network evening news stories (564) featured car bombings,

assassinations, kidnappings or other attacks launched by the terrorists against the Iraqi people or coalition forces, more than any
other topic.

- Even coverage of the Iraqi political process has been negative. More
  stories (124) focused on shortcomings in Iraq's political process—
  the danger of bloodshed during the January elections, political in-
  fighting among politicians, and fears that the new Iraqi constitution
  might spur more civil strife—than found optimism in the Iraqi people's historic march to democracy (92 stories). One-third of those
  optimistic stories (32) appeared on just two nights—January 30 and
  31, just after Iraq's first successful elections.
- Few stories focused on the heroism or generous actions of American soldiers. Just eight stories were devoted to recounting episodes
  of heroism or valor by U.S. troops, and another nine stories featured instances when soldiers reached out to help the Iraqi people.
  In contrast, 79 stories focused on allegations of combat mistakes or
  outright misconduct on the part of U.S. military personnel.
- It's not as if there was no "good news" to report. NBC's cameras
  found a bullish stock market and a hiring boom in Baghdad's business district, ABC showcased the coalition's successful effort to
  bring peace to a Baghdad thoroughfare once branded "Death
  Street," and CBS documented how the one-time battleground of
  Sadr City is now quiet and citizens are beginning to benefit from
  improved public services. Stories describing U.S. and Iraqi achievements provided essential context to the discouraging drumbeat of
  daily news, but were unfortunately just a small sliver of TV's Iraq
  news.[64]

As mentioned earlier, the press was well aware that the Bush administration desperately needed positive news about Iraq; the press also
knew that it was failing to provide that.

The Press as Antidemocratic

Having read this far, you have seen the countless ways in which
the press has injected bias into its reporting about the War on Terror.[65]
In all of these actions, the press violates its own norms for fair reporting. Referring to the standards of objective reporting to which the press
adheres, I think it safe to say that the press failed to provide a truthful,
comprehensive, or intelligent account of the day's events in a fair context. Instead, the press routinely omitted information that was necessary for the American public to make informed decisions, most
importantly, the ideas of the president. Finally, the press failed utterly

to provide full access to the day's intelligence. Although the press does cover breaking events, it presents that information in such a way that portions of that information are withheld if it would hinder the political goals of the press. Moreover, there is little difference in the information presented between one news article and the next, suggesting that the mainstream press overrelies on news wires and other press-generated sources for information. Given that the news organizations included here are supposed to be independent of each other, the level of consistency in both content and point of view is astonishing.

Just because the overwhelming majority of mainstream press outlets engage in biased reporting does not make them antidemocratic. What makes them function to undermine democracy is that they collectively deny Americans information they need to make informed decisions on the policies that affect their lives. The role of the press is to provide this information, and when they continually fail to do so, intentionally or not, they engage in antidemocratic behavior. The mainstream media do not act at all as a source of information, but instead act as a powerful third political party, consciously acting to shape the views of those exposed to its message. This is a grave disservice to Americans, and an outright abandonment of the very reason for the existence of a free press in America.

Notes

Chapter 1　Media Bias and Presidential Justifications for War

1. George W. Bush, Address to the Nation, 11 September 2001, http://www.whitehouse.gov/news/releases/2001/09/20010911-16.html.

2. In this book, I use the term *press* loosely to encompass the news media generally in the sense of the Fourth Estate.

3. This concept is explored further in Robert E. Denton Jr. and Gary C. Woodward, *Political Communication in America*, 2nd ed. (New York: Praeger, 1990); Jeffrey K. Tulis, *The Rhetorical Presidency* (Princeton, NJ: Princeton University Press, 1987); James W. Ceaser, Glen E. Thurow, Jeffrey K. Tulis, and Joseph M. Bessette, "The Rise of the Rhetorical Presidency," in *Essays in Presidential Rhetoric*, ed. Theodore O. Windt and Beth Ingold (Dubuque, IA: Kendall/Hunt, 1983), 3–22.

4. Denton and Woodward, *Political Communication in America*, 199–200.

5. In "Images of Savagery in American Justifications for War," *Communication Monographs* 47 (1980): 279–94, Robert L. Ivie stated that the "enemy [in our case, the Soviets] is portrayed as savage, i.e., as an aggressor, driven by irrational desires for conquest, who is seeking to subjugate others by force for arms" (281). This image is juxtaposed to an image of the United States as a "representative of civilization . . . rational, tolerant of diversity, and pacific" (281).

6. Ivie, "Images of Savagery," 281.

7. Ivie, "Images of Savagery," 284.

8. Robert L. Ivie, "Metaphor and the Rhetorical Invention of Cold War 'Idealists,'" in *Cold War Rhetoric: Strategy, Metaphor, and Ideology*, ed. Martin J. Medhurst, Robert L. Ivie, Philip Wander, and Robert L. Scott (Westport, CT: Greenwood Press, 1990), 103.

9. Robert L. Ivie, "Cold War Motives and the Rhetorical Metaphor: A Framework of Criticism," in Medhurst et al., *Cold War Rhetoric*, 72.

10. Lloyd F. Bitzer, "Rhetoric and Public Knowledge," in *Rhetoric, Philosophy, and Literature: An Exploration*, ed. Don M. Burks (West Lafayette, IN: Purdue University Press, 1978), 74.

11. Bitzer, "Rhetoric and Public Knowledge," 68.

12. Marilyn J. Young and Michael K. Launer, "KAL 007 and the Superpowers: An International Argument," *Quarterly Journal of Speech* 74 (1988): 272.

13. Young and Launer, "KAL 007 and the Superpowers," 289.

14. Bitzer, "Rhetoric and Public Knowledge," 75.

15. Theodore Windt, "The Presidency and Speeches on International Crises: Repeating the Rhetorical Past," in *Essays in Presidential Rhetoric*, ed. Theodore Windt and Beth Ingold (Dubuque, IA: Kendall/Hunt, 1983), 62.

16. Windt, "Presidency and Speeches," 62.

17. Windt, "Presidency and Speeches," 63.

18. Windt, "Presidency and Speeches," 64.

19. Windt, "Presidency and Speeches," 68–69.

20. D. Ray Heisey, "Reagan and Mitterrand Respond to International Crisis: Creating versus Transcending Appearances," *Western Journal of Speech Communication* 50 (1986): 333.

21. Marilyn J. Young and Michael K. Launer, *Flights of Fancy, Flight of Doom: KAL 007 and Soviet-American Rhetoric* (Lanham, MD: University Press of America, 1988); Young and Launer, "KAL 007 and the Superpowers"; Marilyn J. Young and Michael K. Launer, "Superpower Role Reversals: Political Rhetoric Following the Destruction of KAL 007 and the Iranian Airbus," paper presented at the annual meeting of the World Communication Association Singapore, 1989; and Marilyn J. Young, "When the Shoe Is on the Other Foot: The Reagan Administration's Treatment of the Shootdown of Iran Air," in *Reagan and Public Discourse in America*, ed. Michael Weiler and W. Barnett Pearce, 203–24 (Tuscaloosa: University of Alabama Press, 1992).

22. Young and Launer, "KAL 007 and the Superpowers," 289.

23. Andrew A. King, *Power and Communication* (Prospect Heights, IL: Waveland Press, 1987).

24. William A. Gamson, "News as Framing: Comments on Graber," *American Behavioral Scientist* 33 (1989): 157.

25. Gamson, "News as Framing," 157.

26. Paul M. Sniderman, Richard A. Brody, and Philip E. Tetlock, *Reasoning and Choice: Explorations in Political Psychology* (Cambridge: Cambridge University Press, 1991), 52.

27. Thomas E. Nelson, Rosalee A. Clawson, and Zoe M. Oxley, "Media Framing of Civil Liberties Conflict and Its Effects on Tolerance," *American Political Science Review* 91, no. 3 (1997): 567.

28. Robert M. Entman, "Framing toward Clarification of a Fractured Paradigm," *Journal of Communication* 43 (1993): 53.

29. This focusing process of the news media is called by some *second-level effects*. For a selection of recent studies exploring the second-level effect of agenda setting, see Maxwell McCombs, Donald L. Shaw, and David Weaver, *Communication and Democracy: Exploring the Intellectual Frontiers in Agenda Setting Theory* (Mahwah, NJ: Lawrence Erlbaum Associates, 1997); Esteban Lopez-Escobar, Juan Pablo Llamas, Maxwell McCombs, and Federico Rey Lennon, "Two Levels of Agenda Setting among Advertising and News in the 1995 Spanish Elections," *Political Communication* 15 (1998): 225–38; Spiro Kiousis, Philemon Bantimaroudis, and Hyun Ban, "Candidate Image Attributes: Experiments on the Substantive Dimension of Second-Level Agenda Setting," *Communication Research* 26, no. 4 (1999): 414–28; Maxwell McCombs, Esteban Lopez-Escobar, and Juan Pablo Llamas, "Setting the Agenda of Attributes in the 1996 Spanish General Election," *Journal of Communication* 50, no. 2 (2000): 77–92; Sei-Hill Kim, Dietram Scheufele, and James Shanahan, "Think about It This Way: Attribute Agenda-Setting Function of the Press and the Public's Evaluation of a Local Issue," *Journalism and Mass Communication Quarterly* 79 (2002); Joe Bob Hester and Rhonda Gibson, "The Economy and Second Level Agenda Setting: A Time-Series Analysis of Economic News and Public Opinion about the Economy," *Journalism and Mass Communication Quarterly* 80, no. 1 (2003): 73–90; Stephanie Craft and Wayne Wanta, "U.S. Public Concerns in the Aftermath of 9/11: A Test of Second Level Agenda-Setting," *International Journal of Public Opinion Research* 16, no. 4 (2004): 456–63; Spiro Kiousis, "Compelling Arguments and Attitude Strength: Exploring the Impact of Second-Level Agenda Setting on Public Opinion of Presidential Candidate Images," *Harvard International Journal of Press/Politics* 10, no. 2 (2005): 3–27.

30. Anne Johnston, "Trends in Political Communication: A Selective Review of Research in the 1980s," in *New Directions in Political Communication: A Resource Book*, ed. David L. Swanson and Dan Nimmo (Newbury Park, CA: Sage, 1990), 337. Emphasis mine.

31. Gladys Engel Lang and Kurt Lang, "The Media and Watergate," in *Media Power in Politics*, ed. Doris A. Graber (Washington, DC: CQ Press, 1984), 202–9.

32. Mitchell Stephens, *A History of News: From the Drum to the Satellite* (New York: Viking Penguin, 1988), 264.

33. Louis A. Day, *Ethics in Media Communication* (Belmont, CA: Wadsworth, 1991), 32.

34. Robert M. Entman, "Framing U.S. Coverage of International News: Contrasts in Narratives of the KAL and Iran Air Incidents," *Journal of Communication* 41, no. 4 (1991): 7.

35. Entman, "Framing U.S. Coverage," 7.

36. Entman, "Framing U.S. Coverage," 7.

37. Entman, "Framing U.S. Coverage," 6–27. In his 2004 work *Projections of Power: Framing News, Public Opinion, and U.S. Foreign Policy* (Chicago: University of Chicago Press), Robert M. Entman, although inexplicably leaving out

scholarship directly related to his subject matter, does provide a summary of his thoughts on framing and its effect on contemporary U.S foreign policy.

38. Entman, "Framing U.S. Coverage," 21.

39. Jim A. Kuypers, *Presidential Crisis Rhetoric and the Press in the Post–Cold War World* (Westport, CT: Praeger, 1997).

40. This and the subsequent three paragraphs are paraphrased from my essay "Framing Analysis" in *The Art of Rhetorical Criticism*, ed. Jim A. Kuypers (Boston: Allyn and Bacon, 2005).

41. For instance, the *New York Times* stated editorially: "If all sides conclude that the United States and its allies are prepared to apply military force to support a serious diplomatic initiative, the prospects for peace may improve. No one pretends that the latest American plan is a triumph of principle. But it is a workable compromise" ("Force and Diplomacy in Bosnia," 31 August 1995); "Having come this far in brokering a Balkan peace, the United States is obliged to take on a significant share of the peacekeeping operation" ("Peace and Peacekeeping in Bosnia," 6 October 1995); and "America's leading diplomatic role in bringing about a Bosnian peace agreement, as well as its claims to NATO leadership, create a strong obligation to contribute significant forces to peacekeeping" ("Congress Must Vote on Bosnia," 20 October 1995). The *Washington Post* echoed this support: "Finally, after 3½ years of war, NATO planes and U.N. ground troops have replied with heavy and suitable force to a deadly attack seen as coming from the Bosnian Serbs. . . . [It] sets a standard for allied performance anew" ("Answering the Bosnian Serbs," 31 August 1995); and "It would be grotesque, having so far left ground duty to its allies for fear of American casualties, if the United States still did not join the allies after a peace agreement had cut the risk way back" ("A Bosnia Peace Force," 24 September 1995).

42. Jim A. Kuypers, *Press Bias and Politics: How the Media Frame Controversial Issues*. (Westport, CT: Praeger, 2002).

43. Zhongdang Pan and Gerald M. Kosicki, "Framing Analysis: An Approach to News Discourse," *Political Communication* 10, no. 1 (1993): 55–75.

44. Pan and Kosicki, "Framing Analysis," 62.

45. Ben Kauffman, "As You Were Saying . . . Evil Euphemisms Must Not Pass Our Lips Unexamined," *Boston Herald*, 2 May 1999.

46. In fairness to the press, a majority of the papers examined did use these terms. However, enough pejorative examples of naming exist to color the otherwise neutral descriptions.

47. I treat themes as the subject of discussion, or that which is the subject of thought. Within any single news story or broadcast, there is at least one theme, the subject of the report; usually there are several themes. When looking at news reports over a period of time, certain themes recur, each being framed in a particular manner.

48. David Levin, "Framing Peace Policies: The Competition for Resonate Themes," *Political Communication* 22 (2005): 84.

Chapter 2   A New Justification for War?

I wish to acknowledge contributions to this chapter made by Laura Anderson, Evan Fitzpatrick, Elysa Goldman, and Kevin Mazur, all former students of mine at Dartmouth College. Their work and intellectual contributions are greatly appreciated.

1. Theodore Windt, "The Presidency and Speeches on International Crises: Repeating the Rhetorical Past," in *Essays in Presidential Rhetoric*, ed. Theodore Windt and Beth Ingold, 2nd ed. (Dubuque, IA: Hunt, 1987), 126.

2. Master frames are composed of numerous themes, each of which is framed in a particular manner.

3. This chapter and the chapters that follow are at heart comparative framing analyses. I analyze President Bush's speeches, and next subject a selection of press responses to those speeches to the same style of analysis. For this chapter, I examined network news and special reports from ABC, CBS, Fox News Network, and NBC. The newspapers examined were the *New York Times* and the *Washington Post*. In the weeks leading up to the military action against Afghanistan, more than one thousand articles were published in the above papers and over 600 news broadcasts were aired. I did not read them all; instead, the focus was on articles and broadcasts following speeches given by President Bush, and also on articles that reflected best what I saw as the general thrust of press reporting. These reports are the ones whose purpose was to relay the words of the president. There were 88 news articles and broadcast transcripts examined for this chapter: 23 from broadcast news, 45 news articles, 7 editorials, and 13 opinion essays. All press documents in this chapter were retrieved using the Lexis-Nexis database. Unlike the chapters that follow, I have tried to minimize the inclusion of press responses, instead focusing upon statements given by President Bush.

4. George W. Bush, "Remarks by the President after Two Planes Crash into World Trade Center," 11 September 2001, http://www.whitehouse.gov/news/releases/2001/09/20010911.html.

5. George W. Bush, "Statement by the President in His Address to the Nation," 11 September 2001, http://www.whitehouse.gov/news/releases/2001/09/20010911-16.html.

6. George W. Bush, "Remarks by the President in Photo Opportunity with the National Security Team," 12 September 2001, http://www.whitehouse.gov/news/releases/2001/09/20010912-4.html.

7. Bush, "Remarks by the President in Photo Opportunity."

8. Bush, "Statement by the President in His Address to the Nation."

9. George W. Bush, "Remarks by the President upon Arrival at Barksdale Air Force Base," 11 September 2001, http://www.whitehouse.gov/news/releases/2001/09/20010911-1.html.

10. Bush, "Statement by the President in His Address to the Nation."

11. Bush, "Statement by the President in His Address to the Nation."

12. Bush, "Remarks by the President after Two Planes."

13. George W. Bush, "Remarks by the President while Touring Damage at the Pentagon," 12 September 2001, http://www.whitehouse.gov/news/releases/2001/09/20010912-12.html.

14. Bush, "Statement by the President in His Address to the Nation."

15. Bush, "Remarks by the President in Photo Opportunity."

16. Bush, "Statement by the President in His Address to the Nation."

17. Bush, "Statement by the President in His Address to the Nation."

18. Bush, "Statement by the President in His Address to the Nation."

19. Bush, "Statement by the President in His Address to the Nation."

20. Bush, "Remarks by the President in Photo Opportunity."

21. Bush, "Remarks by the President Upon Arrival at Barksdale."

22. Bush, "Statement by the President in His Address to the Nation."

23. Bush, "Remarks by the President in Photo Opportunity."

24. Bush, "Remarks by the President in Photo Opportunity."

25. "Aftermath of the Terrorist Attacks in New York and Washington, DC," *CBS News Special Report*, 11 September 2001.

26. "Attack on America, 11:00 PM," *NBC News Special Report*, 12 September 2001 (emphasis mine).

27. "Aftermath of the Terrorist Attacks in New York and Washington, DC," *CBS News Special Report*, 11 September 2001.

28. Elisabeth Bumiller and David S. Sanger, "A Day of Terror: The President; A Somber Bush Says Terrorism Cannot Prevail," *New York Times*, 12 September 2001.

29. "America under Attack," *ABC News Special Report*, 11 September 2001.

30. "Attack on America, 9:00 PM," *NBC News Special Report*, 11 September 2001.

31. Dana Milbank, "Crisis Brings Shift In Presidential Style," *Washington Post*, 14 September 2001.

32. "The Road Ahead," editorial, *Washington Post*, 13 September 2001.

33. Bumiller and Sanger, "A Day of Terror."

34. "Attack on America, 8:00 PM," *NBC News Special Report*, 11 September 2001.

35. "Terrorism Hits America," Fox News Network, 11 September 2001.

36. "Attack on America, 9:00 PM," *NBC News Special Report*, 11 September 2001.

37. "Special Report: Roundtable," Fox News Network, 14 September 2001.

38. "President Bush's First Win," editorial, *New York Times*, 17 September 2001.

39. See Jim A. Kuypers, *Presidential Crisis Rhetoric and the Press in the Post–Cold War World* (Westport, CT: Praeger, 1997).

40. George W. Bush, "President's Remarks at National Day of Prayer and Remembrance," 14 September 2001, http://www.whitehouse.gov/news/releases/2001/09/20010914-2.html.

41. Bush, "President's Remarks at National Day of Prayer."

42. George W. Bush, "President Bush Salutes Heroes in New York," 14 September 2001, http://www.whitehouse.gov/news/releases/2001/09/20010914-9.html.

43. Bush, "President's Remarks at National Day of Prayer."

44. Bush, "President's Remarks at National Day of Prayer."

45. Bill Broadway, "War Cry From the Pulpit; Some Fear Mix of Patriotism, Religion in Bush's Vow to Rid World of Evil," *Washington Post*, 22 September 2001.

46. "Special Report: America United," Fox News Network, 15 September 2001.

47. "America Mourns, 2:00 AM," *NBC News Special Report*, 15 September 2001.

48. "Special Report: Roundtable," Fox News Network, 14 September 2001.

49. "America Mourns, 4:00 PM," *NBC News Special Report*, 14 September 2001.

50. "America Mourns, 2:00 PM," *NBC News Special Report*, 14 September 2001.

51. "Wartime Rhetoric," editorial, *New York Times*, 19 September 2001.

52. Philip Shenon and Neil A. Lewis, "A Nation Challenged: Safety and Liberty; Groups Fault Plan to Listen, Search and Seize," *New York Times*, 21 September 2001.

53. Maureen Dowd, "Liberties; Old Ruses, New Barbarians," *New York Times*, 19 September 2001.

54. "Intelligence and Terrorism," editorial, *New York Times*, 17 September 2001.

55. Jonathan Krim, "Anti-Terror Push Stirs Fears for Liberties; Rights Groups Unite To Seek Safeguards," *Washington Post*, 18 September 2001.

56. George W. Bush, "Address to a Joint Session of Congress and the American People," 20 September 2001, http://www.whitehouse.gov/news/releases/2001/09/20010920-8.html.

57. Bush, "Address to a Joint Session of Congress."

58. "Lisa Beamer, Wife of Hero Todd Beamer, Tells Her Reaction to President Bush's Speech," *Good Morning America*, 21 September 2001.

59. Howard Kurtz, "Journalists Worry About Limits on Information, Access," *Washington Post*, 24 September 2001.

60. John Kifner, "Aftermath; Forget the Past: It's A War Unlike Any Other," *New York Times*, 23 September 2001.

61. "Calibrating the Use of Force," editorial, *New York Times*, 22 September 2001.

62. Peter Carlson, "The Solitary Vote Of Barbara Lee; Congresswoman Against Use of Force," *Washington Post*, 19 September 2001; John Lancaster and Walter Pincus, "Proposed Anti-Terrorism Laws Draw Tough Questions; Lawmakers Express Concerns to Ashcroft, Other Justice Officials About Threat to Civil Liberties," *Washington Post*, 25 September 2001.

63. Tom Shales, "From President Bush, a Speech Filled With Assurance and Reassurance," *Washington Post*, 21 September 2001.

64. George W. Bush, "Presidential Address to the Nation," 7 October 2001, http://www.whitehouse.gov/news/releases/2001/10/20011007-8.html.

65. Lloyd F. Bitzer, "Rhetoric and Public Knowledge," in *Rhetoric, Philosophy, and Literature: An Exploration*, ed. Don M. Burks (West Lafayette, IN: Purdue University Press, 1978), 87–88.

66. Certainly they are part of the sociocultural background that speakers draw upon to base the arguments in support of their causes.

67. Bush, "Address to a Joint Session of Congress."

68. Bush, "Statement by the President in His Address to the Nation."

69. "Latest Information About the Attack on America," *CBS News Special Report*, 11 September 2001.

70. "After The Attacks: The President; Bush Leads Prayer, Visits Aid Crews; Congress Backs Use Of Armed Force," *New York Times*, 15 September 2001.

71. I have commented on this in other work: "The epistemic status of crisis . . . generates new knowledge; it subverts or contests old knowledge about the situation." Kuypers, *Presidential Crisis Rhetoric*, 26.

72. Marilyn J. Young and Michael K. Launer, Flights of Fancy, *Flight of Doom: KAL 007 and Soviet-American Rhetoric* (Lanham: University Press of America, 1988), 20 (emphasis mine).

Chapter 3   President Bush Speaks to the United Nations

1. George W. Bush, speech to the United Nations, 10 November 2001, http://www.whitehouse.gov/news/2001/11/print/20011110-3.html. Unless otherwise stated, all quotes from President Bush in this chapter come from this speech.

2. There were 72 news articles and transcripts examined for this chapter: 28 from broadcast news, 26 news articles, 11 editorials, and 12 opinion essays. All ABC, CBS, NBC, *New York Times*, *Washington Post*, and *USA Today* documents were obtained using Lexis-Nexis.

3. Rick Lyman, "A Nation Challenged: The Film Industry," *New York Times*, 11 November 2001.

4. "President Bush Shores Up Domestic and World Support for the War Effort," *Early Show*, CBS-TV, 12 November 2001.

5. Philip Shenon, "A Nation Challenged: Law Enforcement," *New York Times*, 12 November 2001.

6. "How the War on Terrorism Is Affecting the Legal System in the U.S.," *CBS Morning News*, 12 November 2001.

7. Kenneth Bredemeier, "Call-Up Law Protects Firms, Military Reservists," *Washington Post*, 12 November 2001.

8. "Netting Bin Laden," editorial, *Washington Post*, 11 November 2001.

9. "President Bush Visits Ground Zero . . . ," *This Week*, ABC-TV, 11 November 2001.

10. "President Bush Calls on the World Leaders to Join the Fight against Terrorism in His Address to the UN General Assembly," *Saturday Early Show*, CBS-TV, 10 November 2001.

11. "Front Lines; Some Things Are Getting Back to Normal," *Sunday Morning*, CBS-TV, 11 November 2001.

12. "Reconsidering Saudi Arabia," editorial, *Washington Post*, 11 November 2001.

13. Kevin Sack, "A Nation Challenged: The Public," *New York Times*, 11 November 2001.

14. John McCain, "Business as Usual," *Washington Post*, 16 November 2001.

15. "Are We There Yet?" editorial, *Washington Post*, 14 November 2001.

16. "President Bush Visits Ground Zero." The portion of this show concerning the comparison with World War II or Vietnam was again aired on 12 November 2001 on ABC's *World News Now*.

17. Lyman, "A Nation Challenged."

18. Alison Mitchell, "A Nation Challenged: The Home Front," *New York Times*, 10 November 2001.

19. Mitchell, "A Nation Challenged."

20. Mitchell, "A Nation Challenged."

21. Richard Cohen, "We Can't Fight Terror Everywhere," *Washington Post*, 13 November 2001.

22. "Vietnam Ghosts," editorial, *New York Times*, 11 November 2001.

23. Alison Stewart, "Newscast: ABC's World News Headlines," *World News Now*, ABC-TV, 12 November 2001.

24. Sack, "A Nation Challenged."

25. Quoted in Sack, "A Nation Challenged."

26. Sack, "A Nation Challenged."

27. "President Bush Visits Ground Zero."

28. "The Battle for Mazur-I-Sharif," editorial, *New York Times*, 10 November 2001.

29. Sack, "A Nation Challenged."

30. "The War So Far," editorial, *Washington Post*, 11 November 2001.

31. "Are We There Yet?"

32. "Are We There Yet?"

33. Sack, "A Nation Challenged."

34. "President Bush Addresses UN General Assembly, Says More than Sympathy Is Needed from All Countries," *NBC Nightly News*, 10 November 2001.

35. "Security Tightens around UN in New York," *Saturday Early Show*, CBS-TV, 10 November 2001.

36. "Secretary of Defense Donald Rumsfeld Discusses the War on Terrorism," *Face the Nation*, CBS-TV, 11 November 2001.

37. "President Bush Shores Up Domestic and World Support."

38. Karen DeYoung, "Bush Urges Coalition to Fulfill its 'Duties,'" *Washington Post*, 11 November 2001.

39. Calum Lynch, "Extraordinary Security Greets U.N. Delegates," *Washington Post*, 11 November 2001.

40. William Raspberry, "Choosing Us or Them," *Washington Post*, 12 November 2001.

41. Richard Holbrooke, "After the Taliban," *Washington Post*, 14 November 2001.

42. "President Bush Addresses UN General Assembly."

43. "President Bush Will Talk to the UN General Assembly, and Tell Coalition Leaders Sympathy Is Great, but the U.S. Wants Them to Commit to Action," *Saturday Today*, NBC-TV, 10 November 2001.

44. "President Bush Addresses the UN on the Threat of Terrorism Worldwide," *CBS Evening News*, 10 November 2001.

45. "President Bush Shores Up Domestic and World Support."

46. Uri Avnery, "To Understand Terrorism, Trace its Bloodline," *USA Today*, 21 November 2001.

47. Philip P. Pan and John Pomfret, "Bin Laden Network's China Connection," *Washington Post*, 11 November 2001.

48. DeYoung, "Bush Urges Coalition."

49. "President Bush Will Talk to the UN General Assembly"; "President Bush Calls on the World Leaders."

50. "President Bush and President Putin Will Meet to Talk about Afghanistan, NATO and U.S. Plans to Build a Missile Defense System," *World News This Morning*, ABC-TV, 12 November 2001; "President Bush Addresses the UN on the Threat of Terrorism Worldwide"; Elisabeth Bumiller, "A Nation Challenged: The President; Bush Chides Some Members of Coalition for Inaction in War Against Terrorism," *New York Times*, 10 November 2001; Bradley Graham and Vernon Loeb, "Rebels' Gains Shift U.S. Focus to the South," *Washington Post*, 13 November 2001; Joan Biskupic and Richard Willing, "Military Tribunals: Swift Judgments in Dire Times," *USA Today*, 15 November 2001.

51. Jim Wallis, "Justice is Still the Goal," *Washington Post*, 14 November 2001.

52. Biskupic and Willing, "Military Tribunals."

53. "End-Running the Bill of Rights," editorial, *Washington Post*, 16 November 2001.

54. Avnery, "To Understand Terrorism."

55. "Anti-Taliban Troops Advancing Forcefully on Kabul . . . ," *Good Morning America*, ABC-TV, 12 November 2001.

56. Elizabeth Becker, "A Nation Challenged: Hearts and Minds—A Special Report," *New York Times*, 11 November 2001.

57. Becker, "A Nation Challenged."

58. "Battle for Mazur-I-Sharif."

59. "Vietnam Ghosts."

60. "Disappearing in America," editorial, *New York Times*, 10 November 2001.

61. Robin Toner and Neil A. Lewis, "A Nation Challenged: Civil Liberties," *New York Times*, 15 November 2001.

62. "End-Running the Bill of Rights," editorial, *Washington Post*, 16 November 2001.

Chapter 4   The State of the Union, 29 January 2002

1. George W. Bush, State of the Union address, 29 January 2002, http://www.whitehouse.gov/news/releases/2002/01/20020129/11.html. Unless otherwise stated, all quotes from President Bush in this chapter come from this speech.

2. There were 110 news articles and transcripts examined for this chapter: 48 from broadcast news, 43 news articles, 6 editorials, and 13 opinion essays.

3. Emphasis mine.

4. "President George W. Bush Addresses the Nation," *Nightline*, ABC-TV, 29 January 2002.

5. "President Bush Gives His State of the Union Address and Senate Majority Leader Tom Daschle Responds," *Good Morning America*, ABC-TV, 30 January 2002.

6. "President Bush Addresses Congress for State of the Union," *CBS News Special Report*, 29 January 2002.

7. "Representative Richard Gephardt Gives the Democrats' Response to the State of the Union Address," *CBS News Special Report*, 29 January 2002.

8. "Sticking with the Fight," editorial, *Washington Post*, 29 January 2002.

9. Judy Keen, "Bush Promotes USA Freedom Corps in South," *USA Today*, 31 January 2002.

10. Steven Erlanger, "U.S. Officials Try to Assure Europeans on NATO," *New York Times*, 3 February 2002.

11. Michael McFaul, "The Other Half of the Job," *Washington Post*, 5 February 2002.

12. "Bush to Focus on War on Terror, Foreign Policy in State of Union Address," *NBC Nightly News*, 29 January 2002.

13. "Discussion of Content of President Bush's State of the Union Address," *NBC News Special Report*, 29 January 2002.

14. "Representative Richard Gephardt Gives the Democrats' Response."

15. "President George W. Bush Addresses the Nation."

16. "Presidential Historian Michael Beschloss Comments on Historic State of the Union Speeches and What Tone the President Might Use as He Addresses the Nation Tonight," *Good Morning America*, ABC-TV, 29 January 2002.

17. "Bush Makes It Clear War on Terrorism Is Not Over, Has Tough Words for Iran, Iraq and North Korea," *NBC Nightly News*, 30 January 2002.

18. "President Bush Delivers State of the Union Address," *The Early Show*, CBS-TV, 30 January 2002.

19. Amy Goldstein and Mike Allen, "Bush Vows to Defeat Terror, Recession," *Washington Post*, 30 January 2002.

20. Judy Keen and Laurence McQuillan, "Country is at 'Unique Moment of Opportunity,' President Says," *USA Today*, 30 January 2002.

21. Laurence McQuillan and Judy Keen, "Bush: 'We Now Press On,'" *USA Today*, 30 January 2002.

22. David E. Sanger, "The State of the Union; The Overview; Bush, Focusing on Terrorism, Says Secure U.S. is Top Priority," *New York Times*, 30 January 2002.

23. "Sticking with the Fight."

24. "Bush's Choice of Guns over Butter is A Risky One," *USA Today*, 29 January 2002.

25. "President Bush's State of the Union Address and the Democratic Response," ABC-TV, 29 January 2002.

26. "Bush to Focus on War on Terror".

27. "Discussion of Content of President Bush's State of the Union."

28. *Today*, NBC-TV, 30 January 2002. This is one of but a handful of news broadcasts or articles that used Iran, Iraq, and North Korea as of *examples* of evil states.

29. "President Bush Delivers State of the Union Address," *The Early Show*, CBS-TV, 30 January 2002.

30. "Highlights of President Bush's State of the Union; Discussion on Key Issues of Bush's Speech," *Good Morning America*, ABC-TV, 30 January 2002.

31. Amy Goldstein and Mike Allen, "Bush Vows to Defeat Terror, Recession," *Washington Post*, 30 January 2002.

32. "President Bush's State of the Union Address Covers War on Terrorism, Recession; House Minority Leader Richard Gephardt Responds to Bush's Address," *World News Now*, ABC-TV, 30 January 2002.

33. "Implications of Bush's 'Axis of Evil' Statement in the State of the Union Address," *CBS Evening News*, 30 January 2002.

34. "President Bush Describes Iran, Iraq and North Korea as Axes of Evil," *World News Tonight*, ABC-TV, 30 January 2002.

35. "Recap of President Bush's State of the Union Address," *World News Now*, ABC-TV, 30 January 2002.

36. "President George W. Bush Addresses the Nation."

37. "Mark Halperin Gives Insight into the Significant Details of President Bush's State of the Union Address," *World News Now*, ABC-TV, 30 January 2002.

38. "Speech Reflects Complex Year Ahead," *USA Today*, 30 January 2002.

39. "George W. Bush's Moment," editorial, *New York Times*, 30 January 2002.

40. Michael R. Gordon, "The State of the Union: Military Analysis; Broadening of 'Doctrine,'" *New York Times*, 30 January 2002.

41. Tom Shales, "A Few Rounds of Applause for George W. Bush," *Washington Post*, 30 January 2002.

42. Karen DeYoung, "Bush Lays Down A Marker for 3 'Evil' States," *Washington Post*, 30 January 2002.

43. "Implications of Bush's 'Axis of Evil' Statement in the State of the Union Address," *CBS Morning News*, 31 January 2002.

44. "Implications of Bush's 'Axis of Evil' Statement," *CBS Morning News*.

45. Barbara Slavin, "Critics Question Tough Talk on Iran, North Korea," *USA Today*, 31 January 2002.

46. James Brooke, "A Nation Challenged: Asian Arena; South Korea and Japan Begin to Sweat After Bush Turns Up the Heat on North Korea," *New York Times*, 31 January 2002.

47. Suzanne Daley, "A Nation Challenged: The Allies; Many in Europe Voice Worry U.S. Will Not Consult Them," *New York Times*, 31 January 2002.

48. Thomas Ricks, "European Security Leaders Alarmed by Bush's Stance," *The Washington Post* (3 February 2002) A16.

49. "The Limits of Power," editorial, *New York Times*, 31 January 2002.

50. "Tough Talk on Rogue Nations Exposes Difficult Choices," editorial, *USA Today*, 1 February 2002.

51. Karen DeYoung and Dana Milbank, "U.S. Repeats Warnings on Terrorism," *Washington Post*, 1 February 2002.

52. "Madeleine Albright Discusses Current Situation with Kidnapped Journalist and Some of President Bush's State of the Union Comments . . . ," *Today*, NBC-TV, 1 February 2002.

53. Barbara Slavin, "Powell: 'Axis of Evil' is Correct," *USA Today*, 4 February 2002.

54. Steven Erlanger, "A Nation Challenged: Diplomacy; Russian Aide Warns U.S. Not to Extend War to Iraq," *New York Times*, 4 February 2002.

55. Thomas Ricks, "U.S. Mission Concerned about NATO Support," *Washington Post*, 4 February 2002.

56. Giandomenico Picco, "Let the Axis Rotate; A Different Approach to Iran Would Better Serve U.S. Interests," *Washington Post*, 10 February 2002.

57. Dana Milbank, "Hitching Civic, Economic Goals to the War," *Washington Post*, 30 January 2002.

58. David S. Broder, "Bush's Focus—And the Country's," *Washington Post*, 31 January 2002.

59. "Expectations for State of the Union and Entrance of Dignitaries," *NBC News Special Report*, 29 January 2002.

60. "President George W. Bush Addresses the Nation."

61. "Sticking with the Fight."

62. "Recap of President Bush's State of the Union Address," *World News Now*, ABC-TV, 30 January 2002.

63. "Budget Takes Ugly Turn: Deficits for Years to Come," *USA Today*, 4 February 2002.

64. "The President's Speech and Reactions to it," *Today*, NBC-TV, 30 January 2002.

65. "Dick Gephardt Responds to State of the Union Address by Calling for Bipartisan Action on the Economy," *CBS Morning News*, 30 January 2002.

66. "President Bush Delivers State of the Union Address, Emphasizing War on Terrorism and Economic Stimulus Plans," *World News This Morning*, ABC-TV, 30 January 2002.

67. John Lancaster and Helen Dewar, "Behind Warmth, Familiar Battle Lines Remain; Domestic Policy Gaps Evident," *Washington Post*, 30 January 2002.

68. Alison Mitchell, "The State of the Union: The Democrats; Gephardt Puts Emphasis on Common Ground on War," *New York Times*, 30 January 2002.

69. "George W. Bush's Moment."

70. E. J. Dionne Jr., "Now, How Do We Pay for It?" *Washington Post*, 1 February 2002.

71. "The Lid is Off," editorial, *Washington Post*, 5 February 2002.

72. Robert L. Borosage, "Rumsfeld's Surrender," *Washington Post*, 7 February 2002.

73. "President Bush Ready to Deliver State of the Union Address Tonight," *Today*, NBC-TV, 29 January 2002.

74. "President Bush's Preparations for the State of the Union; Karen Hughes Gives Insight about the Subjects of the Speech," *Good Morning America*, ABC-TV, 29 January 2002. The interview also carried a rather lengthy quote from Hughes that explained in detail the legal investigation that would make discussion of Enron inappropriate for the State of the Union.

75. "President Bush Prepares for State of the Union Address and Enjoys National Popularity," *World News This Morning*, ABC-TV, 29 January 2002.

76. "President George W. Bush Addresses the Nation."

77. Kevin Phillips, "Integrity and the State of the Union," *New York Times*, 31 January 2002 (emphasis mine).

78. Keen and McQuillan, "Country is at 'Unique Moment.'"

79. Mitchell, "The State of the Union."

80. Elisabeth Bumiller, "The State of the Union: News Analysis; Surer Voice, Bigger Vision," *New York Times*, 30 January 2002.

81. "Discussion of Content of President Bush's State of the Union."

82. "President Bush Addresses Congress for State of the Union."

83. "Enron Donations: Statistical Summary," *Citizen Works: Tools for Democracy*, http://www.citizenworks.org/enrondonations/summary.php.

84. For an example of this and other Democratic involvement, see *OpenSecrets.org*, http://www.opensecrets.org/orgs/summary.asp?ID=D0000001 37&Name=Enron+Corp. Though obviously partisan, another site also provides details concerning Enron donations: see "Democrat Pals," *Stop Democrats*, www.stopdemocrats.com/enron/.

85. Numerous examples exist outside of the elite mainstream news media. For example, see Jerry Seper, "Enron Gave Cash to Democrats, Sought Pact Help," *Washington Times*, 16 January 2002; Patrice Hill, "Enron Cash Got to Bush, But not Results; White House Rejected Pleas for Favorable Legislation," *Washington Times*, 21 January 2002; Ralph Z. Hallow, "DNC Chief Profited from Bankrupt Firm," *Washington Times*, 29 January 2002; and Patrice Hill, "Clinton

Helped Enron Finance Projects Abroad," *Washington Times*, 21 February 2002. *Newsmax.com*, an openly conservative news source, has run numerous articles on the link among Democrats, the Clinton administration, and Enron. For examples, see http://www.newsmax.com/archives/articles/2002/8/12/153512.shtml; http://www.newsmax.com/archives/articles.

Chapter 5　Remarks by the President from the USS *Abraham Lincoln*

1. George W. Bush, address to the nation, 17 March 2003, http://www.whitehouse.gov/news/releases/2003/03/20030317-7.html.

2. George W. Bush, address to the nation, 19 March 2003, http://www.whitehouse.gov/news/releases/2003/03/20030319-17.html.

3. Bush, address to the nation, 19 March 2003.

4. George W. Bush, "President Bush Announces Major Combat Operations in Iraq Have Ended: Remarks by the President from the USS *Abraham Lincoln*," 1 May 2003, http://www.whitehouse.gov/news/releases/2003/05/iraq/20030501-15.html. Unless otherwise stated, all quotes from President Bush in this chapter come from this speech.

5. There were 91 news articles and transcripts examined for this chapter: 39 from broadcast news, 41 news articles, 4 editorials, and 7 opinion essays.

6. Amy Goldstein and Karen DeYoung, "Bush to Say Major Combat Has Ended," *Washington Post*, 1 May 2003.

7. Karen DeYoung, "Bush Proclaims Victory in Iraq; Work on Terror is Ongoing, President Says," *Washington Post*, 2 May 2003.

8. "Content and Strategy of President Bush's Speech Tonight," *CBS Evening News*, 1 May 2003.

9. David E. Sanger, "Aftereffects: The President; Bush Declares 'One Victory in a War on Terror,'" *New York Times*, 2 May 2003.

10. Laurence McQuillan and Richard Benedetto, "Bush Hails Win, Looks Ahead," *USA Today*, 2 May 2003.

11. Barbara Slavin, "U.S. Sees Signs that Syria is Bending," *USA Today*, 5 May 2003.

12. "Many Parallels between President Bush and Bush Sr.," *NBC Nightly News*, 6 May 2003.

13. "Nightline Unfinished Business," *Nightline*, ABC-TV, 1 May 2003.

14. "Nightline Anonymous," *Nightline*, ABC-TV, 2 May 2003.

15. DeWayne Wickham, "Democratic Herd Needs Culling," *USA Today*, 6 May 2003.

16. "White House Communications Director Dan Bartlett Discusses the Current Situation in Iraq and the President's Tax Cut Plan," *The Early Show*, CBS-TV, 1 May 2003.

17. "Dan Bartlett, White House Director of Communications, Discusses President Bush's Speech aboard the USS *Abraham Lincoln,*" *Today,* NBC-TV, 1 May 2003.

18. "Nightline Unfinished Business" (emphasis mine).

19. David E. Sanger, "Bush Begins Campaign to Sell His Economic Program," *New York Times,* 3 May 2003 (emphasis mine).

20. DeYoung, "Bush Proclaims Victory in Iraq."

21. "Unemployment Jumps to 6 Percent on Day After Bush Declares Combat in Iraq Over," *NBC Nightly News,* 2 May 2003 (emphasis mine).

22. "Tax Plan Bush Pushes for Big Cuts," *World News Tonight with Peter Jennings,* ABC-TV, 2 May 2003 (emphasis mine).

23. "Many Parallels between President Bush and Bush Sr." (emphasis mine).

24. Maureen Dowd, "The Iceman Cometh," *New York Times,* 4 May 2003 (emphasis mine).

25. Wickham, "Democratic Herd Needs Culling" (emphasis mine).

26. Walter Shapiro, "Jet Ride Was Smooth, But Tax Cuts Hit Turbulence," *USA Today,* 9 May 2003 (emphasis mine).

27. Mike Allen, "Ship Carrying Bush Delayed Return," *Washington Post,* 8 May 2003 (emphasis mine).

28. Francis X. Clines, "Editorial Observer: Karl Rove's Campaign Strategy Seems Evident: It's the Terror, Stupid," *New York Times,* 10 May 2003 (emphasis mine).

29. *The Chris Matthews Show,* NBC-TV, 4 May 2003 (emphasis mine).

30. *The Chris Matthews Show,* NBC-TV, 4 May 2003.

31. "Rear Admiral John Kelly Discusses President Bush's Visit to the USS *Lincoln,*" *The Early Show,* CBS-TV, 1 May 2003.

32. "Bush's Speech to Mark End of Formal Combat Operations in Iraq," *NBC Nightly News,* 1 May 2003.

33. "President Bush Addresses the Nation from Aircraft Carrier USS *Abraham Lincoln,*" *NBC News Special Report,* 1 May 2003.

34. "Presidential Address: Bush Leaving the *Lincoln* This Morning after Last Night's Address," *Good Morning America,* ABC-TV, 2 May 2003.

35. Laurence McQuillan, "President's Jet Plans are Nixed," *USA Today* (1 May 2003) A5.

36. *Today,* NBC-TV, 1 May 2003.

37. "Dan Bartlett Discusses President Bush's Speech."

38. "President Bush Arrives aboard the USS *Abraham Lincoln* by Fighter Jet," *CBS Evening News,* 1 May 2003.

39. "Nightline Unfinished Business."

40. DeYoung, "Bush Proclaims Victory in Iraq."

41. "A Long Way From Victory," editorial, *New York Times,* 2 May 2003.

42. Clines, "Editorial Observer."

43. *Good Morning America,* ABC-TV, 2 May 2003.

44. "Crew of the USS *Abraham Lincoln* Thrilled to Have President Bush on Board to Give His Speech," *Today,* NBC-TV, 2 May 2003.

45. "Nightline War and Politics," *Nightline*, ABC-TV, 8 May 2003.

46. *The Chris Matthews Show*, NBC-TV, 4 May 2003.

47. "Crew aboard the USS *Abraham Lincoln* Welcomes President Bush with Enthusiasm and Applause," *Today*, NBC-TV, 2 May 2003.

48. Dana Milbank, "For Bush, The Military is the Message for '04," *Washington Post*, 2 May 2003.

49. Sanger, "Aftereffects: Bush Declares 'One Victory.'"

50. Dowd, "Iceman Cometh."

51. "Georges Boulanger," *Encyclopaedia Britannica*, http://search.eb.com.

52. Paul Krugman, "Man on Horseback," *New York Times*, 6 May 2003.

53. "USS *Abraham Lincoln* Sailors Back Home, Bush Exploits War for Photo Op," *World News Tonight with Peter Jennings*, ABC-TV, 6 May 2003.

54. Dana Milbank, "Explanations for Bush's Carrier Landing Altered," *Washington Post*, 7 May 2003.

55. Richard W. Stevenson, "Aftereffects: The President; White House Clarifies Bush's Carrier Landing," *New York Times*, 7 May 2003.

56. "Some in Congress Upset over President Bush's Trip to the USS *Abraham Lincoln*," *CBS Evening News*, 7 May 2003.

57. Allen, "Ship Carrying Bush Delayed Return."

58. Richard Benedetto, "Bush's Jet Landing Raises Criticism," *USA Today*, 8 May 2003.

59. David E. Sanger, "Aftereffects: The President; Bush's Smooth Landing is Followed by Turbulence," *New York Times*, 9 May 2003.

60. Frank Rich, "The Jerry Bruckheimer White House," *New York Times*, 11 May 2003.

61. E. J. Dionne Jr., "The Say-Anything School," *Washington Post*, 13 May 2003.

62. "President Bush Addresses the Nation."

63. "Bush's Speech to Mark End of Formal Combat."

64. "Content and Strategy of President Bush's Speech Tonight."

65. Milbank, "For Bush, The Military is the Message."

66. Tom Shales, "Aboard the *Lincoln*, A White House Spectacular," *Washington Post*, 2 May 2003.

67. Dan Balz and Richard Morin, "Like Father, Bush Gets Postwar Boost," *Washington Post*, 2 May 2003.

68. Sanger, "Aftereffects: Bush Declares 'One Victory.'"

69. "A Long Way From Victory."

70. McQuillan and Benedetto, "Bush Hails Win."

71. Susan Page, "Debate Helps Democrats Show Style Differences," *USA Today*, 5 May 2003.

72. "President Bush Arrives aboard the USS *Abraham Lincoln* by Fighter Jet," *CBS Morning News*, 2 May 2003.

73. "President Bush Out Pushing His Tax Cut Plan and Campaigning for Re-election," *CBS Evening News*, 2 May 2003.

74. "Nightline War and Politics."

75. Shapiro, "Jet Ride Was Smooth."

76. Clines, "Editorial Observer"; Rich, "Jerry Bruckheimer White House."

77. "Misfiring at 'Top Gun,'" editorial, *Washington Post*, 11 May 2003.

78. Balz and Morin, "Like Father, Bush Gets Postwar Boost." A noteworthy exception to this myth of Bush Sr. is Adam Nagourney, "The Nation: Guns, Butter and Hope; Listen Up, Democrats: Why 2004 isn't 1992," *New York Times*, 4 May 2003.

79. "Many Parallels between President Bush and Bush Sr."

80. Ross K. Baker, "Bush Basks in Postwar Glow—But for How Long?" *USA Today*, 12 May 2003.

81. Karen DeYoung, "Pushing Tax Cut Plan, Bush Urges Arkansans to Call Lawmakers," *Washington Post*, 6 May 2003 (emphasis mine).

82. "Many Parallels between President Bush and Bush Sr."

83. Wickham, "Democratic Herd Needs Culling."

84. Don Luskin, "Last Economic Recession Began under Clinton, Despite Rewrites by the Left," *Capitalism Magazine*, 17 May 2004, http://www.CapMag.com/article.asp?ID=3691.

85. Economic Policy Institute, *Job Watch*, 8 July 2005, http://www.jobwatch.org/email/jobwatch_20050708.html.

86. Putnam Investments, "Between the Issues: Portrait of the Recently Retired: Worried about Money, Half Living on Less—And They're Satisfied," *FPA Journal* (15 December 2004), http://wwwfpanet.org/journal/BetweenTheIssues/Contributions/121504.cfm.

87. "Market Commentary, December 31, 2003," *M&T Bank*, http://www.mandtbank.com/personal/invest/december_2003.cfm.

88. DeYoung, "Bush Proclaims Victory in Iraq."

89. "Despite U.S. Military Success, New War Policy Poses Risks," *USA Today*, 2 May 2003.

Chapter 6   President Bush
Addresses the United Nations

1. George W. Bush, address to the United Nations General Assembly, 23 September 2003, http://www.whitehouse.gov/news/releases/2003/08/20030823-4.html. Unless specifically noted, all quotations from President Bush in this chapter are from this speech.

2. There were 72 news articles and transcripts examined for this chapter: 28 from broadcast news, 32 news articles, 5 editorials, and 7 opinion essays.

3. "President Bush Appeals to UN to Help with Rebuilding Iraq," *The Early Show*, CBS-TV, 24 September 2003.

4. Judy Keen, "GOP Insiders Worry that President is Vulnerable," *USA Today*, 24 September 2003.

5. Barbara Slavin, "Global Realities Force Bush to Rethink Strategy," *USA Today*, 23 September 2003. Quote by Leon Fuerth, who was an advisor to Vice President Al Gore during the 2000 election campaign.

6. Elisabeth Bumiller, "The Struggle for Iraq: The President; Bush, at U.N. Defends Policy Over Iraq," *New York Times*, 24 September 2003.

7. "News Summary," *New York Times*, 24 September 2003.

8. "President Bush at the U.N.; Finding a New Path in Iraq," editorial, *New York Times*, 24 September 2003.

9. "A Failed Address," editorial, *Washington Post*, 24 September 2003.

10. Richard Cohen, "Serving Souffle at the U.N.," *Washington Post*, 25 September 2003.

11. "President Bush Appears before UN, Appealing for International Help in Iraq," *CBS Evening News*, 24 September 2003.

12. "President Bush Receives Unenthusiastic Response at UN," *NBC Nightly News*, 23 September 2003.

13. "Richard Haass, Council on Foreign Relations, Discusses Iraq and the United Nations," *Today*, NBC-TV, 23 September 2003.

14. *Special Report*, ABC-TV, 23 September 2003.

15. "President Bush Appears before UN."

16. "President Bush Goes to the UN to Try to Persuade Skeptical World Leaders to Share in the Rebuilding of Iraq," *The Early Show*, CBS-TV, 23 September 2003.

17. "President Bush to Speak at the United Nations Today," *Today*, NBC-TV, 23 September 2003.

18. "Richard Haass Discusses Iraq."

19. "Bush and the World Asking for Help," *World News Tonight with Peter Jennings*, ABC-TV, 23 September 2003.

20. News headlines, *Good Morning America*, ABC-TV, 23 September 2003.

21. "President George W. Bush Discussion on Upcoming Speech to United Nations," *Good Morning America*, ABC-TV, 23 September 2003.

22. Introduction, *Good Morning America*, ABC-TV, 23 September 2003.

23. Slavin, "Global Realities Force Bush to Rethink Strategy."

24. "President Bush Appears before UN."

25. "President Bush Receives Unenthusiastic Response."

26. "President George W. Bush Discussion on Upcoming Speech."

27. Dana Milbank, "At U.N., Bush is Cast in the Unfamiliar Role of Playing Defense," *Washington Post*, 23 September 2003.

28. "Bush Asks UN for Help in Rebuilding Iraq," *CBS Morning News*, 24 September 2003.

29. "News Summary."

30. Noah Feldman, "Democracy, Closer Every Day," *New York Times*, 24 September 2003. Although the general tone concerning Bush's "defiance" is positive, it does support the general press framing of Bush's speech as one of defiance. The major difference here is that the majority in the press framed the defiance in such a way that it was offered as an arrogant, rather than justified, action.

31. Dana Milbank, "At U.N., Bush is Criticized Over Iraq; Annan and Others Decry 'Unilateralism,'" *Washington Post*, 24 September 2003.

32. "A Failed Address."

33. Jim Hoagland, "Ships in the Night at the U.N.," *The Washington Post* 24 September 2003).

34. Bumiller, "Struggle for Iraq."

35. "President Bush to Speak at the United Nations Today."

36. Elisabeth Bumiller, "Iraq and Ailing Economy Leave Bush Aides on Edge, They Say," *New York Times*, 23 September 2003.

37. "President Bush Goes to the UN to Try to Persuade."

38. "President Bush Appeals to UN to Help with Rebuilding Iraq," *The Early Show.*

39. "Bush Asks UN for Help in Rebuilding Iraq," *CBS Morning News.*

40. "General Wesley Clark Discusses Iraq and His Candidacy for the Democratic Presidential Nomination," *Today*, NBC-TV, 24 September 2003.

41. Laurence McQuillan, "Bush Invites Help in Iraq," *USA Today*, 24 September 2003.

42. Felicity Barringer, "The Struggle for Iraq: Reaction; Bush's Remarks Draw Skepticism," *New York Times*, 24 September 2003.

43. Steven R. Weisman, "The Struggle for Iraq: News Analysis; An Audience Unmoved," *New York Times*, 24 September 2003.

44. "President Bush Appears before UN."

45. "President Bush to Speak at the United Nations Today."

46. "Richard Haass Discusses Iraq."

47. "Bush Asks UN for Help in Rebuilding Iraq," *CBS Morning News.*

48. Bill Nichols, "Bush Gives Little Ground in Speech to U.N. Audience," *USA Today*, 24 September 2003.

49. Felicity Barringer, "The Struggle for Iraq: United Nations; Annan Tells General Assembly that U.N. Must Correct its Weaknesses," *New York Times*, 24 September 2003.

50. Barringer, "Bush's Remarks Draw Skepticism."

51. Weisman, "An Audience Unmoved."

52. Milbank, "At U.N., Bush is Criticized over Iraq."

53. Cohen, "Serving Souffle at the U.N."

54. Peter Slevin, "Reluctance to Share Control in Iraq Leaves U.S. on Its Own," *Washington Post*, 28 September 2003.

55. Milbank, "At U.N., Bush is Cast in Unfamiliar Role."

56. "Bush and the World Asking for Help."

57. Other than three additional comments mentioned in the summary of this chapter, this one (from the news headlines on *Good Morning America*, 23 September 2003) was the only reference to any compromise offered by President Bush—and it had its importance quickly minimized.

58. "General Wesley Clark Discusses Iraq."

59. Nichols, "Bush Gives Little Ground in Speech."

60. McQuillan, "Bush Invites Help in Iraq."

61. Barringer, "Bush's Remarks Draw Skepticism."

62. Slevin, "Reluctance to Share Control in Iraq."

63. "President Bush at the U.N.; Finding a New Path."

64. I found only four exceptions to this in the press response covered in this chapter: George Stephanopoulos's introduction on *Special Report*, ABC-TV, 23 September 2003; news headlines, *Good Morning America*, 23 September 2003; "A Kinder, Gentler Bush Appeals to U.N. for Iraq Aid," *USA Today*, 24 September 2003; and Feldman, "Democracy, Closer Every Day." A fifth might possibly include David E. Sanger in the *New York Times* writing that President Bush was "making a plea for the United Nations to take a bigger role in Iraq" ("The Struggle for Iraq; The Mood; Bush's Day at the U.N.: It's Chilly, Still, There," *New York Times*, 24 September 2003).

65. "President Vladimir Putin Doesn't Give Bush What He Wants in the Rebuilding Efforts in Iraq," *CBS Evening News*, 27 September 2003.

66. "War on Iraq to be Central Issue of 2004 Presidential Race," *Today*, NBC-TV, 24 September 2003.

67. Clyde Haberman, "Calm Meadow Intersects Risky World," *New York Times*, 23 September 2003.

68. Elisabeth Bumiller, "White House Letter; President Bestows Nicknames and Gets Star Treatment, but No Aid," *New York Times*, 29 September 2003.

69. Helen Dewar and Vernon Loeb, "In Senate, Kennedy Fuels Sharp Debate," *Washington Post*, 24 September 2003 (emphasis mine).

Chapter 7   President Bush Commemorates Veterans Day

1. George W. Bush, Veterans Day address, 11 November 2005, http://www.whitehouse.gov/news/releases/2005/11/20051111-1.html. Unless specifically noted, all quotations from President Bush in this chapter are from this speech. There were 56 news articles and broadcast transcripts examined for this chapter: 34 from broadcast news; 14 news articles; 1 editorial; 7 opinion essays.

2. Emphasis mine.

3. Emphasis mine.

4. There were 56 news articles and broadcast transcripts examined for this chapter: 34 from broadcast news, 14 news articles, 1 editorial, and 7 opinion essays.

5. Linton Weeks and Peter Baker, "Bush Spars With Critics of the War; Exchanges With Democrats Take Campaign-Style Tone," *Washington Post*, 12 November 2005.

6. "White House Defending Itself Against Criticism of Iraq War," *The Early Show*, CBS-TV, 11 November 2005.

7. "Fractured GOP Moves on Divergent Paths; Strategies for Next Year Undergo Revision as Public Approval Ratings Drop," *Washington Post*, 13 November 2005.

8. "President Bush to Give Veterans Day Speech Today in Pennsylvania," *Today*, NBC-TV, 11 November 2005.

9. Richard W. Stevenson and David S. Cloud, "His Image Tarnished, Bush Seeks to Restore Credibility," *New York Times*, 11 November 2005.

10. *CBS Evening News*, 11 November 2005.

11. Introduction, *NBC Nightly News*, 11 November 2005; "Republicans and Democrats Resume Dispute over Iraq War," *NBC Nightly News*, 11 November 2005.

12. Richard W. Stevenson, "Bush Contends Partisan Critics Hurt War Effort," *New York Times*, 12 November 2005.

13. "Controversy over U.S. Involvement in Iraq War Continues; President and Others Defend Their Stand," *CBS Evening News*, 11 November 2005.

14. Frank Rich, "'We Do Not Torture' and Other Funny Stories," *New York Times*, 13 November 2005.

15. Frank Rich, "Dishonest, Reprehensible, Corrupt," *New York Times*, 27 November 2005.

16. News headlines, *Good Morning America*, ABC-TV, 12 November 2005.

17. *Saturday Today*, NBC-TV, 12 November 2005.

18. "Skewed Intelligence or Not, War Was A Mistake," *USA Today*, 16 November 2005.

19. "Another Poll Out Shows President Bush's Poll Numbers Still Dropping," *NBC Nightly News*, 12 November 2005.

20. Weeks and Baker, "Bush Spars with Critics of the War."

21. "Fractured GOP Moves on Divergent Paths."

22. "President Bush Lashes Back at Critics of Iraq War Policy," *The Saturday Early Show*, CBS-TV, 12 November 2005.

23. *CBS Evening News*, 11 November 2005.

24. "War over the War Fighting in Washington," *World News Tonight*, ABC-TV, 17 November 2005.

25. Jill Lawrence, "Politicians Across Spectrum State their Case on Iraq," *USA Today*, 21 November 2005.

26. "Dan Bartlett, Counselor to the President, Discusses the War in Iraq and Democratic Accusations," *Today*, NBC-TV, 14 November 2005.

27. Weeks and Baker, "Bush Spars with Critics of the War."

28. Weeks and Baker, "Bush Spars with Critics of the War."

29. "President Bush Defends U.S. Military in Iraq, Says Critics Had Same Access to Intelligence He Did," *NBC Nightly News*, 14 November 2005.

30. "Debate over Total U.S. Troop Withdrawal from Iraq," *The Early Show*, CBS-TV, 18 November 2005.

31. "Important Veteran Congressman Says It's Time for the U.S. to Get Out of Iraq," *CBS Morning News*, 18 November 2005.

32. This is seen even in a comparatively detailed *Washington Post* article that highlighted the efforts of Democrats to obtain copies of all Presidential Daily Briefings having to do with Iraq. The simple point brought out by Dan Bartlett—that Congress was fully briefed and provided with a comprehensive report (no less nuanced information than that contained in the PDBs)—was noticeably absent from this report. Instead, the report devolved into charge-countercharge, this time with Democrats pictured as on the offensive. See Walter Pincus, "Lawmakers Focus on Daily Brief in Prewar Intelligence Debate; Kennedy Pushes for Access to Bush's Classified CIA Reports," *Washington Post*, 19 November 2005.

33. Stevenson, "Bush Contends Partisan Critics Hurt War Effort."

34. "Lawmakers Debate Reasoning behind Iraq War," *NBC Nightly News*, 13 November 2005.

35. "Ongoing Debate over Iraq between Republicans and Democrats Getting Very Partisan and Nasty," *NBC Nightly News*, 19 November 2005.

36. "Congress Finally Debates War But Finds No Easy Solution," editorial, *USA Today*, 21 November 2005.

37. Eugene Robinson, "No Way Out for Bush and Co." *Washington Post*, 22 November 2005.

38. Rich, "Dishonest, Reprehensible, Corrupt."

39. "War over the War Fighting in Washington."

40. "Debate over Total U.S. Troop Withdrawal."

41. Julie Chen, "War of Words in Washington over the Iraq Policy Continues to Rage On," *The Early Show*, CBS-TV, 18 November 2005.

42. "Important Veteran Congressman Says It's Time."

43. "Debate on Capitol Hill over the Iraq War," *NBC Nightly News*, 20 November 2005.

44. "Iraq War Debate Continues," *The Osgood File*, CBS-Radio, 18 November 2005.

45. Andrea Stone, "Murtha: Troops' Pain, Not Politics, Behind Stance," *USA Today*, 18 November 2005.

46. Dave Moniz, "Democrat Hawk Wants Pullout," *USA Today*, 18 November 2005.

47. Frank Rich, "One War Lost, Another to Go," *New York Times*, 20 November 2005.

48. "Democrat Representative John Murtha Saying It's Time for Troops to Come Home From Iraq," *Today*, NBC-TV, 18 November 2005.

49. Stone, "Murtha."

50. "Ongoing Debate over Iraq between Republicans and Democrats."

51. Stevenson, "Bush Contends Partisan Critics Hurt War Effort."

52. Stevenson, "Bush Contends Partisan Critics Hurt War Effort."

53. "Republicans and Democrats Resume Dispute."

54. "President Bush Defends His Iraq War Policy in Veterans Day Speech, Taking Anti-War Democrats to Task," *Saturday Today*, NBC-TV, 12 November 2005.

55. Weeks and Baker, "Bush Spars With Critics of the War."

56. Stevenson, "Bush Contends Partisan Critics Hurt War Effort."

57. Stevenson and Cloud, "His Image Tarnished."

58. "Another Poll Out."

59. E. J. Dionne Jr., "Another Set of Scare Tactics," *Washington Post*, 15 November 2005.

60. "President Bush Passionately Defends His Iraq War Policy in a Veterans Day Speech," *The Saturday Early Show*, CBS-TV, 12 November 2005.

61. "Skewed Intelligence or Not." This may have been made in reference to "the latest *USA Today* poll" that found "a record 60% of those surveyed . . . said the war wasn't 'worth it.'" See Susan Page, "American Attitudes on Iraq Similar to Those in Vietnam," *USA Today*, 16 November 2005.

62. "War over the War Fighting in Washington."

63. "Debate over Total U.S. Troop Withdrawal."

64. Rich, "One War Lost."

65. There are numerous polls in this time frame that demonstrate the uptick; see http://www.washingtonpost.com/wp-dyn/content/article/2005/12/19/AR2005121900924.html for one example.

Chapter 8   News Media Reporting of the War on Terror

1. Robert E. Denton, "Rhetorical Challenges to the Presidency," paper presented at the annual convention of the Southern States Communication Association, New Orleans, 1 April 2000, p. 5.

2. Jim A. Kuypers, *Press Bias and Politics: How the Media Frame Controversial Issues.* (Westport, CT: Praeger, 2002). See specifically the concluding chapter and the discussion concerning omission of information.

3. See David A. Snow and Robert D. Benford, "Master Frames and Cycle of Protest," in *Frontiers in Social Movement Theory*, ed. Aldon D. Morris and Carol M. Mueller (New Haven, CT: Yale University Press, 1992), 133–55. See also D. S. Myers, "Framing National Security: Elite Public Discourse on Nuclear Weapons during the Cold War," *Political Communication* 12 (1995): 173–92.

4. David Levin, "Framing Peace Policies: The Competition for Resonate Themes," *Political Communication* 22 (2005): 84.

5. Thomas Patterson, "The News Media: An Effective Political Actor?" *Political Communication* 14 (1997): 445.

6. The American Society of Newspaper Editors Statement of Principles, then known as the Canons of Journalism, was adopted in 1922. It was revised in 1975, renamed the Statement of Principles, and updated in 2002. It can be viewed in its entirety at http://www.asne.org/kiosk/archive/principl.htm.

7. Code of Ethics, Society for Professional Journalists, http://www.spj.org/ethics_code.asp.

8. I have focused on the ideas most germane to this study; for the complete listing of the Associated Press's code of ethics, last updated May 2004, see http://www.asne.org/ideas/codes/apme.htm. The numbers assigned in the text are mine.

9. Code of Ethics and Professional Conduct Radio-Television News Directors Association, http://www.rtnda.org/ethics/coe.shtml. The numbers assigned in the text are mine.

10. I have focused on the ideas most germane to this study; for the complete listing, please see, "Eugene Meyer's Principles for the *Washington Post*," *Washington Post*, http://www.washpost.com/gen_info/principles/index.shtml.

11. *Ethical Journalism: A Handbook of Values and Practices for the News and Editorial Departments* (New York: New York Times, 2004). Available online at http://www.nytco.com/company-properties-times-coe.html.

12. One should differentiate between news sources that do not purport to be objective and those that do. Talk radio, for example, is overwhelmingly Right-leaning in America. Yet talk radio hosts provide *commentary* and do not purport to being objective in how they present the news; instead they publicly announce that they are providing political interpretations of facts.

13. Gary C. Woodward, "Narrative Form and the Deceptions of Modern Journalism," in *Political Communication Ethics: An Oxymoron?*, ed. Robert E. Denton Jr. (Westport, CT: Praeger, 2000), 127.

14. For example, consider this headline: "Behind the Show of Bipartisanship: Muted Dissent; Crisis-Inspired Unity Shows Signs of Crumbling as Democrats Air Concerns Over Bush Response" (John F. Harris, *Washington Post*, 17 December 2001). The main point of the story suggests that some "Democrats, and even some Republicans, have expressed concern that the necessity to give broad powers to the White House could go too far, robbing what they said was Congress's constitutional authority to appropriate money and hold the administration accountable for policy decisions it makes to meet the crisis."

15. Linton Weeks and Peter Baker, "Bush Spars With Critics of the War; Exchanges With Democrats Take Campaign-Style Tone," *Washington Post*, 12 November 2005.

16. Dan Balz, "Bush Faces Dual Challenge on Iraq," *Washington Post*, 25 November 2005.

17. "Debate over Total U.S. Troop Withdrawal from Iraq," *The Early Show*, CBS-TV, 18 November 2005.

18. "Howard Fineman, *Newsweek*, Discusses the War in Iraq," *Today*, NBC-TV, 25 November 2005.

19. "White House Defending Itself against Criticism of Iraq War," *The Early Show*, CBS-TV, 11 November 2005.

20. Richard W. Stevenson, "Bush Contends Partisan Critics Hurt War Effort," *New York Times*, 12 November 2005.

21. "President Bush Lashes Back at Critics of Iraq War Policy," *The Saturday Early Show*, CBS-TV, 12 November 2005.

22. Frank Rich, "One War Lost, Another to Go," *New York Times*, 20 November 2005.

23. Eugene Robinson, "No Way Out for Bush and Co.," *Washington Post*, 22 November 2005.

24. Robinson, "No Way Out for Bush."

25. Frank Rich, "'We Do Not Torture' and Other Funny Stories," *New York Times*, 13 November 2005.

26. Michael Ryan, for instance, examined only editorials published between September 12, 2001, and the Afghanistan invasion that appeared in the ten most circulated U.S. papers. He wrote that the editorials matched the narrow Bush framing and also that the "causes of the attacks and the alternative remedies . . . were not addressed meaningfully. Even the scope of the problem was not well defined, for government and media frame-makers defined the problem exclusively in terms of military retaliation and US interests." See Michael Ryan, "Framing the War against Terrorism: U.S. Newspaper Editorials and Military Action in Afghanistan," *Gazette: The International Journal for Communication Studies* 66 (2004): 378. See also Douglas Blanks Hindman, "Media System Dependency and Public Support for the Press and President," *Mass Communication & Society* 7, no. 1 (2004): 29–42.

27. Karen Callaghan and Frauke Schnell, "Assessing the Democratic Debate: How the News Media Frame Elite Policy Discourse," *Political Communication* 18 (2001): 203.

28. Marilyn J. Young and Michael K. Launer, "KAL 007 and the Superpowers: An International Argument," *Quarterly Journal of Speech* 74 (1988): 272, 289.

29. Dana Milbank, "For Bush, The Military is the Message for '04," *Washington Post*, 2 May 2003.

30. "President Bush Lifts Sanctions against Iraq; Asks UN to Do the Same," *CBS Morning News*, 8 May 2003.

31. Elisabeth Bumiller, "The State of the Union: News Analysis; Surer Voice, Bigger Vision," *New York Times*, 30 January 2002.

32. Dana Milbank, "Hitching Civic, Economic Goals to the War," *Washington Post*, 30 January 2002.

33. "Top Officials Say It May Take Months to Win Agreement on New UN Resolution for Iraq," *NBC Nightly News*, 24 September 2003.

34. "War on Iraq to Be Central Issue of 2004 Presidential Race," *Today*, NBC-TV, 24 September 2003.

35. Introduction, *Special Report*, ABC-TV, 23 September 2003.

36. Introduction, *Special Report*, ABC-TV, 23 September 2003.

37. For additional examples of sandwiching, see Kuypers, *Press Bias and Politics*, 210–12.

38. Richard Benedetto, "Bush's Jet Landing Raises Criticism," *USA Today*, 8 May 2003.

39. Glenn Kessler, "A Vague Pitch Leaves Mostly Puzzlement," *Washington Post*, 24 September 2003.

40. Kessler, "A Vague Pitch."

41. Dana Milbank, "At U.N., Bush is Criticized Over Iraq; Annan and Others Decry 'Unilateralism,'" *Washington Post*, 24 September 2003.

42. "White House Communications Director Dan Bartlett Discusses the Current Situation in Iraq and the President's Tax-Cut Plan," *The Early Show*, CBS-TV, 1 May 2003.

43. "Some in Congress Upset over President Bush's Trip to the USS *Abraham Lincoln*," *CBS Evening News*, 7 May 2003.

44. "Senator Bob Graham Discusses Why He Wants to Be the U.S. president and What He Would Do if He Won," *Today*, NBC-TV, 7 May 2003.

45. "Howard Dean Reactions to President Bush's U.N. Speech," *Good Morning America*, ABC-TV, 24 September 2003.

46. "Push polling" involves the attempt at influencing the opinion of poll respondents with the polling question. This can take various forms. For example, a push poll could be used to bring to mind a particular issue. Such a question might take the following form: "Please rank the following candidates as you think of the issue of national security." Another form associates negative qualities with a candidate or politician: "Would you be more or less likely to vote for George Bush if you knew he was a draft dodger?"

Other abuses of polling exist. See Ted J. Smith III and J. Michael Hogan, "Public Opinion and the Panama Canal Treaties of 1977," *Public Opinion Quarterly* 51 (1987): 5–30.

47. "Karen Tumulty and Doyle McManus Discuss Presidential Politics," *Face the Nation*, CBS-TV, 11 May 2003.

48. "Skewed Intelligence Or Not, War Was A Mistake," *USA Today*, 16 November 2005.

49. "Senator Joe Biden Speaks about Bush Administration's Iraq Policy," *The Osgood File*, CBS-Radio, 22 November 2005.

50. Dana Milbank, "Opening the Door to Debate, then Shutting It," *Washington Post*, 22 November 2005.

51. Robinson, "No Way Out for Bush."

52. Rich, "'We Do Not Torture' and Other Funny Stories."

53. This type of press bias is called "bias by omission" by Brent H. Baker. Baker documents well and thoroughly the practices of the major network news organizations in his book *How to Identify, Expose and Correct Liberal Media Bias* (Alexandria, VA: Media Research Center, 1994). For additional information on bias by omission, see Kuypers, *Press Bias and Politics*, 215–35.

54. Robert M. Entman, "How the Media Affect What People Think: An Information Processing Approach," *Journal of Politics* 51, no. 2 (May 1989): 367.

55. Bradley Graham, "Clark Wants More Foreign Aid, New Department to Handle It," *Washington Post*, 29 September 2003.

56. Helen Dewar and Vernon Loeb, "In Senate, Kennedy Fuels Sharp Debate," *Washington Post*, 24 September 2003.

57. Peter Slevin, "Reluctance to Share Control in Iraq Leaves U.S. on Its Own," *Washington Post*, 28 September 2003.

58. For an investigation of differences and similarities between print and broadcast news coverage of the 9/11 terrorist attacks, see Xigen Li and Ralph Izard, "9/11 Attack Coverage Reveals Similarities, Differences," *Newspaper Research Journal* 24, no. 1 (2003): 204–19.

59. "Secretary of State Colin Powell Discusses the War on Terrorism," *Meet the Press*, NBC-TV, 11 November 2001 (emphasis mine).

60. "Secretary of Defense Donald Rumsfeld Discusses the War on Terrorism," *Face the Nation*, CBS-TV, 11 November 2001.

61. For example, see Brigitte Lebens Nacos, *The Press, Presidents, and Crises* (New York: Columbia University Press, 1990).

62. For more on this practice, see Kuypers, *Press Bias and Politics*, 19, 86, 199, 246.

63. Michael Kelly, "All-Negative, All the Time," *Washington Post*, 14 November 2001.

64. Rich Noyes, "TV's Bad News Brigade: ABC, CBS and NBC's Defeatist Coverage of the War in Iraq," Media Research Center, 13 October 2005, http://www.mrc.org/SpecialReports/2005/pdf/TVs_Depressing_Iraq_News.pdf.

65. The remarks in this summary section apply fully to the three major news networks and the three major newspapers covered in this study. However, I am strongly inclined to believe that they apply equally to the whole of the mainstream news media in America. See Kuypers, *Press Bias and Politics*, for similar results derived from examination of 116 different mainstream news media sources.

Index

9/11, 1–6, 17–22, 24, 26, 28, 30–34, 36, 38, 43–48, 51, 53, 55, 69–71, 82, 96–97, 101, 114, 118, 140, 169n29, 194n58

agenda extension, 9–10, 136
agenda setting, 9–11, 135–36, 152–53, 169n29
al Qaeda. *See* Qaeda, al
axis of evil, 54–55, 58–64, 70, 72, 144–45, 147, 178n33, 179nn43–44, 53, 56

bin Laden, Osama, 23, 27, 36, 45, 49, 56, 104, 162, 175n8, 176n47
Bitzer, Lloyd L., 30, 168nn10–11, 14, 174n65
Bush Doctrine, 58, 76, 80, 94–95, 97, 110, 178n40

Clinton administration, 5, 12–13, 63, 73, 96, 180n85, 184n84
Cold War rhetoric, 3, 56, 168nn8–9, 168n21, 170n39
crisis atmosphere, 3, 6, 20, 31–32, 34, 40, 151–52

crisis rhetoric, 4–6, 12–13, 18, 170n39, 171n1, 172n31, 174n71, 191n14, 194n61

Day, Louis A., 10, 169n33

Enron, 51, 55, 65, 68–70, 73, 144–46, 161, 180n74, 180n83, 180n85

frame: master, 19, 22, 28–30, 33, 48, 70, 136, 171n2, 190n3; war on terror, 19, 21, 27, 29, 32, 36, 41, 46–50, 52, 57, 70, 77, 94, 110, 114–15, 142, 144, 146, 151–52
frames, definition of, 7–15, 125
framing, 7–15, 17, 21–24, 26, 30–34, 136; war on terror, 47–50, 70–73, 94–97, 109–12, 129–34, 140–52
framing analysis, 8, 10, 140; comparative, 11–12, 15

Hussein, Saddam, 14, 61, 75–76, 81, 94, 100–101, 110, 119–20, 126, 142, 146, 154

ideology, terrorist, 77, 114–17, 150
intelligence, prewar, 101, 114, 120–26, 130–32, 141, 148–50, 158–59, 173n54, 188n18, 188n29, 189n32, 190n61, 193n48
Iran, 54, 58–64, 177n17, 178n28, 178n34, 179n45, 179n56

Launer, Michael K., 32, 168nn12–13, 21–22, 174n72, 192n28

mainstream media, 2, 7, 10, 18, 111, 135, 137, 139, 152, 161–63, 165, 180n85, 194n65
mainstream press. *See* mainstream media
master frame. *See* frame: master
media bias. *See* press: bias
metanarrative: Cold War, 2–6, 30–32; definition of, 2–3, 30; new, 6–7, 19, 117, 151–52
Murtha, John, 127–31, 150–51, 189n45, 189n48

North Korea, 12–13, 54, 58–64, 177n17, 178n28, 178n34, 179nn45–46

Oklahoma City bombing, 38

Pearl Harbor, 31
poll data, 132–34, 150, 152, 158, 188n19, 190n61, 190n65, 193n46
preemption, 37, 39, 61–62, 71, 97, 155
preknowledge, 6–7, 32–34, 151; stable, 18, 33
press: agenda of, 136, 142; antidemocratic nature of, 164–65; bias, 2, 10–12, 15, 70, 96, 112, 136–39, 170n42, 190n2, 193n53; editorial opinion, 163; ethics, 137–40; neutrality, 10, 48, 137–40; objectivity, 10, 135, 140, 142,

163–64; opposition, 39, 46, 48, 57–58, 95, 120–24, 137, 140, 142, 144, 146, 149, 151
press practices, biased: agenda setting, 152–53; exclusion of material, 143, 159–61, 190n2, 193n53; hearsay, 161; leading with negative, 156–57; priming, 153–54; pushing polls, 158, 193n46; sandwiching, 155–56, 192n37
priming, 9, 136, 153–54
public knowledge, 3, 5–7, 12, 17, 19, 21, 30–34, 116–17, 151, 168n10, 174n65

Qaeda, al, 27, 29, 45, 57, 59, 77, 79, 81, 97, 104, 111, 114–17, 123, 131

"rally 'round the president," 18, 25, 33, 142
reporting, interpretive, 86, 106
rhetorical presidency, 2, 167n3
rhetorical situation, 6, 18

speeches: 9/11, on or after, 17–22, 142–43; State of the Union, January 2002, 51–73, 144–46; United Nations, November 2001, 35–50, 143–44; United Nations, September 2003, 99–112, 146–49; USS *Abraham Lincoln*, 75–97, 146–47; Veterans Day, November 2005, 113–34, 149–51; West Point, 71
strategy, war on terror, 113–19, 129–37, 149–51

Taliban, 23, 29, 35, 39–40, 43, 49, 57, 162, 176n41, 176n55
talk shows, 162
terror attacks, 18, 20
terrorist ideology. *See* ideology, terrorist

themes, 14–15, 18–19, 22–25, 32–33, 136, 170n47, 170n48, 171n2, 190n4; apology, 106–7, 142–51; appeals for help from United Nations, 105–6; axis of evil, 58–64, 142–51; carrier arrival, 86–92, 142–51; civilization vs. barbarism, 33, 36–37, 52–53, 77–80, 99–103, 113–17, 142–51; defiant president, 106, 142–51; domestic issues, 82–85, 142–51; economy, 64–67, 142–51; Enron, 68–70, 142–51; freedom vs. tyranny, 21, 23, 25, 29, 31, 33, 36–37, 53, 77–80, 142–51; good vs. evil, 21, 23–25, 27–28, 33, 36–37, 52–53, 77–80, 142–51; intelligence, prewar, 121–26; Iraq war, 77–82, 99–105, 113–17, 142–51; Murtha, John, 127–29, 189n45, 189n48; nature of the enemy, 21–22, 24–25, 27–29, 36, 38–39, 44–45, 54, 77–80, 99–103, 113–17, 142–51; nature of the war, 27, 36, 38–40, 46–47, 53–58, 77–80, 99–103, 113–17, 142–51; patience, 42–44, 77–80, 142–51; plan, no, 126–27; president, critical comments of, 119–20; purpose of speeches, 77–80, 99–103, 117–20, 142–51; reelection speech, 92–94; role of United Nations, 99–103, 142–51; strategy, comprehensive U.S., 117–19; Top Gun, 86–92, 146–47, 184n77; working with other nations, 36–37, 46, 54–55, 77–80, 142–51; World War II or Vietnam, 41–42, 142–51; uncompromising president, 108–9; unilateral action, 107–8

themes, summary of, 47–50, 70–73, 94–97, 109–12, 129–34, 142–51

totalitarian, 27, 31, 115, 117

weapons of mass destruction (WMD), 39, 45, 54, 59–62, 79–80, 100–103, 110–11, 116, 118, 120, 146, 148, 152, 154,

Windt, Theodore O., 167n3, 168nn15–19, 171n1

Young, Marilyn J., 21–22, 32, 168nn12–13, 174n72, 192n28

About the Author

Jim A. Kuypers is assistant professor of political communication at Virginia Tech. He is the author of two important works in presidential communication and press bias: *Presidential Crisis Rhetoric and the Press in a Post–Cold War World* and *Press Bias and Politics: How the Media Frame Controversial Issues*. He is the recipient of the American Communication Association's Outstanding Contribution to Communication Scholarship Award, the Southern States Communication Association's Early Career Research Award, and Dartmouth College's Distinguished Lecturer Award.